Person-Centred Therapy

Person-Centred Therapy

A European Perspective

edited by

Brian Thorne and Elke Lambers

SAGE Publications

London • Thousand Oaks • New Delhi

First published 1998

SAGE Publications Ltd
6 Bonhill Street
London EC2A 4PU

SAGE Publications Inc.
2455 Teller Road
Thousand Oaks, California 91320

SAGE Publications India Pvt Ltd
32, M-Block Market
Greater Kailash – I
New Delhi 110 048

British Library Cataloguing in Publication data

A catalogue record for this book is available
from the British Library

ISBN 0 7619 5154 7
ISBN 0 7619 5155 5 (pbk)

Library of Congress catalog card number 98–61238

Typeset by Mayhew Typesetting, Rhayader, Powys
Printed in Great Britain by Biddles Ltd, Guildford, Surrey

Contents

Notes on Contributors   vii

Preface   x

Acknowledgements   xii

1   The Person-Centred Approach in Europe: Its History and
    Current Significance   1
    Brian Thorne

Part I   Theory   11

2   Person-Centred Theory as a System of Meaning   11
    Martin Van Kalmthout

3   Unconditional Positive Regard and its Spiritual Implications   23
    Campbell Purton

4   'On Becoming a Person-Centred Approach': A Person-Centred
    Understanding of the Person   38
    Peter F. Schmid

5   Personality Change and the Concept of the Self   53
    Martin Van Kalmthout

6   From Non-Directive to Experiential: A Paradigm Unfolding   62
    Germain Lietaer

7   'Face to Face' – The Art of Encounter   74
    Peter F. Schmid

8   Empowerment or Collusion? The Social Context of
    Person-Centred Therapy   91
    Sarah Hawtin and Judy Moore

9   On the Development of the Person in Relationships   106
    Eva-Maria Biermann-Ratjen

10 Incongruence and Psychopathology   119
    Eva-Maria Biermann-Ratjen

Part II Practice   131

11 Focusing: Interpersonal and Intrapersonal Conditions of
    Growth   131
    Mia Leijssen

12 Client-Centred Therapy for Adolescents: An Interactional
    Point of View   159
    Lidwien Geertjens and Olga Waaldijk

13 A Person-Centred Perspective on Leadership and
    Team-Building   176
    Leif J. Braaten

14 'Anchorage' as a Core Concept in Working with Psychotic
    People   195
    Dion Van Werde

15 The Relevance of a Phenomenological Attitude when Working
    with Psychotic People   206
    Chris Deleu and Dion Van Werde

16 Empathy and Empathy Development with Psychotic Clients   216
    Ute Binder

    Postscript: Person-Centred Therapy: An International Force   231
    Brian Thorne

    Appendix: European Associations, Societies and Training
    Institutes for the Person-Centred Approach   232

    Index   240

Notes on Contributors

The editors

Brian Thorne is Professorial Fellow and Director of the Centre for Counselling Studies at the University of East Anglia, Norwich, England. He is also a Professor of Education in the College of Teachers. A founder of the Norwich Centre, the first person-centred counselling agency in Britain and a co-director of Person-Centred Therapy (Britain), Brian is a Fellow of the British Association for Counselling and a major contributor to the professional literature. He is co-author (with Dave Mearns) of *Person-centred Counselling in Action* (Sage, 1988) and author of *Carl Rogers* (Sage, 1992).

Elke Lambers is a Dutch clinical psychologist living and working in Scotland. She completed her training as a person-centred therapist with the Dutch Rogerian Society (now VCgP) in the early 1970s. She has worked as a therapist in adult psychiatry both in Holland and in Scotland and for 14 years she was a counsellor in higher education. She currently works in private practice as a therapist, supervisor and trainer. She was a co-founder of FDI (Britain) and as a co-director of PCT (Britain) she has been involved in the training of person-centred therapists since 1985. Her current work includes person-centred supervision training and advanced training for person-centred therapists. She has a particular interest in the development of a person-centred theory of psychopathology. Elke is a Fellow of the British Association for Counselling and plays an active part in the development of counselling in Britain.

The contributors

Eva-Maria Biermann-Ratjen studied psychology at the Universities of Berlin, Munich and Hamburg. Since 1965 she has worked as a clinical psychologist and lecturer at the University Hospital of Hamburg-Eppendorf, Klinik für Psychiatrie und Psychotherapie. She is a client-centred therapist and trainer in the Gesellschaft für wissenschaftliche Gesprächstherapie and has published extensively.

Ute Binder is a clinical psychologist and client-centred psychotherapist who has worked since 1970 with Dr Johannes Binder in a community-based practice in Frankfurt-on-Main. The focus of her work is on psychotherapy with severely disturbed persons and she has published widely on client-centred work with psychiatric patients and on the further development of the concept of empathy and its applications.

Leif J. Braaten earned his PhD at the Department of Psychology in the University of Chicago in 1958 where he was sponsored by Dr Carl Rogers and his person-centred staff. After four years at Cornell University, he returned to Norway in 1964 as a Professor of Clinical Psychology at the Institute of Psychology in the University of Oslo and has taught client-centred theory and practice there ever since.

Chris Deleu studied psychology at the Catholic University of Leuven and since 1975 he has practised individual and group therapy at St Camillus psychiatric hospital near Ghent, Belgium. In addition to his client-centred training, he has specialized in short-term biographical therapy and in phenomenological perception-training for patients suffering from psychosis or personality disorders.

Lidwien Geertjens lives in Amsterdam and has a master's degree in clinical psychology. She has had both client-centred and psychoanalytical psychotherapy training. She has worked as a psychologist-psychotherapist in both inpatient and outpatient clinics for adults and adolescents and is currently employed as a psychotherapist and supervisor in the adolescent unit of a psychiatric hospital. She is also a trainer and supervisor for postgraduate courses in child and adolescent psychotherapy.

Sarah Hawtin works at the University of East Anglia (UEA) as a part-time educational counsellor and is also attached to a general medical practice in Norwich. In addition she is a trainer for the UEA Diploma in Counselling. Her central interests are the philosophical and spiritual implications of person-centred counselling.

Mia Leijssen is professor at the Catholic University of Leuven and teaches client-centred and experiential psychotherapy to students of clinical psychology at both undergraduate and postgraduate levels. She has a practice in individual and group psychotherapy at the University's Counselling Centre.

Germain Lietaer studied as a post-doctoral fellow with Carl Rogers at the Centre for Studies of the Person in La Jolla in 1969–70. He is a full professor at the Catholic University of Leuven and teaches client-centred/experiential psychotherapy and process research in psychotherapy. He is also a staff member of a three-year part-time postgraduate training programme in client-centred/experiential psychotherapy at the same university. Professor Lietaer has published widely; he is chief editor (with J. Rombauts and R. Van Balen) of *Client-centred and Experiential Psychotherapy in the Nineties*

(Leuven, Belgium: Leuven University Press) and co-editor (with L.S. Greenberg and J. Watson) of the *Handbook of Experiential Psychotherapy: Foundations and Differential Intervention* (New York: Guilford, 1998).

Judy Moore studied and taught English literature before training as a counsellor within the person-centred approach. She has counselled at the University of East Anglia since the mid-1980s and has been a trainer on the university's full-time Counselling Diploma since 1993. She has recently become Director of Counselling at UEA.

Campbell Purton is a counsellor at the Counselling Service of the University of East Anglia, Norwich and teaches philosophy at the Wensum Lodge Adult Education Centre in the same city. He has contributed articles to philosophical and counselling journals, together with several book chapters in the same fields. His particular interests at present include the emotions of self-assessment, such as shame, Buddhist approaches to psychotherapy and the philosophical work of Eugene Gendlin.

Peter F. Schmid is a person-centred psychotherapist, practical theologian and pastoral psychologist. He is an Associate Professor at the University of Graz, Styria, and teaches at several Austrian and German universities. He is a co-founder of the Austrian person-centred association IPS (APG) and of the international society PCA (Person-Centered Association in Austria). He is a person-centred psychotherapy trainer and his current interests include person-centred anthropology, encounter groups and the integration of body work into person-centred practice. He has published many books and articles on the person-centred approach and its foundations, theory and practice.

Martin Van Kalmthout is an Associate Professor in Clinical Psychology at Nijmegen University in Holland. He has published widely on the history and foundations of psychotherapy. In addition to his university work he maintains a private psychotherapy practice.

Dion Van Werde is a psychologist and person-centred psychotherapist. He is a staff member and trainer with the European Pre-Therapy Training Institute (inspired by the work of Dr Garry Prouty) which is based at the St Camillus psychiatric hospital near Ghent in Belgium. At the same hospital he has inaugurated and currently works on a person-centred ward for treating psychotic people according to pre-therapy principles.

Olga Waaldijk is a Dutch child-and-adolescent psychotherapist who has worked in a children's home and in the adolescent unit of a psychiatric hospital. She has been much involved in the training of child and youth psychotherapists and in the professional organization of therapeutic services for young people since 1983.

Preface

There are still many mental health specialists in Britain who apparently believe person-centred therapy to be an essentially American import that arrived in the 1960s and, despite its initial impact, has never become firmly rooted in British soil.

We believe that, in many cases, this ignorance is feigned rather than real and springs from vested interests. Perhaps it is simply not politic for the psychiatric establishment, the analytical societies and the currently much-favoured cognitive behavioural therapists to acknowledge or to admit into full consciousness that person-centred counselling, far from being a transitory American import, is well established in Britain, has large numbers of accredited practitioners who see many hundreds of clients each week, and currently boasts three professors in British academia – more than any other therapeutic orientation.

A principal aim of this book is to demonstrate that what is true of Britain is equally true of many other European countries. What is more, there is nothing to suggest that the approach has reached the limit of its development and influence within the European continent. On the contrary, the collapse of the Soviet bloc has seen increasing interest in the approach in Eastern Europe, while in the West person-centred therapists have established themselves as a powerful force within the mainstream of therapeutic activity in several countries. The contributors to this book, drawn from six different European person-centred communities, provide ample evidence of the health of the approach and of its continuing vitality in both theory and practice. Most significantly, they also demonstrate that person-centred therapy is by no means an alien import. On the contrary, the approach to which Carl Rogers and his associates gave a new coherence and inspiringly original formulations has its roots deep in European culture and history. To read many of the chapters in this book is to realize that, in many ways, the person-centred approach has 'come home' and that it may now be Europe's task to ensure that its revolutionary legacy is not lost to the world.

Many British readers will find parts of the book somewhat daunting. Person-centred practitioners in Britain are not on the whole accustomed to wrestling with some of the deeper philosophical issues the approach raises and which to a large extent determine or threaten its internal coherence.

Nor are they familiar with the application of the approach to psychopathological difficulties and to the accompaniment of persons who are institutionalized or suffering from severe mental disturbance. We have deliberately not attempted to make life easy for our readers by oversimplifying in translation contributions from German, Austrian and Belgian colleagues who are working at the cutting edge of both theory and practice. The translations retain the sense of struggle and complexity that is characteristic of the work of those who are not content to remain within the safe confines of past theory and practice, and who know that to stand still is to betray an approach whose very key is to remain open to experience, despite the confusion and challenge this engenders.

Brian Thorne
Elke Lambers

Acknowledgements

Those of us for whom English is our maternal or adopted tongue often fail to realize how frustrating it can be to endure the superior attitude that implies that nothing of importance is ever written in any other language. We wish to pay particular tribute therefore to the linguistic abilities of many of our non-British contributors who were able to produce working manuscripts that did not require Herculean editorial revision. We also gratefully acknowledge the work of Elisabeth Zinschitz, person-centred therapist and professional translator, who did so much to bring the contributions of Peter Schmid and Ute Binder to their English fruition. We know that there are other anonymous linguistic consultants who equally deserve our thanks.

There are many who have been involved in the word-processing of the various contributions to this volume, but particular thanks are due to Christine Jope and Jane Ramsbottom of the University Counselling Service of the University of East Anglia, Norwich, for their meticulous work in wrestling with the complexities of compatible discs at different stages of the book's evolution.

1 The Person-Centred Approach in Europe: Its History and Current Significance

Brian Thorne

In the summer of 1997 the Fourth International Conference on client-centred and experiential psychotherapy took place in Lisbon, Portugal. The previous three had been in Leuven, Belgium (1988), Stirling, Scotland (1991) and Gmunden, Austria (1994). The Lisbon conference saw the birth (ten years after Carl Rogers's death) of the World Association for Person-centred Counselling and Psychotherapy and the delegates voted over-whelmingly that the next international conference should be held in Chicago as the appropriate venue both to mark the millennium and to acknowledge the 'home' of the approach.

The person-centred community in Portugal is currently not large but, as in neighbouring Spain, the influence of Rogers and person-centred ideas is growing and therapeutic practitioners with a clearly defined allegiance to the approach are increasing as training opportunities become more numerous. In Eastern Europe, too, the approach is gaining ground with the demise of the Soviet bloc and the emergence of more democratic regimes. Even in the former Yugoslavia, torn apart as it has been by hatred and violence, psychologists and others are eager to become acquainted with Rogers's writings and the application of the person-centred approach both in therapy and in other fields. When Rogers himself visited Poland in 1979 he spoke to audiences thirsting for the liberation of the individual spirit and, although there is currently no professional association committed to the person-centred approach and no formal training programme, Rogers's work is well known and contributes richly to the creative eclecticism which characterizes the present Polish psychotherapeutic scene. When he died in February 1987 Rogers was about to embark on a second trip to Russia, and a recent visit which I received in Norwich from a psychology student from the University of St Petersburg provided evidence that his ideas have not fallen on stony ground.

In the former Czechoslovakia the first reference to client-centred psycho-therapy appeared in a psychology textbook written by Stanislav Kratochvil in 1966. Kratochvil subsequently studied in the USA, where he met Rogers, and on his return to his homeland spent many uncomfortable years as an external assistant at Brno University before being fired in 1978 because of his lack of support for Marxist ideology and his informal teaching style (deCarvalho and Cermák, 1997). Since the revolution of 1989 Kratochvil has been fully rehabilitated as Professor of Clinical Psychology, and person-centred theory and practice now flourish in both the Czech and Slovak Republics. The first formal Rogerian group was the Rogers Psychotherapeutic Association presided over by Vladimir Hlavenka who in the dying months of the old regime organized the first person-centred workshop in Czechoslavakia with Chuck Devonshire from the USA as the principal facilitator. Hlavenka now leads the Person-Centred Approach Institute – Ister in Slovakia, while in the Czech Republic there are institutes in Prague and in Brno. What is more, the person-centred approach is currently taught in both the Faculty of Letters and the Faculty of Medicine at the Charles University in Prague.

These developments demonstrate the continuing capacity of the person-centred approach to win new adherents and to respond to the needs of professionals and their clients in many European countries, both East and West. Such developments are but the latest evidence of the vitality of the approach on the European continent. This book has as its aim the presentation of some of the innovative ideas and practical applications which are the outcome of the committed work of European scholars and practitioners at a time when the growing power of insurance companies to determine potential clientele, the emergence of new and often restrictive national mental health policies and a move towards the 'manualization' of therapeutic procedures are creating both philosophical and practical difficulties for person-centred practitioners in many parts of the world, not least in the USA where the work of humanistic therapists in general is under threat from such developments.

Contributors to the present volume are drawn for the most part from those countries where the approach has been a significant force for some 20 years or more. By far the largest professional association of person-centred practitioners is to be found in Germany where the Gesellschaft für wissenschaftliche Gesprächspsychotherapie (GwG), founded in 1970, now has some 7,300 members and constitutes the largest professional body of psychotherapists and counsellors in the country. The psychologist, Reinhard Tausch, was responsible for establishing the first training programme in client-centred therapy at the University of Hamburg in the 1960s and in the 30 years since then the approach has become firmly established within the universities so that today it is represented in 76 per cent of psychology departments. The approach is in no way confined to a narrow emphasis on one-to-one psychotherapy but its relevant application to group work, social education, personal development, pastoral work and many other fields is acknowledged through training programmes and special interest groups. In Germany, too, much innovative work is taking place in the applicability of the approach to work with children and adolescents as well as with old people and those suffering from serious psychiatric disorders. As a result person-centred practitioners are currently to be found in a wide variety of settings including schools, hospitals and churches as well as clinical units specializing in marital or family therapy, crisis intervention, and many other specialist areas. At postgraduate level, too, there are courses leading to qualifications for those wishing to be more effective supervisors or trainers. The powerful presence of the approach within the university system also ensures a solid base for both outcome and process research studies.

There are those who would claim that the very success of the approach in Germany has led to a certain rigidity or conformism – a kind of 'respectability' which threatens to stifle creativity. It is well known that Rogers himself viewed with some anxiety what he perceived to be an increasing 'dirigisme' in the GwG in the early 1980s and Reinhard Tausch, too, has had his difficulties with the direction of the Association in recent years. However justified some of these misgivings might have been, there can be no doubt that the spread of person-centred ideas and practice in Germany has been extensive and shows little sign of abating. The chapters by Eva-Maria Biermann-Ratjen and Ute Binder in this present book provide powerful evidence of the major contribution of German scholars and practitioners to the understanding of personality development and to the growing effectiveness of the approach with the seriously disturbed.

It was no accident that the First International Conference took place in Belgium. As early as 1949 Professor J.R. Nuttin of the Catholic University of Leuven was writing in one of his books of 'non-directive therapy'. Fifteen years later it was Nuttin who was chiefly responsible for the intro-duction of the first formal postgraduate training in the client-centred approach within the Faculty of Psychology at Leuven. In the intervening years, J. Rombauts became the first Belgian student to complete a thesis on Carl Rogers's theories (1957), R. Van Balen was installed as the first client-centred student counsellor (1959), Rombauts went to work with Rogers, Gendlin and Truax at Wisconsin (1962–3) and returned to Belgium equipped to launch the first training programme with Nuttin's encourage-ment in 1964.

Carl Rogers himself visited Leuven in 1966 and lectured to a large audience at the university. His visit followed closely on the founding of the Centrum voor Client-centered Therapie en Counseling and served to inspire and invigorate the young staff of the centre. Three years later, Germain Lietaer went to work with Rogers at La Jolla for a year (1969–70) and in 1974 a Flemish client-centred society was founded whose influence and membership have grown constantly over the past 20 years. For French-speaking Belgians the situation has been less favourable because of a lack of regular and well-established training opportunities in the universities, but a French-speaking association has also been founded and there are notable proponents of the client-centred tradition within its ranks. For the Flemish Society recent years have been marked by close and cordial co-operation with colleagues in the Netherlands and there have been several successful joint conferences and publications. Germain Lietaer, the long-standing Director of the Leuven Centre, has himself been a source of inspiration for many practitioners and it was thanks to his dynamic leadership that the First International Conference was launched and proved to be such a pivotal event in the development of the approach in Europe. The present book contains contributions both from Lietaer and from his close professional colleague at Leuven, Mia Leijssen, who has been a major influence in introducing the work of Gendlin and focusing to European practitioners. The rich application of person-centred theory and practice is further exemplified by chapters by Dion Van Werde and his colleague, Chris Deleu, who provide a fascinating insight into highly innovative work with psychotic persons within a conventional hospital setting. Van Werde and Deleu are close associates of Dr Garry Prouty and their work is a striking example of the European application of ideas and practices developed in more recent years in the country of the approach's origin. They also provide further evidence that person-centred therapy in Belgium is alive and well and can look forward to a balanced and creative future both within the university context and within clinical settings.

In the same year that Rogers's ideas were being introduced into Belgium by Nuttin (1949), there appeared in the Netherlands an article by Van Lennep entitled 'The Development of Clinical Psychology in the United States' in which the writer presented the main ideas posited by Rogers in his first book *Counseling and Psychotherapy* (1942). Four years later, in 1953, the psychiatrist, Kamp, gave a lecture for the Dutch Association for Psychotherapy in which he attempted to explain the main principles and implications of 'client-centredness'. Interest in the approach rapidly increased and this was much aided by training courses directed by Ella Goubitz who had studied with Rogers between 1950 and 1952. Prior to Kamp's lecture, Toine Vossen had already started a client-centred child therapy course in Nijmegen and the 1950s saw the first steps towards the creation of an association for client-centred therapy mainly thanks to the initiatives of Cremers and Jan Dijkhuis. This association was formally established in 1962 and immediately began to offer its own training programme for potential members. Radical aspects of the programme were obligatory sensitivity training and the requirement to conduct several therapeutic processes under supervision. With the passage of time, the training programme has become more complex and demanding so that today it takes some five or six years to complete the curriculum largely as part of a postgraduate psychotherapy training provided by Regional Institutes for Postgraduate Training and Education. What is highly significant is the fact that client-centred therapy stands alongside psychoanalysis, behaviour therapy and systems therapy as one of the four mainstream therapies in which trainees can choose to specialize during their basic professional training. This indicates the current secure position of the person-centred approach within the spectrum of therapeutic orientations in the Netherlands. This is crucial in a country where psychotherapy is now subject to legal statute and where the completion of postgraduate training is a requirement for registration as a psychotherapist by the Ministry of Health.

Interestingly, in the early years client-centred therapy was applied mainly in the treatment of vulnerable and underprivileged people such as those in psychiatric hospitals and delinquent and disenchanted youth. This is no longer the case, and among the 950 or so members of the client-centred association there are many who operate outside the structures of institutional life and who provide help for those who are wrestling with a wide variety of issues both within clinical settings and outside them. Person-centred scholars are also concerned to relate the theory of the approach to wider existential questions and to an understanding of human development and personality formation. The contributions to this book from Martin van Kalmthout of the University of Nijmegen provide excellent examples of Dutch practitioners' willingness to battle with issues of meaning and personality change without losing sight of the day-to-day challenges of clinical practice. The contribution from Lidwien Geertjens and Olga Waaldijk reflects the long-standing interest of Dutch practitioners in the problems of adolescence and is also an example of a willingness to be open to other orientations.

In Great Britain the ideas of Carl Rogers first surfaced in the context of the work of the Marriage Guidance Council (now called Relate) during the late 1950s and early 1960s. In the mid-1960s client-centred therapy was first taught in British universities, mainly by visiting Fulbright professors from America, as part of the core curriculum for those training to become school counsellors at the Universities of Keele and Reading. The surge of interest in humanistic psychology in general which swept London at the end of the 1960s resulted in the emergence of a loosely knit network of persons mainly in education and social work for whom Rogers became a principal source of inspiration. In 1974 Rogers himself had been invited to Britain but his wife's grave illness at the time made him cancel the visit which had been initiated by a young psychologist from Scotland, Dave Mearns, who had studied with Rogers at La Jolla in 1971–2.

Over 200 people had signed up for the workshop at which Rogers was to appear but this number fell to a mere 90 when it became known that Rogers himself would not be coming. The event went ahead nonetheless and a key figure was Dr Charles (Chuck) Devonshire from the College of San Mateo in California, Director of the Centre for Cross-Cultural Communication and a close associate of Rogers. It was thanks to the co-operative efforts of Devonshire, Mearns, Elke Lambers, a Dutch client-centred therapist living in Scotland, and myself that the Facilitator Development Institute (British Centre) came into being in 1975, and for the following decade provided annual summer residential workshops for members of the helping professions who wished to learn more of person-centred theory and practice especially with reference to small and large group work.

In 1976 the British Association for Counselling was founded and its first executive committee contained both person-centred practitioners and others sympathetic to the approach. The growth of the BAC in the past 20 years has been immense and its membership now totals some 15,000. Of these a significant number describe themselves as person-centred practitioners and many have held or currently hold key positions in the Association. Dave Mearns is the present Chair of the Association's Professional Committee and Elke Lambers was for many years Chair of its Accreditation Committee.

In 1985 Mearns, Lambers, Thorne and William Hallidie Smith developed the work of the Facilitator Development Institute by offering the first full-scale training for person-centred therapists, and the Institute (renamed Person-Centred Therapy, Britain in 1988) continued to offer such training until 1997. During the same period Devonshire was energetically developing training programmes throughout Europe and his Person-Centred Approach Institute International began to offer a British programme in 1987. A splinter group from Devonshire's original staff team subsequently founded the Institute for Person-Centred Learning and all three of these private institutes continue to offer professional training at a basic or advanced level.

In contrast to the American experience where client-centred work first established itself in the universities but, with Rogers's disenchantment with the university system, then moved outside, the British movement has been in the reverse direction. While other private training institutes now offer programmes in person-centred therapy (most notably Metanoia in London) there can be no doubt that the major advances in theory, training, research and practice are to be found in the Universities of Strathclyde (in Glasgow), East Anglia and Keele where Mearns, Thorne and John McLeod (a graduate of the first Facilitator Development Institute programme) all hold chairs in counselling or counselling studies. As there are currently only four such chairs in British universities, this is a significant power base for the person-centred approach in Britain. Graduates from these university-based training programmes as well as those from the private institutes now form the bulk of the membership of the British Association for the Person-Centred Approach (BAPCA) which was founded in the late 1980s in order to give the approach its own unique voice in the British therapeutic world. In Scotland, too, the Association for Person-Centred Therapy (Scotland) has a membership of about a hundred therapists and owes much of its vitality to the work of Person-Centred Therapy (Britain) and the Counselling Unit in the University of Strathclyde where opportunities for post-diploma training are now offered.

The British contributors to the present book all work in the University of East Anglia, with Purton and Moore having trained originally in the private sector, and Hawtin having received her professional training in the university of which she is now a staff member. Their backgrounds in philosophy and English literature give their contributions the freshness which often typifies the work of British authors in this field where first degrees in psychology are not a prerequisite for professional training and advancement.

Mention has already been made of the commitment of Dr Chuck Devonshire to the development of the person-centred approach throughout Europe and there needs to be a generous acknowledgement of his formidable accomplishments in this endeavour. Both through his Centre for Cross-Cultural Communication and through the creation of various facilitator development institutes, Devonshire was instrumental in introducing person-centred ideas and practice to countless European nationals in the 1970s and 1980s. The founding of the Person-Centred Approach Institute International (with its original headquarters in Lugano) was jointly undertaken by Devonshire and Rogers himself, who continued to participate in its training programmes until shortly before his death in 1987. The Institute is committed to the training both of person-centred therapists and those who wish to apply the approach in other settings – most notably education and youth work. Its influence has been crucial in those countries where there was little 'indigenous' knowledge of Rogers's work or where there had previously been little or no opportunity for formal training in the approach. Italy, Greece and, to a lesser extent, France are countries where without Devonshire's energetic contribution the approach would be far less well known than it currently is. All three countries now have thriving institutes and/or associations and in France the journal *Mouvance Rogérienne*, founded in 1994 and edited by Micheline Bezaud, is proving an excellent channel of communication. Amazingly, too, in France the former senior official in the Ministry of Education, André de Peretti, who was mainly responsible for Rogers's controversial visit to France in 1966, remains a powerful advocate of the person-centred approach and actively contributes to the professional literature and to experiential workshops and conferences. Both de Peretti and the distinguished scholar, Max Pagès, continue in their old age to give person-centred ideas credibility in a country where psychoanalysis exercised a governing influence until comparatively recently. In Greece, a recent development has been the recognition of the training course offered by Polly Iossifides and her colleagues at the Centre for Education in the Person-Centred Approach, by the University of Strathclyde in Scotland as a graduate diploma course equivalent to the qualification received by British students studying at Strathclyde. This is perhaps the most notable example yet of cross-cultural co-operation within the European continent serving the best interests of high-quality training in the person-centred approach. Without the original enthusiasm of the indefatigable Dr Devonshire it is doubtful if such an outcome could ever have come about. It was Devonshire, too, who from the outset invited into the directorship of the Person-Centred Approach Institute International a charismatic and forceful Italian, Alberto Zucconi, and the two of them were primarily responsible for the introduction into Italy of person-centred training during the 1980s. In 1986 Professor Aldo Dinacci founded the Istituto di Psicologia della Persona et della Personalita and this institute in recent years has introduced Italian therapists to the work of Gendlin and Prouty.

In Scandinavia Rogers's ideas are widespread but there is, as yet, no formal person-centred assocation committed to systematic training and scholarly research. In December 1997, however, I had the pleasure of presenting a paper and leading a seminar in London for a group of Norwegian scholars and practitioners, led and inspired by Ragnvald Kvalsund of the University of Trondheim, who have a deep interest in Rogers's ideas and particularly in the relevance of person-centred practice to new forms of spiritual expression in contemporary society. Norway is also the home of Professor Leif Braaten who has held a chair in psychology in the University of Oslo since 1964 and has been the chief representative of the person-centred approach in Norway and Scandinavia throughout the whole of that time. Braaten studied with Rogers in Chicago from 1955 to 1959, having previously rejected the mainstream psychoanalytical approach in Norway as uncongenial to his temperament. After a period as an associate professor at Cornell University he returned to his native country and has continued to uphold the person-centred tradition among a group of colleagues committed to the psychodynamic approach. It says much for them that Braaten has flourished in this environment and has produced a series of books on client-centred counselling, students' emotional problems and, more specifically, on group work and its applications which have had a significant impact on the Scandinavian academic scene. Braaten's contibution to this book explores some of his more recent work on the use of groups in the development of leadership skills and team-building for managers within industrial and other settings. It is a fine example of how one person with a deep commitment to the approach can exercise considerable influence within his academic and social community.

Austria boasts no fewer than three registered person-centred associations which offer training in person-centred therapy and are recognized by the Austrian Ministry of Health. Such recognition has become a critical matter since the introduction of the Law of Psychotherapy (1990) which defines, among other things, mininum training standards and licensing requirements. This law has influenced the whole professional field profoundly and the person-centred community has not been exempt. There is now more formalism and competitiveness and the baleful effect of 'market forces' has induced a commercial orientation which often sits uncomfortably with person-centred values.

Carl Rogers himself visited Austria in 1981 and 1984 and lectured at the University of Vienna as well as participating in workshops and holding discussions with prominent representatives of the major therapeutic schools. Since that time the Reverend Doug Land, a close associate of Rogers, has frequently visited Austria and spent lengthy periods of time there. In 1990, too, the two largest training associations – the Österreichische Gesellschaft für wissenschaftliche, klientenzentrierte Psychotherapie und personorientierte Gesprächsführung (OeGWG), founded in 1974 and the Arbeitsgemeinschaft für personenzentrierte Psychotherapie und Gesprächsführung und Supervision (APG), founded in 1979 – combined to organize a joint conference near Vienna to celebrate the fiftieth anniversary of the founding of client-centred therapy. This major event, with presentations from Hans Swildens of the Netherlands, Germain Lietaer of Belgium and myself, gave ample evidence of the health and vigour of the approach in Austria. It was therefore not surprising when it was the Austrian contingent which, the following year at the Second International Conference in Scotland, emerged as the organizers designate for the 1994 conference. The resulting event at Gmunden provided further evidence of the confidence of Austrian person-centred practitioners who now form one of the largest groups of licensed psychotherapists in the country. Peter Schmid has been a prime mover of the approach for many years and has contributed handsomely to the professional literature. His varied academic background in psychology and theology is very much in evidence in his deeply reflective chapters on the person and on encounter in the present book.

The lack of Swiss contributors to this volume is no reflection on the vitality of the approach there. The first pioneers in the early 1970s received their training from Reinhard Tausch in Hamburg and were certified by the German GwG. In 1979, however, the Swiss Association for Client-Centred Psychotherapy was founded and since that time has been highly active in offering training programmes both for aspiring psychotherapists and for others wishing to apply the approach in different professional fields. The Association has also been powerfully influential in achieving recognition of the approach within the national context. It currently has some 550 members, of whom 140 are certified client-centred psychotherapists, and it also publishes a quarterly journal *Brennpunkt* which often contains articles culled from the international person-centred community.

So rapid and dynamic is the spread of the person-centred approach throughout Europe at the present time that I am conscious of the likely incompleteness, inaccuracy and inadequacy of the above overview. It will also assuredly be out of date by the time this book is published. For British readers, however, an important purpose will have been achieved if they are disabused of the idea that the person-centred approach is a fragile sapling among the sturdy trees of the psychodynamic and cognitive behavioural traditions. The strength and vitality of the developments throughout the European continent (and the historical rootedness of many of them) demonstrate that Rogers's ideas are in no way alien to the European spirit but owe much to European philosophies and religious streams of thought. (This is particularly illuminated by Peter Schmid's contributions to the present volume.) What is more, at a time when psychotherapy and coun-selling have yet to achieve a paradigm for the field, there is much evidence to suggest that the person-centred framework of thought with its emphasis on relationships, the self-concept and the internal locus of evaluation may be better positioned to provide such a paradigm than most of its current rivals. As the new millennium approaches, person-centred practitioners have every reason to be proud of what has been achieved in the European context and to feel hopeful for the future.

Acknowledgements

I am particularly grateful to the following for their generous assistance in providing information for this introductory chapter:

Micheline Bezaud	–	France
Leif Braaten	–	Norway
Czeslaw Czabala	–	Poland
Aldo Dinacci	–	Italy
Robert Hutterer	–	Austria
Polly Iossifides	–	Greece
Dora Iseli-Schudel	–	Switzerland
Václav Lepičovský	–	Czech Republic
Marlis Pörtner	–	Switzerland
Thomas Reckzeh-Schubert	–	Germany
Roelf Takens	–	Netherlands
Richard Van Balen	–	Belgium

Reference

deCarvalho, R.J. and Čermák, I. (1997) 'History of humanistic psychology in Czechoslovakia', *Journal of Humanistic Psychology*, 37 (1): 110–30.

PART I

THEORY

2 Person-Centred Theory as a System of Meaning

Martin van Kalmthout

The central objective of this chapter is to explore whether person-centred theory has a contribution to make to resolving the old issue of life's meaning. Related questions to be addressed pertain to the advantages and disadvantages of taking person-centred theory as a system of meaning and not just a therapeutic method.

Questions about the meaning of life are no longer the exclusive domain of philosophy and religion but have become legitimate issues for empirical research and theorizing in the social sciences (Baumeister, 1991; Debats, 1996). In psychotherapeutic practice these questions are also an increasing part of the therapeutic agenda (Yalom, 1980). This state of affairs is certainly related to the decline of traditional religions, which do not seem to be able to provide modern men and women with a convincing system of beliefs. Jung was one of the first psychotherapists to suggest that psychology, and especially psychotherapy, might replace religion by offering a new system of meaning. This view of the function of modern psychotherapy is especially characteristic of humanistic psychotherapies, which provide many people with new meanings and values. Such psychotherapeutic approaches go far beyond the treatment of symptoms/conditions and offer a complete view of human nature and the good life.

Although many psychotherapists would prefer to present their approach as based on a neutral scientific method, closer scrutiny shows that psychotherapeutic systems – just like religious ones – contain either an implicit or an explicit system of values that provides an answer to the age-old question of the meaning of life (Bergin, 1980). This might even be true for the more technically oriented psychotherapies such as behaviour therapy, which have their own worldview, rightly designated by Woolfolk and Richardson (1984) as 'the behavioural Weltanschauung'. One way of looking at the relation between psychotherapies and religious or philosophical systems is, therefore, to consider them functionally equivalent as far as the question of the meaning of life is concerned (Kilbourne and Richardson, 1984). That is to say that they serve the same function in so far as both provide a way of viewing the meaning of life for members of contemporary society.

The question of the meaning of life can be understood in different ways by different people. One meaning, which is common among psychotherapists, refers to the personal significance of life (or the lack of it). This is to say that life may take on a particular meaning or significance for a particular individual given certain values, endeavours and experiences. When these are lacking (for example, absence of a good job or a satisfying relationship), life may become meaningless for that person. For others, life may also be meaningful (or meaningless) for quite different reasons. The statement 'To me life is worthwhile for this or that reason' reflects the unique significance of the question to each individual in the search for meaning.

A second meaning, which is common among religious people, concerns the purpose of all life and the cosmos. The statement 'The meaning of all life is this or that' reflects this all-encompassing, general perspective. For example, the meaning of life is to reach point Omega, as proposed by Teilhard de Chardin.

In the present chapter, the response of person-centred theory to both these questions will be considered. By person-centred theory, I mean – for simplicity's sake – the theory developed by Carl Rogers in his main statements (Rogers, 1951, 1959, 1961, 1980a).

Clinical practice and the meaning of life

Most professional clinicians today are not particularly willing to include questions about the meaning of life in a consideration of the work they are doing. They appear to limit themselves to the treatment of symptoms or to working with well-defined clinical disorders. This situation is in part the result of economic pressures and in part reflects the current intellectual *Zeitgeist* in which no-nonsense thinking and a highly technical approach to the treatment of psychological problems dominate. In such a climate, questions regarding the meaning of life are relegated to other domains and are seen as the province of other professionals including ministers of religion, gurus, shamans, and various types of healers. Nevertheless, clinicians are confronted by questions about the meaning of life, whether they like it or not. The following vignettes serve to illustrate this point.

She was a 22-year-old girl, good looking, and intelligent. In the last three years, she had suffered several psychotic episodes for which she was treated in hospital.

During one of these episodes, she tried to commit suicide. During another, she went to the police station to report her parents for having tortured her. This had not in fact happened but was an expression of the way in which she had been treated emotionally as a child. She was a typical example of parentification. As the oldest daughter, she had taken care of the family while her mother (and later her father) was ill. In her present life, she was unable to undertake higher education (and eventually a job) or to develop social relationships. This was made all the more dramatic by the fact that she intensely desired both of these things. After several years of trying to do so in vain, she came to me and said that she no longer wanted to live in this way and was looking for professional help in order to terminate life.

She was a 60-year-old woman, very proper, referred to me by her general practitioner because of serious depressive symptoms. She was ashamed of her present state and did not like psychotherapists. She asked for some advice and did not want to go too far or 'too deep into the past'. It turned out that she had lost all purpose in life since her children had left home and her husband had retired. The latter had, with the best of intentions, taken over a lot of her housekeeping activities. She no longer saw a useful function for her life and longed to end it.

He was an 18-year-old boy who could not make a decision about his future education or jobs. He enjoyed life in terms of sports, friends, and other leisure activities but he did not like going to school or studying. It was nevertheless important to him to earn money and thus participate in society. He was not able to discipline himself enough, and he could not find what really interested him. He used to talk philosophically about society and life but was now quite sceptical about both. In fact, he was very uncertain about himself and felt that his future in society was very grim. He could not find a meaningful perspective for moving on and giving shape to his life.

At the age of 30, she lost her husband to cancer. At his instigation and although they knew his cancer was terminal, they had decided to have a child. She does not find her life together with her son very pleasant. At the same time, she feels ashamed of these feelings and condemns herself for having them. In fact, she had never aspired to become a mother. What she wanted was to live her own life and have her own profession. She is clearly not able to live such a life now and feels extremely constrained by her present situation. She also feels guilty towards her son and her deceased husband. These feelings of guilt block her from giving shape to her life according to her own standards, and depression and a lack of meaning in life are the result.

Many more examples could be provided in which the question of the meaning of life comes up in a very concrete and urgent form. Generally speaking, psychotherapists will be guided by their own theoretical framework in approaching such existential problems, and this implies the formulation of the presenting problems in their own language, in order to treat them in familiar ways. The values and the worldview of the psychotherapist will play a role right from the beginning and will determine his or her course of action. Psychotherapists generally have an implicit or explicit image of the goal to be striven for and how that goal should be reached. This is certainly the case for person-centred therapists, as will be seen in the next section.

Person-centred theory and the meaning of life

What, according to person-centred theory, is the meaning of life? As indicated before, there are two aspects to this broad question: (1) What is the meaning of life for me ('personal meaning')? (2) What is the meaning of life in a more general, absolute sense ('cosmic meaning')?

Personal meaning

Basic to person-centred theory is the conviction that personal experience is the highest authority (Rogers, 1961: 23). Rogers generally hypothesized that children introject the values of others in order to gain positive regard. Problems arise when they start to view these introjected values as their own. They can then become alienated from their own, inner, organismically based valuing process. They thus learn to have a basic *dis*trust of their own experiencing as a guide to behaviour (Rogers, 1964: 162–5). The goal of therapy is to reverse this pattern and help the client to select his or her own values. The locus of the evaluating process is not to be found in external values, authorities or institutions (including psychotherapeutic schools) but within oneself. The postulate of the actualizing tendency constitutes the foundation of a trust in the organismic self, which – contrary to the values of the conditioned self with all the conditions of worth imposed from the outside – is wiser than the intellect.

The basic tenet of person-centred theory places the person-centred therapist in a paradoxical position. On the one hand, the therapist will never seek to guide the client to a particular value or goal. On the other hand, the therapist is explicitly and actively guiding the client towards contact with his or her inner, organismic self and away from external authorities (including person-centred therapy itself as an external value-system). In other words, the therapist is actively trying to facilitate the client's movement from the outer world of the conditions of worth into the inner world of the organismic valuing process (Van Kalmthout, 1995). For that reason, it is not correct to say that person-centred therapy is a neutral therapeutic technique or method. On the contrary, and as Rogers often emphasized, person-centred theory is first and foremost a basic philosophy or way of being. On the other hand, clients are not seduced or manipulated into a particular belief-system but are offered the climate in which to take the risk of experiencing reality as it is to them. In this sense, person-centred theory is not just a theory but a description of what it means for every individual to trust the experience of his or her subjective reality.

According to person-centred theory, the answer to the question of the meaning of life is first and foremost the product of the personal experience of each individual: every individual has to find out for himself or herself what the meaning of life is. The basic philosophy of the person-centred approach nevertheless has an explicit process for resolving this question, namely that everybody should actualize his or her real self and move away from the prison of the conditions of worth into alignment with the actualizing tendency. The foregoing is summarized in the following well-known statement from Rogers: 'The best way I can state this aim of life, as I see it coming to light in my relationship with my clients, is to use the words of Søren Kierkegaard – to be that self which one truly is' (1961: 166). This sentence implies a move away from façades, oughts, meeting expectations, and pleasing others. It means the positive movement towards self-direction, process, complexity, openness to experience, acceptance of others and trust of self. Again, according to Rogers:

> It seems to mean that the individual moves toward *being*, knowingly and acceptingly, the process which he inwardly and actually *is*. He moves away from being what he is not, from being a facade. He is not trying to be more than he is, with the attendant feelings of insecurity or bombastic defensiveness. He is not trying to be less than he is, with the attendant feelings of guilt or self-depreciation. He is increasingly listening to the deepest recesses of his physiological and emotional being, and finds himself increasingly willing to be, with greater accuracy and depth, that self which he most truly is. (1961: 176)

In this way, person-centred theory holds that each individual person, following the unique path of his or her life, touches upon the same general meaning of life. That is why Rogers could state that the most personal is the most general (Rogers, 1961: 26).

Cosmic meaning

The following statement by Rogers also provides an answer to the question of cosmic meaning:

> I am suggesting that this view contains the seeds of a philosophical approach to all of life, that it is more than a trend observed in the experience of clients. (1961: 180)

Person-centred theory, as formulated by Rogers, can be generalized even further, from the individual client to all of humankind and to life itself in all of its manifestations, both organic and inorganic. This view of Rogers is most explicitly expressed in a chapter in his book *A Way of Being* (Rogers, 1980b). In addition to the actualizing tendency as a characteristic of organic life, Rogers also postulates the formative tendency, as a characteristic of the universe as a whole. He emphasizes that the two tendencies are the foundation blocks of the person-centred approach and the theoretical base for the building of a true humanistic psychology.

With the formative tendency, Rogers suggests that the meaning of life is to be found in the cosmos and for individuals in their participation in this evolutionary life flow. In living his or her personal, organismic, experiential process, the individual already takes part in the stream of life. Being part of the species, he or she experiences that which is, firstly, common to all of humanity and, secondly, common to all living organisms and even to matter. This organismic experience can provide a feeling of unity with all that exists. That is, going deep into this bodily experience, one can come into contact with the universal laws of nature and thus feel part of a universal order. This means that the personal is a kind of window on the universal. By moving away from the outer world (of the conditions of worth) into the inner world (of the organismic life flow), there is a union with the universal very much like the mystic's experience of unity with all that there is (Van Belle, 1980, 1990; Van Kalmthout, 1995).

Person-centred theory has all of the characteristics of a philosophy of life or worldview, with a clear view of life's meaning. Although person-centred theory stresses personal meaning, Rogers formulated outspoken views on the general meaning of life and of the cosmos.

Advantages and disadvantages of taking person-centred theory as a system of meaning

The advantage of taking person-centred theory as a philosophy of life and not just a psychotherapeutic approach is open to question. The opponents of the philosophy of life view will point to the risk that the theory construed in this way will foster a quasi-religious movement or encourage the development of a sect with all the dangers of dogmas and rituals. This would exclude, they fear, a genuinely scientific approach and reduce the theory to the level of faith, magic and religion (O'Hara, 1995; Vitz, 1994).

Person-centred theory, like other psychotherapeutic approaches, certainly runs the danger of becoming a dogmatic, ritualized system of belief. Other psychotherapeutic approaches, such as psychoanalysis, have become orthodoxies used to convert clients to a particular therapeutic faith. It should be noted, however, that person-centred theory is first and foremost a way of being that provides the climate for every individual to find out for himself or herself what it means to live life to the full. It is an experiential, open-ended approach to life in which the personal experience of the individual is considered the highest authority. Contrary to traditional religion, no external authorities are recognized, not even the organized system of person-centred therapy. This fundamental tenet prevents dogma, moralism and pre-programmed approaches to life while emphasizing the experience of what and who one really is.

One clear advantage of conceptualizing person-centred theory as a philosophy of life is that the adherents are motivated to live this way of being themselves. It is incongruent to live differently from what one preaches. As a person-centred therapist or teacher, one cannot be neutral or indifferent to the basic values and goals of person-centred theory. The theory constitutes a living part of one's personal life: 'It means taking a stand and affirming values' (Thorne, 1991: 113). It also implies, as Rogers has stated, a lifelong journey. This way of being is not for the faint-hearted but for those who seriously want to endeavour to live life in all its complexity. We might well assume that this seriousness of intent will make all the difference to the therapist's life and to each and every one of his or her relationships, including the client–therapist relationship.

In present-day clinical practice, clinicians are often preoccupied with the treatment of well-described symptoms and psychological disorders. As already suggested, they appear to be more symptom oriented than person oriented. Psychotherapy is construed as a technical procedure aimed at the reduction or removal of symptoms. This is, in fact, a medical/psychiatric approach to psychological problems and to life. And within such an approach, there is no place for questions regarding life itself: Who am I really? What is the meaning of my life? What do I value the most in life? What is the origin or purpose of life? As a system of meaning, person-centred theory does not exclude these questions. On the contrary, every human experience, whether psychological, interpersonal, existential or religious, can be the focus of person-centred exploration. This is certainly of great value to all those clients who do not want to limit their exploration to medically defined categories. Such a view of the goals of psychotherapy, however, can only be practised in the light of an experientially based philosophy of life and manner of living. All of this is not to say that the ultimate questions should be immediately raised with every client and the particular conditions/symptoms of the client ignored. Client-centredness prevents such a stance. The person-centred therapist is aware of all the complexities of life and is prepared, in following the actual experience of clients, to help them see and experience as far as possible and desired the deeper levels of their symptoms. This is the critical extra dimension that person-centred therapy as a basic philosophy of life has to offer and to which symptom-oriented psychotherapies attach no significance.

This raises a final question in regard to the taking of person-centred theory as a system of meaning: should the concept of cosmic meaning, as conceptualized by Rogers, be included in person-centred theory and be seen as a legitimate concern in therapy? This may well depend upon whether it makes any difference to the actual practice of psychotherapy. If so, it should definitely be taken on board (as Thorne, 1991, 1992 has proposed). If not, cosmic meaning should be considered superfluous. Whatever the content of a particular view of cosmic meaning, the experience of unity with all that there is stands as a central issue. Most people today – including both clients and therapists – have little sense of being connected to life and the cosmos.

They have succeeded in developing autonomy but nevertheless feel estranged, lonely, and afraid of death. Most psychotherapeutic systems, and person-centred therapy in particular, have made an important contribution to furthering the development of autonomy. At the same time, however, such systems have basically failed to foster feelings of belonging and connectedness. Rogers seems to have felt this one-sidedness and as a result tried to redress the balance. His formative tendency is conceptualized as the cosmic source of the actualizing tendency, which is at work within the individual. Whether this conceptualization is true or not does not seem to be of particular significance. What is important is the fact that this view of life places the individual with his or her personal problems in a much wider context which can then be explored in the same way as the context of interpersonal relationships has been explored. It is hard to resist the thought that person-centred theory might well be a good candidate for helping modern man and woman in their search for cosmic meaning, because it represents a secular, innerworldly, almost biological view of humanity and the cosmos, without any of the overt trappings of religion or mysticism.

Discussion

It should be noted that the view presented here of person-centred theory as a way of being is not in keeping with the stance of those person-centred theorists and practitioners who, in line with the present climate of no-nonsense thinking, see it as no more than a psychotherapeutic approach or method. I am convinced, however, that in adopting this narrow perspective they miss not only the essence of the approach but also hinder its further development as a modern system of meaning. In my opinion, person-centred theory should be taken out of its limited psychotherapeutic context and placed within the wider scope of the philosophical traditions of personalism, humanism and existentialism (Schmid, 1991; Van Deurzen-Smith, 1988; Van Kalmthout and Pelgrim, 1990).

The later development of person-centred theory by Rogers in the direction of a way of being (including cosmic meaning) has been rejected by many of his followers. One representative example is Van Belle who stated:

> By moving from a way of doing to a way of being Rogers may have exceeded the bounds of therapeutic thought and may have given us a philosophy of life, a worldview or even a religion instead. (1990: 54)

I agree with Van Belle on this point, especially with his analysis that this later move was prefigured in Rogers's earlier writings, in which a preference for attitude rather than technique, for being and becoming rather than doing, is already evident. It demonstrates that it is more accurate to conceptualize Rogers's contribution as a system of meaning rather than as a therapeutic technique. I disagree with Van Belle, however, when he suggests that this means the ending of Rogers's role as the defender of individual persons, or inevitably implies a world-avoiding fundamentalistic view, not unlike the Christian version of Rogers's own parents (Van Kalmthout, 1995). In fact Rogers extended his approach to include experiences which in the past may well have been considered the exclusive domain of religion, but which are nowadays considered part of everyone's experience, whether one sees oneself as religious or not.

There are other person-centred therapists who favour the view that person-centred theory should include cosmic meaning. For example, Thorne has expressed the following point of view:

> Fifty years from now it is likely that Rogers will be remembered not so much as the founder of a new school of psychotherapy but as a psychologist whose work made it possible for men and women to apprehend spiritual reality at a time when conventional religion had lost its power to capture the minds and imagination of the vast majority. (1992: 105–6)

To him this does not mean that person-centred therapy inevitably becomes a dogmatic creed, where there is no place for personal autonomy. On the contrary:

> The most far-reaching of Rogers' many contributions may well turn out to be this assurance that in order to affirm our natures we do not have to put on the straitjacket of a common creed or shared dogma but can celebrate the mysterious paradox of our uniqueness and our membership one of another. (Thorne, 1992: 107)

Another example is Leijssen (1995), who has explored the possibility that the experiential process of focusing is for certain clients a doorway to cosmic meaning. By going deeply into the unique and personally 'felt sense' within the body, one may well tap into a deeper cosmic process. The resulting participation in this universal process is not the result of a formulated faith or theory, but of the client's unique process of experiencing. This process is therefore seen as a universal way to cosmic meaning, and has many well-known parallels in religious traditions.

Sommeling (1996) is another person-centred therapist who sees a bright future for person-centred theory and therapy as a system of meaning, with the potential to be of great help to modern men and women in their search for an answer to the meaning of life. He proposes that religion should be conceptualized very broadly. It is not a separate domain, but can embrace all levels of reality. In therapy this view is operative right from the beginning and makes client and therapist sensitive to what is authentic and what is really of ultimate importance. Sommeling suggests that we would do well to avoid the term 'religious' altogether, since it is misleading to many modern men and women because of its dogmatic and authoritarian associations. He is nevertheless of the opinion that religious experience in the true sense of the word adds a deeper dimension to the intrapsychic, interpersonal and even existential aspects of our problems. As this deeper level of our existence is intrinsically part of our experience, it is also rightly part of the domain of person-centred theory and therapy.

A number of students of psychotherapy have been interested in the relation between psychotherapy and systems of meaning, and have studied it as natural scientists. One prominent exponent of such an approach is Jerome Frank in his landmark study on the commonalities of all systems of healing, whether they be from the West or the East, 'primitive', scientific, magic, religous or otherwise (Frank, 1974). To this respected and influential student of psychotherapy it is evident that there is much in common between psychotherapies and systems of meaning:

> The suffering of many persons who seek psychotherapy includes some degree of spiritual malaise or existential anxiety, so psychotherapy cannot avoid issues concerning the meaning of life and other questions usually considered the exclusive province of philosophy or religion. Successful psychotherapy, along with other changes in the patient's values, often includes development of a more optimistic view concerning the meaning of existence. In this sense its results resemble those of a religious conversion. This may be characterized as a change in the person's attitudes towards God or the Universe, with concomitant changes in his attitudes toward himself and the people significant to him. (Frank, 1974: 79)

Luckmann (1967), a sociologist, is another natural scientist who has studied religion and systems of meaning in a scientific way. He is the inventor of the concept of 'the invisible religion'. According to him, modern systems of meaning have replaced the old religions, which no longer inspire modern man and woman in their search for meaning. Typical characteristics of such modern 'religions', according to Luckmann, are the centrality of self-realization, subjective experience, innerworldliness, and the absence of institutionalization. These secular systems, like religions in the past, reflect humankind's universal endeavour to give meaning to life and to answer the basic questions about life and the cosmos, the so-called 'ultimate concerns'. Person-centred theory is, in my opinion, a good example of what Luckmann calls the 'invisible religion'. To name Rogers 'a mystic – albeit an anti-religious one' (O'Hara, 1995: 41) is in line with this view.

This does not mean that science has no contribution to make to person-centred theory. It does mean, however, that a natural tension exists between science and the deepest human longings, and that this is inevitably so. Reduction of person-centred theory to either the scientific or the religious would be a serious error: the theory has to be put to the test continuously, scientifically and experientially (O'Hara, 1995). The search for meaning, for what is authentic and true, for what is really important, and for who we really are, never ends.

One important caveat in taking person-centred theory as a modern system of meaning needs to be emphasized. Like all systems of meaning it is culturally and historically determined and therefore inevitably one-sided and limited (Van Belle, 1980). To be fully aware of this is the best possible antidote to the theory becoming a dogmatic system of belief.

References

Baumeister, F. (1991) *Meanings of Life*. New York: Guilford.

Bergin, A. (1980) 'Psychotherapy and religious values', *Journal of Consulting and Clinical Psychology*, 48: 95–105.

Debats, D. (1996) 'Meaning in life: psychometric, clinical and phenomenological aspects'. Thesis, University of Groningen.

Frank, J. (1974) *Persuasion and Healing: A Comparative Study of Psychotherapy*. New York: Schocken Books.

Kilbourne, B. and Richardson, J. (1984) 'Psychotherapy and new religions in a pluralistic society', *American Psychologist*, 39: 237–51.

Leijssen, M. (1995) 'Focusing: psychotherapeutisch proces en religieuze ervaring', *Tijdschrift voor Psychotherapie*, 21: 24–36.

Luckmann, T. (1967) *The Invisible Religion: The Problem of Religion in Modern Society*. New York: Macmillan.

O'Hara, M. (1995) 'Rogers as scientist and mystic', *Journal of Humanistic Psychology*, 35 (4): 40–53.

Rogers, C. (1951) *Client-centered Therapy: Its Current Practice, Implications, and Theory*. Boston: Houghton Mifflin.

Rogers, C. (1959) 'A theory of therapy, personality, and interpersonal relationships, as developed in the client-centered framework', in S. Koch (ed.), *Psychology: A Study of a Science*, Vol. 3. New York: McGraw-Hill. pp. 184–256.

Rogers, C. (1961) *On Becoming a Person*. Boston: Houghton Mifflin.

Rogers, C. (1964) 'Toward a modern approach to values: the valuing process in the mature person', *Journal of Abnormal and Social Psychology*, 68: 160–7.

Rogers, C. (1980a) *A Way of Being*. Boston: Houghton Mifflin.

Rogers, C. (1980b) 'The foundations of a person-centered approach', in *A Way of Being*. Boston: Houghton Mifflin. pp. 113–36.

Schmid, P. (1991) *Person-zentriert: Grundlagen von Theorie und Praxis*. Mainz: Grünewald.

Sommeling, L. (1996) 'Wat als eerste komt', *Tijdschrift voor Psychotherapie*, 22: 38–46.

Thorne, B. (1991) *Person-centred Counselling: Therapeutic and Spiritual Dimensions*. London: Whurr.

Thorne, B. (1992) *Carl Rogers*. London: Sage.

Van Belle, H. (1980) *Basic Intent and Therapeutic Approach of Carl R. Rogers*. Toronto: Wedge.

Van Belle, H. (1990) 'Rogers' later move towards mysticism: implications for person-centered therapy', in G. Lietaer, J. Rombauts and R. Van Balen (eds), *Client-centered and Experiential Psychotherapy in the Nineties*. Leuven: Leuven University Press. pp. 47–57.

Van Deurzen-Smith, E. (1988) *Existential Counselling in Practice*. London: Sage.

Van Kalmthout, M. (1995) 'The religious dimension of Rogers' work', *Journal of Humanistic Psychology*, 35 (4): 23–39.

Van Kalmthout, M. and Pelgrim, F. (1990) 'In search of universal concepts in psychopathology and psychotherapy', in G. Lietaer, J. Rombauts and R. Van

Balen (eds), *Client-centered and Experiential Psychotherapy in the Nineties*. Leuven: Leuven University Press. pp. 381–96.

Vitz, P. (1994) *Psychology as Religion: The Cult of Self-worship*, 2nd edn. Grand Rapids, MI: Eerdmans, Carlisle: Paternoster Press.

Woolfolk, R. and Richardson, F. (1984) 'Behavior therapy and the ideology of modernity', *American Psychologist*, 39: 777–86.

Yalom, I. (1980) *Existential Psychotherapy*. New York: Basic Books.

3 Unconditional Positive Regard and its Spiritual Implications

Campbell Purton

Aimer un être, c'est lui dire: 'Toi, tu ne mourras pas.'

Gabriel Marcel

In this chapter I want to explore some important but little-discussed aspects of what is involved in the therapeutic condition which Rogers called 'unconditional positive regard' (UPR). Of the three core conditions UPR is the one which seems most open to criticism or even to ridicule. For while empathy and congruence are often not easy qualities to embody, there is nothing in principle which makes the effort absurd. In the case of UPR the situation is arguably different. For a start, 'unconditional positive regard' is a technical term, rather than a naturally existing phrase whose normal use in the language could be explored as we might explore, say, the use of the term 'genuineness'. With an invented phrase like UPR there is less certainty that the phrase corresponds to anything real at all. Nor does the fact that its component terms have established meanings prove that *it* has a clear meaning. (Consider the analogous example that although 'loose' and 'adjective' have established meanings, it does not follow that 'loose adjective' has a clear meaning.)

The puzzle of UPR

In the case of UPR, Rogers and person-centred writers generally do make use of other terms as near-equivalents in meaning (for example 'acceptance', 'prizing', 'respect' and 'warmth'), but then a different difficulty arises: these terms differ in meaning among themselves. Consider for instance 'respect' and 'warmth'. The dictionary suggests for 'respect': '1. Admiration felt towards a person or thing that has good qualities or achievements; politeness arising from this. 2. Attention, consideration.' But for the relevant kind of use of 'warm' we read: '1. Enthusiastic, hearty. 2. Kindly and affectionate'. It seems that 'respect' is a term with definite ethical or value-oriented implications: the respected person must be seen as having good qualities, and given that they have these qualities they deserve our respect. 'Warmth', on the other hand, seems to have much less of an ethical tone; whether it is right or valuable to be warm with someone is more a matter of the context and of what that person (at that time) wants. Some people thrive on hearty enthusiasm and affectionate hugs; others find a certain coolness to be refreshing. Rogers in giving alternative terms was undoubtedly trying to find the best words to convey an attitude which he had identified as therapeutic; I am suggesting, however, that just what that attitude is requires further exploration.

A more substantial concern about UPR is that on reflection it may seem not only that, as an invented phrase, UPR might not have a determinate meaning, but that its component terms almost guarantee that it is a meaningless notion. One surely has positive regard for things which are seen as in some way good or appealing, negative regard for things bad or unlikeable. 'Unconditional positive regard' seems to mean positive regard for things whether they are good or not, which seems either incomprehensible or to involve a sort of mad sentimentality. (Consider the corresponding phrase 'unconditional negative regard' – if comprehensible at all such an attitude would seem to involve a mad degree of cynicism.) So we are led to the uncomfortable thought that UPR may not be so much a vague or indeterminate phrase like 'loose adjective', but more of a contradiction in terms, like 'square circle'.

There is enough here at least to raise doubts about the notion of UPR, and such doubts often half surface in discussions of the topic amongst counsellors. It is sometimes said, for example, that UPR is very difficult to maintain for long, that it is all very well within the limits of counselling sessions, but cannot possibly be adopted in life generally, that it is difficult to adopt the attitude while being honest about one's own values, and so on. These 'difficulties' and feelings of unease arise from very deep-rooted issues which I aim to explore in this chapter. My conclusion will be that the notion of UPR cannot be salvaged unless we adopt a particular view of the person which it is natural to call a 'spiritual' view. In this way my discussion links with one trend within the person-centred school of thought. It is well known that Rogers in the course of his life moved away from a religious worldview, and person-centred theory, while not necessarily hostile to such a view, is not generally seen as having any implications of a religious kind. On the other hand, late in his life Rogers (1980, 1986) seems to have turned somewhat towards a 'spiritual' view of the world, and some writers in the person-centred tradition have seen this not just as something idiosyncratic to Rogers, but as a natural development in the evolution of person-centred theory.[1] The arguments I present here can be seen as supporting the latter view.[2] I seek to show that the concept of unconditional positive regard cannot properly be employed without taking a view of the person that is essentially 'spiritual'. This is, of course, a provocative claim, but if it is false then I hope that an examination of the arguments that lead me to it may at least bring to light important aspects of what we are up to when we, as counsellors, try to foster an attitude of unconditional positive regard towards our clients.

Unconditional valuing

The crucial thing about UPR seems to be the notion of the unconditional valuing of a person. In Rogers's view it is conditional valuing of people (especially by parents) which tends to give rise to a self-concept which is out of step with the person's own experiencing. In the simplest possible terms, the child feels that they are accepted/respected on condition that they are such-and-such (honest, kind, polite, etc.); also, although this is less often remarked on, the child may feel *more* accepted when they are *more* polite, for example. Since the need for acceptance and respect is strong and universal in human beings, the child is faced with a dilemma whenever their own feelings do not coincide with the 'conditions of worth' that are implicit in the parents' attitude. The effectiveness of counselling, in Rogers's view, derives from the fact that it provides a setting in which conditions of worth are not laid down. That is, the counsellor tries to adopt an attitude in which he or she respects the client whether or not the client has certain qualities, and whether or not the client has any quality to any particular degree. The ideal counselling attitude is one of absolute respect, not respect that is relative to the way the client happens to be. The theory, at least, is that if the counsellor honestly respects the client abso-lutely, whatever feelings or attitudes the client has, then the client will no longer need to pretend to be other than they are, and will be released into being fully themselves, into being fully authentic.

The concept of unconditional respect is central to Rogers's theory of therapy, but it is also, as I have indicated, a deeply puzzling notion. Normally we respect someone for some particular characteristics which they have, and which we see as good. We speak of deserving respect and earning respect, all of which seems to show that respect is normally an attitude which is conditional on a person being a particular way. Respecting someone seems to be in that way similar to liking them: if they change we may well not like them so much (or may like them better). Prizing and valuing seem to be similar sorts of notions – we prize or value people (or things) for their characteristics, and their capacities to meet our needs, and if these characteristics change then there is no necessary expectation that the prizing or valuing will continue. The only near-synonym of 'unconditional positive regard' which does seem to allow fairly naturally for the uncon-ditional aspect is 'love', but this is unhelpful unless we are clearer about what 'love' means than we are about what 'unconditional positive regard' means! However, since some of what I say in this chapter may raise doubts about whether UPR is possible at all, it may be worth remembering that we do sometimes at least see love as unconditional, or not grounded in any reasons. It doesn't sound odd to hear someone say 'I don't know why I love you', whereas the remark 'I don't know why I respect you' at least requires some kind of special context or explanation in order to be intel-ligible. Some people experience the unconditional form of love in connec-tion with their children: there are parents who can honestly say 'Whatever you do, whatever you become, I will still love you.' Of course, someone may say this, and then when the testing time comes find that their love falters. That is possible, but the continuation of this sort of love regardless of all circumstances also seems possible. The concept of love (one sort of love) allows at least for this as a possibility, whereas it seems clear that the concept of liking does not. The reader may be relieved (or disappointed) to know that I will not mention love again until the very end of my discussion; but I think it is important, in reflecting on the rather artificial-sounding notion of UPR, that we do have a familiar, well-established notion that is logically very similar to it. If it should come to seem that UPR really is an unacceptable or unintelligible notion, then we will have to look very hard at the notion of love, in the relevant sense, as well.

The difficulty about the unconditionality of UPR, or 'unconditional respect' as I shall usually call it, is one of which most client-centred counsellors are acutely aware; that is, how, with certain clients, can one possibly embody the core conditions of congruence and unconditional respect at the same time? An answer which is quite often given in this context is that one can accept (respect)[3] the client while not accepting (respecting) the client's actions. I think there is something in this, but in a way it just raises our problem in a different form, namely, how is it possible to think of the *person* as separate from what they do? Of course, we can separate 'the person' from particular things they do, as when we make allowances for bad behaviour ('She is really a fair-minded person, but she has been under a lot of pressure lately'). We may even separate 'the person' from certain of their character traits ('He is really a considerate person in spite of his short temper'). Yet these sorts of cases get us no further in the direction of *unconditional* respect. For in these cases we are saying, in effect, that we respect or value the person for what they are 'on the whole' or 'for the most part', and that this overall respect for their good qualities (their 'redeeming features') allows us to tolerate certain 'lapses' or 'difficult bits of their personality'. Unconditional respect, by contrast, would make no reference to what the person is like 'on the whole'; unconditional respect must allow for the case where a person has no redeeming features, no characteristics which deserve our respect.

The dilemma could be put like this: either the person does deserve our respect, in which case they must be in some way respectworthy and our respect must be conditional upon them being that way; or, the person does not deserve our respect, in which case our respect (if we do feel it), is inappropriate. The sort of inappropriateness we have here can, I think, be identified as *sentimentality*, an emotional attitude in which positive feeling clouds rational perception of a genuinely negative situation. (Not the case of the parent who loves their child in spite of everything but, for example, the case of seeing the child as honest while knowing, really, that he is not.) So another way of putting my central question would be: is unconditional respect necessarily a sentimental attitude? In brief, my answer will be: not necessarily, but the conditions for it not being sentimental involve a view of human beings that is essentially spiritual. In other words I shall argue that unless we see people as essentially spiritual beings UPR *is* sentimental.

Aspects of the self

I will begin my main discussion by distinguishing some different aspects of 'the person' or 'self'. UPR involves the possibility of respecting a person in spite of all the empirical evidence showing that they are unworthy of respect. There is some sort of distinction being made here between the 'essential self' (which is worthy of respect) and the 'empirical self' (which is not), and this distinction needs to be explored. Consider first two different situations, those of Anneka and of Theodore:

Anneka is someone who naturally has a rather directive, bossy side to her personality. She enjoys telling people what to do. Her parents are very tolerant, accepting people, except when it comes to bossiness, which they do not approve of at all. Anneka learns to disguise her bossiness but the self-deception becomes hard to maintain. Unable to understand her own feelings and behaviour, she seeks counselling help. With the help of the counsellor she comes to acknowledge her bossy side, and indeed comes to think that it is not altogether a bad characteristic to have. Amongst other things she joins the Territorial Army and there finds plenty of scope for ordering people around without any need to feel guilty about it. She is able to respect herself in spite of her bossy tendencies, through growing to have some positive regard for what she naturally is. It could be said that Anneka solves her problem by integrating the previously rejected tendencies into her personality as a whole.

This is a happy ending, but is such an ending always possible?

Theodore has suppressed his awareness that he has a cruel streak to his nature, that he can actually enjoy inflicting pain. (Conditions of worth in his kind, gentle family don't allow acknowledgement of cruel tendencies.) In counselling he comes to acknowledge his cruel streak. Knowing how Anneka successfully handled her problem, Theodore considers the possibility of taking up some occupation where he can harmlessly indulge his cruelty – perhaps he should train as a dentist? But on reflection this feels quite wrong: it would be unethical to enjoy causing pain to his patients, even if the pain were an unavoidable conse-quence of dental treatment. He doesn't want to be that sort of person. Theodore does not wish to integrate his cruel tendency: he wants it not to be there. The tension of this situation could of course lead to him suppressing awareness of his cruel impulses again, but he does not want to return to such a condition of incongruence either. So it seems he has to live with the knowledge that to some extent he is not the sort of person he would like to be.

But what if someone is not prepared to accept that they are 'not the sort of person they want to be'? What way forward is possible for someone who

(a) is no longer able to deceive themselves about their inclination to *X*,

(b)   is unable to see *X*ing as integratable behaviour; that is, as acceptable at least in certain circumstances,

(c)   is unable to accept themselves as they are?

The most obvious way would be to accept that although one's character is flawed it doesn't have to remain flawed. I accept that I have a reprehensible inclination to *X*, but I see this as something I can work on, something I can change in myself. I identify with the part of myself that desires the change; I side against the cruel bit of me. I don't want to integrate it; I want to eliminate it. But am I not then mutilating myself, killing what is a genuine, though unlikeable part of myself? This seems to go against self-acceptance, against unconditional respect for myself; for *this is the way I am*.

However, an interesting response is possible here: what if I say 'This cruel bit is *not* really part of me; it is alien to me. Hence in getting rid of it I am not mutilating myself, but removing something which I see as analogous to an alien growth, or a distortion of my "essential nature".' If I say this I am making a distinction between what belongs to my 'essential nature', and what does not so belong. My cruelty, my desire to cause pain, I see as a desire that is external to, or a distortion of, my essential self.

Note that the distinction being made here is different from that between 'self-concept' and 'real self' which is the only distinction that is relevant in the case of Anneka. Anneka initially felt she was an amiable sort of person. She then realized that she had an intolerant, bossy side to her nature, and came to see that the wholly amiable Anneka was a distorted picture of her real self. She subsequently found a niche in the Territorial Army where her 'bossy' behaviour seemed harmless and even valuable, and thus was able to live fully in an authentic and undistorted way at last. The initial part of the story is the same in the case of Theodore, who realizes that his wholly kind persona or self-concept is a distorted version of his real self, which contains a cruel streak. However, Theodore cannot and does not wish to integrate his cruelty, to accept it as an essential part of his nature. The question now is whether it makes any sense for Theodore to see the 'real self' that he has discovered as a distortion of some still deeper self, which he calls his 'essential self'. That is, does it make sense for Theodore to say that while he really has a cruel streak, this cruel streak is not an essential part of his nature? If this option is not open to him, then Theodore will either have to resign himself to being a cruel person, or return to a state of incongruence, or remain alienated from part of himself. But to make the move of saying that he is not 'essentially' cruel is fraught with possibilities of renewed self-deception, and also runs the risk of conceptualizing the 'essential self' as an unchanging entity, thus going against Rogers's conception of the self as a flux, as an embodiment of an 'actualizing tendency'. What can it mean for a person to claim that they are not 'essentially' that which they undeniably are? And how can a person 'have an essential self' while not being identified with a fixed, unchanging entity? These are the questions which will occupy me in the rest of the chapter.

'Essential self' and 'original innocence'

First let me mention a possibility which may initially seem attractive, but which does not really get us anywhere. It is the possibility of identifying the 'essential self' with a person's 'original self'. For instance, I may suppose that I was kind as a child, but then experienced life situations that led me to develop a hard, cruel streak as a survival strategy. Or, I may suppose that I was naturally kind, but my father had a cruel streak and I introjected this aspect of his character. Or I may have been influenced by reading Rousseau, or other Romantic thinkers who see early childhood as a state of innocence which is gradually corrupted by the societies in which we live ('the noble savage'). Can I then not identify my 'essential self' with my 'original self', and see certain aspects of my empirical self as distortions of my original self?

There are two difficulties with this sort of view. One is that it simply may not be true in the particular case in question. For it surely could turn out that my cruel streak was *not* developed as a defence strategy or introjected from anyone; perhaps I was just born like that. Without some theological or anthropological theory of 'primal innocence' there is no guarantee that one's original state was innocent; to assume this could well just be wishful thinking.

The second, and perhaps decisive, objection is that even if people do begin life in a state of innocence, this innocence may be manifestly destroyed through subsequent events. To say that a person was once innocent is not to say that they are in *any* sense innocent now. Life may not have distorted my nature, but changed it. To say that I am not essentially cruel on the grounds that I was once not cruel is no more intelligible than saying my car is essentially rust-free, on the grounds that it was once rust-free.

Yet while the 'original innocence' view doesn't stand up to close examination, as a picture or a myth it does seem to catch something of the feel of the 'essential self', the self in its primal state where it is unclouded, undistorted by extraneous defects. The question is whether this picture must remain just a picture (which will draw from the tough-minded the charge of sentimentality), or whether we can exhibit certain features of the human situation which show how the picture has a genuine use, and is not a matter of sentimental imagining.

First- and second-order desires

Let us return to the point that 'Theodore is cruel, but he would like not to be'. He identifies with the part of himself which wants to change, siding against the cruel bit. He would like to eliminate the cruel streak. It is undeniable that human beings are capable of wanting not to have the desires they have, and of wanting to have desires they don't have. Such desires about one's own desires have been termed by Harry Frankfurt

(1971) 'second-order desires'. (For simplicity I shall refer mostly to 'desires', but second-order aversions or fears should be understood to be included as well.) The capacity to have second-order desires is, Frankfurt argues, a characteristic which we do not share with the animals, and if this is so it would not be surprising if this capacity were fairly central to the notion of a personal as distinct from an animal self. Part of what is involved in being a person is that one can, as it were, stand back and evaluate one's own desires and fears. A person, for this reason, cannot be seen as simply the sum of the first-order desires and other propensities which they happen to have.

This, I think, is what really lies behind our feeling that in wishing to eliminate his cruel streak, Theodore is not mutilating himself. The wish to remove the cruel streak is a second-order desire characteristic of Theodore as a person, while the cruel streak itself is a first-order desire. The conflict which Theodore experiences is not a conflict between two first-order desires, such as the conflict between wanting to go to a party and wanting to have an early night; it is a conflict between a person and one of his first-order desires.

The distinction here is not merely an academic one. Especially striking examples arise in the case of addictions, where the addict is not balancing his craving for a drug against his other desires, but simply wishes to be free of the craving. The craving is, in Frankfurt's (1976) terminology, an 'external desire'. Similarly the person who has an irrational fear of spiders seldom wishes to integrate this fear into the rest of her life; she wants to be free of it. But it is not only in cases like these that the issue of 'external desires' arises. It is a familiar and pervasive aspect of all our lives. I think for instance of a client I once had who was involved in a relationship from which he could not free himself. At first it seemed to me that his situation could be characterized as one in which he had two desires in conflict with each other: a desire to stay with the girl, and a desire to get her out of his life. But when I reflected his account back to him in these terms he quickly put me right, saying that he wouldn't want to waste our time just dithering between the options: he knew what he wanted, which was to get away from her. His problem was not that of deciding what he wanted most, but that of overcoming a desire he did not want to have at all. He did not experience this desire as intrinsic to his nature; the desire was an 'external desire'. The problem, however, is that external desires may still be deeply embedded.

Let us suppose that Theodore's cruel streak really is deeply embedded in him. It is not a superficial bit of conditioning, reaction formation or introjection. It connects in deep and complex ways with all sorts of other attitudes and desires which he has. It is in an important sense part of his nature, and precisely that is what constitutes his painful moral situation. Now can we say all this and still maintain that his cruelty is external to him, a distortion of what he essentially is? It seems that we can, on condition that there is in Theodore some desire to be different from the way he is (something that may show up not only in what he honestly says, but in his feelings of regret, guilt, remorse, etc.). Our attitude to Theodore is likely to be radically different if we see him as having some desire to change. If he clearly has this second-order desire to change then our attitude towards him may be not very unlike the attitude we might have towards someone who is excessively timid, but bravely tries to overcome their fears. We regret the timidity, but respect them for trying to overcome it. The more we appreciate how hard Theodore struggles against his cruel impulses, the more we respect him.

It seems then that our respect for a person is bound up with our view of them as having the capacity to evaluate and struggle with their first-order desires and aversions. However, Frankfurt's terminology of 'second-order' desires, although useful in introducing the topic, can now be misleading. It suggests that first-order and second-order desires are more similar than they really are. A second-order desire is not just another desire which a person 'has' – it is that person's evaluation of their own desires. Consider the person who wants a cigarette but doesn't want to want it. 'Wanting a cigarette' is simply a desire, a state of mind that has arisen. But 'wanting not to want it' means something like 'reflecting that on balance this isn't good for me'; it expresses an evaluative choice, not a desire in the ordinary sense. We could say that the difference between first- and second-order desires is really that between desires and values, and this helps to make it clearer how respect becomes appropriate for beings who have second-order desires. Such beings are those who reflect in terms of values, who reflect in terms of which desires are worthwhile and which are not. In short, any being of this sort is a moral agent, and while we may disagree with the content of their morality, we respect them for their engagement in the moral world.

The question arises of whether a person could grow up without developing any second-order propensities to evaluate their first-order self. It is tempting to say that this is an empirical question which can only be answered by psychological or sociological surveys, but I doubt whether this is correct. Given the social context of personal life, with the crucial importance that other people play in the development of a child,[4] it is hard to see how a human being could develop as a person without acquiring some sense of their desires and behaviour being open to assessment, as being possibly, and in various ways, 'bad' or 'good'. Such evaluative awareness of oneself may not be very explicit, but I agree with Frankfurt that something of *this* kind of self-awareness, this having of second-order attitudes, is part of what is involved in a distinctively personal consciousness. We see (some) animals as having desires and fears, but we don't see them as being able to reflect on those desires and fears with a view to whether they should act on them or not. (I mean this as a remark about our concept of an animal as distinct from our concept of a person; if evidence should accumulate that dolphins, for example, reflect on their desires, then I would count dolphins as non-human persons.)

Let me now summarize what I hope to have shown, before drawing the rather surprising implications for spirituality which I believe to follow.

We began with the question of how UPR is possible, given that what a person does may not be worthy of respect. It began to seem possible that UPR is a downright sentimental attitude: i.e. one that involves feelings that are inappropriate to their object, an attitude involving emotional dishonesty. If Jones acts in a way that we cannot respect, how can we honestly say that we respect him? The only way through this seemed to be by distinguishing Jones's essential self from his empirical self, and although this distinction was not easy to elucidate, I argued that the distinction can be made once we appreciate that our respect for a person is linked with their second-order rather than with their first-order propensities. Simply by being a person Jones has the capacity to stand back from himself (from his first-order self), and reflect on and evaluate his desires and aversions. In so far as Jones enjoys a personal form of consciousness at all he engages in this sort of activity to some extent, however faint and flickering it may be. But this sort of activity, this orientation towards the question of what is good or valuable, is worthy of respect. Hence any being of a personal nature is worthy of respect, regardless of the nature of their first-order self. This, in my view, is why unconditional respect is an appropriate attitude to persons. Strictly speaking, the respect is not unconditional (all unsentimental respect is conditional upon its object being in some way good), but given that the being that is respected is a person, no further conditions are required. *People* unconditionally deserve our respect.

The implications for spirituality

In getting this far we have introduced a conception of the person which sees people as beings different in kind from animals. Animals have desires, but people can take up attitudes towards the desires they have, and it is this which introduces the attitude of unconditional respect which is peculiarly appropriate to persons. Now this much seems to me quite consistent with a humanist, rather than a spiritual, approach to persons. People are not just animals, because they have second-order desires, the existence of which is bound up with the peculiarly social nature of the human form of life. But there seems to be nothing here beyond what can be elucidated in humanist terms. I think that this first part of the argument can stand on its own, and it may be as far as we can go. However, there is a possible development of the argument which, if valid, leads to the conclusion not only that persons are deserving of unconditional respect, but that the nature of beings who are deserving of unconditional respect is inevitably a spiritual nature.[5] By a spiritual nature I mean what I think has traditionally been meant by this, namely, that the nature of persons cannot be wholly elucidated in terms of their lives 'in this world', that there is a dimension to personal existence that goes 'beyond this life'.

For this final development of the argument I need to return to the point that the reason that unconditional respect is appropriate to persons, is that persons are the sort of being who can assess and struggle with their first-order propensities, their desires, their fears. Respect is due for the first-order propensities and the actions that spring from them, only in so far as those propensities have been developed through effort that is worthy of respect.

The unconditional respect which it is appropriate to feel towards people is thus linked not so much with what they empirically do and are, but with their second-order desires to change (or maintain) what they do and are. Now 'desire' is a rather vague term, and it needs to be made clear that the kind of desire in question must involve a genuine hope rather than merely an idle wish. If Theodore's 'desire' to eliminate his cruel streak amounts only to him saying to himself, 'Ah, it would be nice not to have these cruel impulses, but there it is, the leopard can't change its spots', then I think our (appropriate) response to this would not be one of respect at all. We can't appropriately respect someone's resignation to continue with their cruel behaviour. In short, it is not enough for respect that the person should dislike an aspect of themselves, or have some ideal of being different; what is needed is some attempt at, or at least some hope for, change – however fleeting.

Now if someone is to make the attempt to change, or at the very least hope for change, they must believe that it is possible for them to change. (Logically one cannot attempt to do, or hope for, something one believes to be impossible.) Sometimes this belief or hope will be quite a reasonable one. If Theodore's cruel streak is not very deeply embedded, then he may well have reason to hope that in due course, and with effort, he will succeed. But what if the cruelty *is* deeply embedded? It is this case which is the interesting one, since it is here that we encounter the most acute moral difficulty: the person who knows that they have a deeply embedded trait which they nevertheless regard as external to, or a distortion of, their essential nature. If they are to see the trait as such a distortion they must have some hope of eliminating it, but they may also (correctly) believe that the years left to them in this life cannot possibly be enough for them to do so. It would seem to follow that if they are to see the trait both as deeply embedded *and* as a distortion of their essential self then they must see their existence as somehow extending beyond their present life.

An analogy may help here. What we are trying to do is make sense of the claim that a person who manifestly is, for example, cruel, is not 'really' or 'essentially' cruel. But the situation is not like the one we had with Anneka: Anneka is not really the compliant person she appeared to be. 'Not really' means here that when we look more closely we see that her compliant nature is a kind of deception. She is not what she seems. An analogy would be that we first see Anneka at the Territorial Army cabaret and notice that she has red hair. But then someone points out that it is just an effect of the lighting; it is an illusion. Really, her hair is blonde. The

case we are concerned with is not like that at all. It is in no ordinary sense
an illusion that Theodore is cruel. The analogy would rather be: we see
Theodore in the dentist's waiting room under normal lighting, and we
notice that he has red hair. But then someone points out that his hair 'is
not really red, it is dyed'. The redness of Theodore's hair is in no ordinary
sense an illusion, yet it makes perfectly good sense to say that his hair is not
really red. It makes sense, that is, because of a whole context that is being
taken for granted: if we accept the point about Theodore's hair not really
being red it is because we believe that he did not originally have red hair,
and that the red will soon grow out. The fact is that in the present
Theodore's hair is, by all ordinary criteria red, so that if in spite of this we
say it is not 'really' red, we must be assuming something about the past or
the future which makes sense of our assertion. Similarly, if by all ordinary
criteria Theodore in the present is cruel, but we assert that he is not 'really'
cruel, we must be assuming something about the past or the future of
Theodore which makes sense of this assertion. But we have seen that
innocence in the past is not enough; the only possibility remaining seems to
be a future in which Theodore has overcome his cruelty, and if the cruelty
is deeply embedded in his character, that future cannot arrive within the
span of his present life.

As one further way of looking at it, consider the case of someone for
whom we find it difficult to take up an attitude of unconditional respect.
Consider Hitler, for example. Since Hitler was a person, and persons are
worthy of unconditional respect, it follows that Hitler was worthy of
unconditional respect. But if the whole truth about Hitler is constituted by
the details of his empirical biography, unconditional respect seems out of
place. There must therefore be more to Hitler than his empirical biography.
It seems that unconditional respect for Hitler can only mean respect for
what Hitler potentially is: it means not writing him off, in spite of there
being no empirical reasons for supposing that Hitler can ever realize his
authentic spiritual nature. The empirical biographical truth about Hitler
cannot be the whole truth if unconditional respect is appropriate to people
generally.

Since this conclusion may seem surprising (and no doubt, to some,
totally bizarre), it will be helpful to review what is involved. The starting
point is our need to distinguish between 'essential self' and 'empirical self'
if we are to be able to take up (unsentimentally) an attitude of unconditional respect towards a person. We cannot unconditionally and unsentimentally respect the empirical selves of most people, including of course
ourselves. (Let us leave aside here the possibility of saints or fully enlight-
ened beings!) So we picture it like this: we respect not the empirical self we
see before us but the essential self of which the empirical self is a distorted
form. But if this picture is to make any sense we must see it as possible for
the distortions to be removed; yet that, in the case of even moderately
embedded traits, involves there being more possibilities available for
change than this life can provide. Hence if we are to respect a person

unconditionally *and* unsentimentally, we must see their development as containing possibilities which go beyond the possibilities of their present empirical existence.

Needless to say, the argument does nothing to establish how or even in what sense persons extend beyond their empirical lives. The conclusion of the argument is only that somehow it must be so, but nothing follows about how we should picture its being so; whether, for example, in terms of purgatory, or repeated lives on earth, or life in some other dimension of reality. A character in one of Iris Murdoch's novels remarks in this connection, 'These are images, the truth lies beyond' (Murdoch, 1978: 384). I think that we reach the limits of discursive language here and have no option but to employ images and pictures. The truth of the matter is expressed in the pictures, and perhaps can *only* be so expressed.[6]

This matter of the expression of the truth in pictures is also relevant to the doubt I raised earlier concerning whether talk of an 'essential self' goes against a 'process view' of the self. While not having space to go into this in the detail it deserves, I would say that we need to see people as being wholly respectworthy irrespective of what they empirically are (this is precisely the attitude of unconditional respect), and that it helps us to do this if we picture them as having, now, an 'essential self' to which our respect may be directed. But this 'essential self' is not an empirical reality, a real unchanging entity. Empirically, the self is a flux, but that is not the whole truth for anyone who adopts an attitude of unconditional respect towards a person.[7] The remainder of the truth is not empirical at all; it is a matter of faith, of hope, of the spiritual imagination.

Conclusion

I would emphasize that, even if it is valid, my argument does not prove that human beings are spiritual entities who in some way extend beyond the limits of their empirical lives. The most it can show is that if we adopt an attitude of (unsentimental) unconditional respect towards a human being then we are *ipso facto* seeing them as having an essential self of which their empirical self is a distorted form; and if the last bit of the argument is valid what also follows is that we are *ipso facto* seeing their essential self as unlimited by the temporal confines of their present life. Those who welcome a spiritual attitude towards human beings may be pleased with this conclusion. Those who regard a spiritual view of life as false will, if the argument is valid, need to work it backwards. From their basic belief that human beings are not spiritual entities extending beyond their empirical lifespan, they will deduce that adopting an attitude of unconditional positive regard towards them is sentimental.

The argument, if valid, makes life difficult only for those who would like to hold on to the idea of unconditional positive regard (or, let us finally risk saying, to the idea of love in the relevant sense), without seeing human beings as spiritual entities. I hope that it could make life a bit easier for those who, like myself, want to be able to see human beings as spiritual entities, yet do not like sentimentality or disregard for rational argument. For if the argument is valid it means we can, rationally and without sentimentality, assert with Gabriel Marcel's Antoine: 'To love someone is to say to them, "You will not die".'[8]

Notes

1 See Thorne (1992: 105–7).

2 In developing these arguments I am much indebted to a series of interrelated papers by Harry Frankfurt (1971, 1976, 1987) and Terence Penelhum (1971, 1979, 1984). But in connection with the last part of the argument I also have had in mind Plato's view of the soul as the moral part of the person which cannot be harmed by death (e.g. Crito, 47e; Gorgias 521–2); Gabriel Marcel's 'Value and immortality' (in Marcel, 1962) and his *The Mystery of Being* (1960) Part 2, Ch. 9; also a remark of Wittgenstein's reported by Norman Malcolm (1958: 71): 'a way in which the notion of immortality can acquire a meaning is through one's feeling that one has duties from which one cannot be released, even by death.'

3 I do not really think that 'respect' and 'acceptance' are equivalent terms, but the distinction is not very relevant here. I have discussed the distinction briefly in an earlier paper (Purton, 1996).

4 I have discussed the essentially social nature of personal existence in relation to counselling theory elsewhere (Purton, 1993).

5 The argument is essentially that of Penelhum (1979, 1984).

6 See Wittgenstein (1966: 70–1).

7 The issues here have been discussed for many centuries in Buddhist Mahayana philosophy (see for example Hookham, 1991). On the level of 'ordinary truth' the self is a flux, is 'empty' of any real independent existence. But such talk of 'emptiness' by some Buddhist philosophers (the 'Emptiness-of-self' school) can be misleading, and subversive of the idea of spiritual progress towards enlightenment. So it is said by other philosophers (the 'Emptiness-of-other' school) that (on the level of 'absolute truth') the essential Buddha-nature is eternally there in all beings, and that the Buddha-nature is not *itself* empty of real existence; rather, it is empty of everything *else*. Now this would seem to bring back the notion of a real, unchanging self (*atman*) that Buddhism has always denied, but it does not have to have this implication if it is understood as a picture, an imaginative construction, a way of seeing things adopted for a spiritual purpose.

8 This koan-like remark by Antoine in Marcel's play *Le Mort de demain* (in Marcel, 1931, Act 2, Scene 6, p. 161) is one to which he often refers in his philosophical writings. For example Marcel (1960, Vol. 2: 68–9, 171; 1962: 147; 1965: 103). I am grateful to Anne Marcel for tracking down this reference for me.

References

Frankfurt, H. (1971) 'Freedom of the will and the concept of a person', *Journal of Philosophy*, 68: 5–20.

Frankfurt, H. (1976) 'Identification and externality', in A.M. Rorty (ed.), *The Identities of Persons*. Berkeley, CA: University of California Press. pp. 239–51.

Frankfurt, H. (1987) 'Identification and wholeheartedness', in F. Schoeman (ed.), *Responsibility, Character and the Emotions: New Essays in Moral Psychology*. Cambridge: Cambridge University Press.

Hookham, S.K. (1991) *The Buddha Within*. Albany, NY: State University of New York Press.

Malcolm, N. (1958) *Ludwig Wittgenstein: A Memoir*. Oxford: Oxford University Press.

Marcel, G. (1931) *Trois Pièces*. Paris: Plon.

Marcel, G. (1960) *The Mystery of Being*. Chicago: Henry Regnery.

Marcel, G. (1962) *Homo Viator*. New York: Harper Torchbooks.

Marcel, G. (1965) *Being and Having*. London: Collins Fontana.

Murdoch, I. (1978) *The Sea, The Sea*. London: Chatto & Windus.

Penelhum, T. (1971) 'The importance of self-identity', *Journal of Philosophy*, 68: 667–78.

Penelhum, T. (1979) 'Human nature and external desires', *The Monist*, 62: 304–18.

Penelhum, T. (1984) 'Religious belief and life after death', in W.L. Gombocz (ed.), *Philosophy of Religion (Proceedings of the 8th International Wittgenstein Symposium, Part 2)*. Vienna: Holder-Pichler-Temsky. pp. 37–45.

Purton, C. (1993) 'Philosophy and counselling', in B. Thorne and W. Dryden (eds), *Counselling: Interdisciplinary Perspectives*. Milton Keynes: Open University Press. pp. 152–70.

Purton, C. (1996) 'The deep structure of the core conditions: a Buddhist perspective', in R. Hutterer, G. Pawlowsky, P. Schmid and R. Stipsits (eds), *Client-centered and Experiential Psychotherapy: A Paradigm in Motion*. Frankfurt: Peter Lang. pp. 455–67.

Rogers, C.R. (1980) 'Growing old: or older and growing', in *A Way of Being*. Boston: Houghton Mifflin. pp. 70–95.

Rogers, C.R. (1986) 'A client-centered/person-centered approach to therapy', in I.L. Kutash and A. Wolf (eds), *Psychotherapist's Casebook*. San Francisco: Jossey-Bass. pp. 197–208.

Thorne, B. (1992) *Carl Rogers*. London: Sage.

Wittgenstein, L. (1966) *Lectures and Conversations on Aesthetics, Psychology and Religious Belief*. Oxford: Blackwell.

4 'On Becoming a *Person*-Centred Approach': A Person-Centred Understanding of the Person

Peter F. Schmid

> In these days most psychologists regard it as an insult
> if they are accused of thinking philosophical thoughts.
> I cannot help but puzzle over the meaning of what I observe.
>
> Carl Rogers (1961b: 163)

For the person-centred approach it is of decisive significance to reflect in a fundamental way on which conception of man its theory and practice should be based and to establish in this way a basic anthropological stance.[1] If we do not do this we will inevitably be exposed to the legitimate reproach that we are merely, as person-centred practitioners, acquiring clinical skills as techniques.

The name of the approach contains the term 'person', which is reason enough to ask what this actually means. Even if the name may first have originated for pragmatic reasons (that is, to find a comprehensive term for clients, pupils, communication partners, group members, etc.; in other words, for possible new fields of application), Rogers also deliberately chose it because of its essential meaning (cf. Kirschenbaum, 1979: 424). For, unlike other psychotherapeutic and social-psychological interpretations, the person-centred approach takes a radical look at the human being as a person.

The shift of paradigms in philosophy and psychology

The traditional, problem-centred approach in psychology and psychotherapy ultimately aims at controlling the world and other people; according to this approach, the therapist, the educationalist, the group leader, the pastoral worker or the social worker is an expert who, on the basis of skills and knowledge, can say more or less 'where we should go'. Anyone who subscribes to a person-centred approach, however, is convinced of and thus has faith in the fact that every human being possesses the capacity to shape his or her own life and that the main objective of every form of aid should be to support this capacity, that is to promote human freedom and auto-nomy. This, however, is not to be seen only as an ultimate aim and, so to speak, as the optimal status 'post therapy' – as many adherents of other approaches object, who say that in the last analysis independence is also what we aim for, but first the crisis must be eliminated, a problem must be solved, an illness must be cured, and then the 'cured patient' can be considered 'normal' again and left to their own devices. An approach which takes man – in all stages of life – really seriously as a person believes that all human beings are themselves capable of determining the direction, the nature and the quantity of their change in a constructive way, and they are believed to have this capacity because of the tendency of life to develop and to extend its possibilities – if the person is offered at least the minimum of suitable interpersonal conditions.

What sounds so simple and obvious turns out, on closer examination, to be a revolutionary change in the philosophy of interpersonal relationships, as well as in the way they are handled in practice. Philosophy took a long time to consider man of sufficient value to be worth asking questions about (Kant was the first to take the step beyond ontology towards anthropology) and only in the twentieth century has philosophy really become serious about the fact that man can never include himself in his questions without entering into dialogue with his own kind. Psychology has not even now really undertaken this paradigm shift. Likewise, psychotherapy still con-siders its task as one of diagnosis and interpretation. This is exactly what Carl Rogers spoke out against. The person-centred approach does not ask, as objectifying philosophy did for many centuries and subsequently psy-chology and psychotherapy did and still do, *what* man is, and accordingly does not orientate its practice of assistance towards *treating* a human being as an object. It asks, as does personalism (the philosophy of dialogue), following a shift of philosophical paradigms, *who* man is, and consequently considers it to be its goal to *encounter* a human being as a fellow man. This takes into account that such a question always includes the person asking and that he or she is always inextricably involved. Strictly speaking, the question as to who man is can also no longer be phrased in a general way; on the contrary, the appropriate question would be put in concrete terms: 'Who are you?' This question, however, asks about the personhood of a particular human being. Thus, 'person' is not the concrete term for a general notion, but always refers to someone unique.

Use of the word and etymology: what is the meaning of the term 'person'?

The use of the word 'person' is not standardized, either in everyday language (person is contrasted with an object or the society at large; it refers to a numbered individual, not to mention the legal and grammatical meanings), or in philosophy, as will be shown in what follows, or in psychotherapy (the Jungian term 'persona' stands for 'mask of the mind' and is thus the very opposite of what is meant by the term 'person' in humanistic psychology or in personalistic forms of depth psychology with their conception of progressive personalization).

Etymologically, the word probably originates from the Etruscans via the Latin *persona*: tomb paintings have been found depicting a man looking like a demon and wearing a mask. Next to it the word 'phersu' is written. Depending on whether one applies the word to the mask – which is probably wrong – or takes it to be the name of the demon – probably right – one can find different interpretations: it indicates either the mask or the one wearing it. A similar case is the Greek word *prósopon*, from which 'person' can be derived, according to another interpretation. Originally, it meant 'face' (as in Aristotle and the Bible) and, derived from that, the mask of an actor who 'pulls a face'; here one has to consider, however, that in Greek theatre the mask did not, as we assume nowadays, serve to hide, but to reveal (the personified god). This is how 'person' gained the meaning of the one who played a role in the theatre (that is the scroll on which the poet had written the part of the actor). Nowadays the word is still used in a similar way (cf. the characters and their actors). Later, in Roman times, 'persona' was also used for the (social) 'role in life'.

The philosophical conception of the person

But how was this expression adopted by philosophy? The colloquial term which denotes the relationship in the social structure was first introduced by theologians to their terminology when, seeking to understand the events of Jesus' life, they aspired to define more precisely the relationship between him, God, whom he called his father, and his spirit (the Holy Ghost). Reflecting on this, the Fathers of the Church – the first of whom was Tertullian (who died after AD 213) – used the Roman relationship term 'persona' in their doctrine of the Trinity and formulated the concept of 'one God in three persons' in order to accentuate equality (unlike the monarchianistic position in which priority was given to the Father). Therefore up to the present day the notion of person as a professional term has been characterized by two still relevant factors: it has been used to define an empirical fact, and from the very beginning it has aimed at characterizing equality (cf. Schmid, 1998).

This, however, did not really solve the problem, but intensified the conflict: did the theologians mean that there were three gods, three individuals (as we naturally assume nowadays, if we talk about three persons – for instance in a boat)? Or does the term mainly accentuate their relationship to each other? What is the crux of being a person? The individual component? The relationship? It is this very question that has preoccupied 2,000 years of philosophy. Two traditions emerged, an individualistic one and a relationalist one.

The person as an independent being

The individualistic (or substantialistic) conception of the person was first defined by Boëthius (AD 480–525): 'Persona est rationalis naturae individua substantia [the person is the indivisible substance of a rational being].' Substance derives from *sub-stare* which literally means 'achieving a standing position from below', or standing by oneself, being based upon oneself, and thus implies autonomy and independence – or, to be precise, indivisible independence (*in-dividuum*), that which ultimately cannot be divided, shared, communicated. In this tradition we find Thomas Aquinas with his conception of the person as 'distinctum subsistens [sub-sistence that differs from others]', that is something that has been erected on a supporting foundation and is supported from within, is consisting-of-itself. Also part of this tradition is the Enlightenment (Locke, Leibnitz), which accentuates self-confidence, and Kant who emphasizes the status and dignity of the person who may not be used as a mere device, but who is an end in himself or herself deserving freedom and therefore capable of being held responsible. Edmund Husserl (who also takes the social environment into account), Dietrich von Hildebrand (who includes the development of the person in his reflections), Max Scheler (the person as an act in the realization of values), Helmut Plessner (corporality and self-reflection as characteristics of the person) and many others also subscribe to an individualistic conception of the person. This becomes explicit in existential philosophy: Heidegger, Jaspers and – particularly relevant – Søren Kierkegaard (1813–55) stress man's responsibility, man who experiences himself in his existence, his *Dasein*, in his individual uniqueness and non-transferability, in his potential for choice and for freedom and for whom it is essential 'to be that self which one truly is' (Kierkegaard, 1924: 17) – a quotation with which Carl Rogers (1961b: 163, 166) prefaces a chapter about genuineness. Therefore, whoever associates person with independence and uniqueness, freedom and dignity, unity, sovereignty and self-determination, responsibility, human rights, etc., sees himself or herself in the tradition of such an individualistic conception of the person. That is what is meant when man is defined as a person, starting from the moment of conception and regardless of his or her physical or mental health and development. Being a person therefore means being-from-oneself (*Aus-sich-Sein*) and being-for-oneself (*Für-sich-Sein*).

This conception of the person is especially influential in the (early) period of Carl Rogers's thinking during which, based on the actualizing tendency, he mainly understands man from the individualistic point of view and consequently sees therapy as a process of the development of personality with its emphasis on confidence in the organism, a realistic self and, above all, positive regard and empathy as beneficial conditions. As an ideal notion of the mature human being Rogers coins the phrase 'fully functioning person', which is similiar to Maslow's 'self-actualizing human being'. Kant's anthropological, theoretical and practical conception of the person left its traces in respect of the person and his or her inner valuing process, and in the rejection of means and methods. Husserl's '*Umweltlichkeit* [environmentalism]', which forms a person out of the ego, and his scientific conception can be found in Rogers's phenomenological understanding of the person in a dynamic interaction with the environment, which promotes or restricts growth, and ultimately in the formulation of helpful conditions for therapeutic personality change (Rogers, 1957). The idea – derived from existential philosophy – of the existence of man as a fulfilled actualization of being a person as opposed to being threatened by anxiety and death, which in the here and now of the present leads to freedom and to a decision, represents a fundamental element of humanistic psychology. The existence of the therapist becomes a co-existence (being-with, *Mitsein*) with the existence (being-here, *Dasein*) of the Other.[2] Heidegger's distinction between a solicitude generating dependence (*einspringende Fürsorge*) and a solicitude which makes the person needing help free to care for himself or herself (*vorausspringende Fürsorge*) can almost be considered the philosophical point of departure for the non-directive, client-centred approach, which sharply contrasts the person-centred practice with the problem-centred one.

Person as being in relationship

As the initiators of the relationalistic tradition, we find the Fathers of the Church. In patristic theology the person is understood as being in relationship. God's being is relationship, is pure being related, *esse ad*. According to Augustine (AD 354–430), a constituent element of man's being a person is self-knowledge in the dialogue which goes beyond the Self – to be more precise, in the inner dialogue. Here man experiences that God is nearer to him than he himself is; he experiences himself as being addressed by God as Thou. Richard of St Victor (died AD 1173) then defines person as 'naturae intellectualis existentia incommunicabilis [incommunicable existence of an intellectual nature]'. Here, person is not conceived as a *sub*-sistence, but as an *ek*-sistence, as coming into being from outside (*ex*), through others, as standing opposite to others (and hence as inexchangeable, *incommunicabilis*). Therefore, a person is he or she who has become himself or herself precisely through others. A constituent element of the person is his or her originating relationship – for example the relationship between the child and its mother. Phenomenology, existentialism and the philosophy of values (*Wertphilosophie*) emphasize that as a subject the person is beyond any objectification. In particular, however, personalism (also called 'dialogical thinking'), which emerged as a reaction to system philosophy, to the objectification of modern life and to the worldview represented by the mechanistic natural sciences, stresses that thinking in terms of subject and object is not applicable to the person. Johann Gottlieb Fichte had already suggested: 'Man only becomes a human being when he finds himself among human beings – if there are human beings at all, then there must be several of them', Kant's contemporary Friedrich Heinrich Jacobi had written: 'Without a Thou, the I is impossible', and Hegel again had placed the person in the context of the doctrine of the Trinity: through devotion to another human being one finds oneself in the Other. The personalistic philosophers, first and foremost Martin Buber (1878–1965), constantly underline the dialogical existence of man: 'The I is developed through the Thou. While becoming an I, I say Thou. All real life is encounter' (Buber, 1974: 18). The fundamental fact of existence is 'the human being together with other human beings'; 'the person emerges while entering into a relationship with others' (Buber, 1982: 164). Here we have arrived at Rogers's second 'favourite philosopher', one by whom he himself was significantly inspired (cf. Rogers and Buber, 1994). The 'I–Thou relationship' of dialogue, which Rogers often quotes – in Buber's philosophy it often stands in opposition to the objectifying 'I–It relationship' including perception, feelings and thoughts – is characterized by immediacy, that is devoid of any 'media' (means), and by presence, therefore it always occurs in the present moment. 'Between the I and the Thou there is no purpose. All means are obstacles. Only wherever all means are disintegrated, does encounter take place' (Buber, 1974: 78f.). Emmanuel Lévinas (1905–95), the 'Other-oriented thinker' who has yet to be discovered by the person-centred approach, interprets the fact that the person depends on relationship in an even more radical way than Buber: the foundation of self-awareness is not reflection (by the I facing the Thou), but the predetermined experience of relationship (Thou–I instead of I–Thou). As such, the Other is not an alter ego, but remains a mystery and hence a continuous challenge. He 'descends upon us', for which Lévinas uses the metaphor of 'visage', evoking the origin of the term 'person'. This visage addresses us and its need challenges us. This is why ethics is the foundation of every philosophy and why responsibility – Lévinas calls it '*diakonia* [service]' which precedes every dia-logue – is the fundamental category of being a person: from the encounter arises the obligation to respond. Unlike Buber, Lévinas doesn't stop at the duality of the I–Thou relationship, because there is not only one Thou: the Other always exists only in the (at least potential) presence of a third one, from which it follows that action is no longer self-evident and the latitude of freedom emerges. So, 'the Others' exist and instead of duality, the pair, I and Thou, now the tri-unity, the group, We, become the fundamental elements of interpersonality (see Chapter 7 on encounter in this book). Love becomes shared love (*condilectio* = with-love) where two persons harmoniously love a third one. Teilhard de Chardin's (1881–1955) conception of personalization (becoming a person) also belongs to this relationalistic tradition. Teilhard refers to the ability of the person to transcend, and he understands personalization as an evolution of the person linked to the socialization of humanity, leading to the coincidence of the personal and the universal. One is reminded instantly of Rogers's assertion that the most personal is the most general (1961b: 26).

So, whoever understands the person through relationship, through dialogue, through partnership, through connection with the world, through the condition of being dependent on others, through interconnectedness, whoever sees him or her in the totality of the community, as basically unavailable, whoever emphasizes that man is person as far as he has a relationship with others, follows the tradition of the relationalistic (transcendent) conception of person. Being a person thus means being-from- and -in-relationship (*Aus- und In-Beziehung-Sein*), being through others.

This conception of man as a person particularly characterizes Rogers's later work, where he understands the human being as 'person to person', as being relational, in a group and in community, because of his or her interconnectedness. Consequently, mutual encounter is a decisive element in therapy and personal development, and Rogers now considers genuineness as a pre-eminent facilitative condition. Like Augustine, Rogers knows that self-knowledge originates from dialogue, that becoming a self is based on listening (to oneself and to the Other). The person is brought to fruition in dialogical encounter: anyone who becomes him/herself while encountering others becomes a person. In such a conception, which assumes that the individual as well as the individual relationship is embedded in the community, lies the foundation for the discovery of the group as a salutary field in personal development. Teilhard's conception of a personalization of the entire creation in the direction of future perfection and Rogers's conception of a formative tendency, together with his references to spirituality, point to considerable similarities, as do Rogers's conception of therapy in accordance with the encounter concept and Lévinas's interpretation of ethics as the primary philosophy that recognizes the obligation of responsibility deriving from the primordial experience of relationship and the perception of the Other as a continuous challenge.

Sovereignty *and* commitment

In the substantialistic as well as in the relationalistic conceptions of the person we find important approaches which make it impossible for any current point of view to regress to earlier conceptions. The substance-oriented conception of the person of Boëthius and Thomas Aquinas emphasizes the independence of the person, his capacity to understand himself, to possess himself and to act freely. The conception of the Fathers of the Church, which aims at relationality, is directly oriented towards relationship and being related; where it concerns man, it refers to the dialogical situation of coming to himself as an I because he is addressed as a Thou. Being a person originates from and takes place in the person opposite, that is in the encounter. If the substantialistic approach underlines what the person is, then the relationalistic approach accentuates how this person has become a person (cf. Wucherer-Huldenfeld, 1978: 86). From the very beginning man is an individual person and from the very beginning he is related in personal community with others. It is only through the relationships with other persons that he develops and actualizes his being as a person: he becomes a personality.

The attempt to grasp man as a person thus means that he has to be understood equally as a distinctive independent being (the individualistic aspect of the conception of the person) and as a being who originated and originates from a loving encounter (the relationalistic aspect). His nature can neither be understood only through his being-from-himself and his being-for-himself, nor merely through the being-from-relationship and the being-in-relationship. The sovereignty – and therefore freedom, respect and dignity of the person, his non-transferability and indivisibility, his corporeality and uniqueness, his capacity for self-reflection and self-experience, as well as commitment – and therefore his orientation towards relationships, his dependence on others, his fundamental concentration on community, his capacity for dialogue, partnership and I–thou relationship, his striving for transcendence – are intrinsically part of what it means to speak of a human being as a person. Neither conception of the person excludes the other as long as neither of them is defined as absolute. Essential elements of the person are independence *and* dependence on relationships, sovereignty *and* commitment, autonomy *and* solidarity. Only in the dialectic of both interpretations, which for a long time were considered to be and apparently were incompatible, not in an 'either–or', but in a 'both–and', does the mystery of the person become accessible to whoever allows himself or herself to become involved in a personal encounter instead of remaining at a distance in objectifying observation. A conception gained from these two perspectives of the person contrasts with an individualistic-privatistic conception of the human being just as it does with a collectivistic one.

The person as a response: a conception of the person based on experience

The question about the person is therefore more than the answer to the question about the 'what' of man in general. It is the question about the 'who' of the one that is addressed as Thou in the relationship – and hence the question is directly related to experience. The answer to the question of what the person is is therefore to be sought in the direction of the answer to the dialogical question 'Who are you?' (The question 'who?' includes the question about 'whence' and 'whither'.)

These denote the two most important principles of the person-centred image of the human being: we live through *experience*, and we live in *relationships*. Both have to do with being a person as well as with becoming a person; they supplement and depend on each other: we are and become persons through the experience of and in the relationship – through the experience we are having at the very moment (awareness in the present) and biographical experience (the developmental aspect of becoming a person), in our current relationships (the interpersonal aspect of being-a-person-in-a-relationship), as well as in the history of our relationships (persons are what they have become and may become in relationships). Thus, we become what we are: persons. In the beginning there was experience. The importance of experience to the development of the conception of the person has already been emphasized: by reflecting historical experience in the relationships with Jesus, man developed a new conception of himself. Experience always stands at the beginning of philosophizing. The relationship aspect of the person is closer to experience (while the individualistic aspect is more abstract). The person-centred approach can only accept a conception of the person which is continuously correlated with experience. For Carl Rogers (1961b: 22f.) experience was always the highest authority.

So, what from the very beginning is man's experience of being a human being? What is his experience of becoming a human being, of his incarnation? To find an answer to this question one has to go back to the origin of development: to the newborn baby, indeed, even to the unborn baby. Man already finds himself addressed – even before he himself can speak; as Thou, even before he can say I; as a loved person, even before he can love. Man's primordial situation is a dialogical one. Therefore the person can be considered a response in an act of communication into which man is born. (From this, again, derives his respons-ability and here there is also again an ethical foundation for person-centred behaviour as behaviour springing from encounter.[3]) This leads to an understanding of the person as a relational becoming-identity:

> As a person man is what he is – from the (development-) psychological point of view – through communication. He acquires his distinctive independence through the loving encounter with his parents or other persons he can relate to, which enables him to become someone who loves and encounters others.
>
> As a person man is – from the philosophical point of view – the response to the word that is addressed to him. And here lies his responsibility, contingent on his freedom and his status as a fellow man which takes place in history: through his ongoing self-actualization in the community with other people, that is his actualization of being a person, the person becomes what he is.[4]

Rogers's conception: person-centredness versus alienation

The roots of Carl Rogers's conception of man can already be found in Socrates's thinking: in *Daimonion* the idea of the good core in every person is described which has to be revealed. This assumes that every human being carries the source of all knowledge and ability within himself. These can be tapped by a method called maeutics, a kind of game of questions and answers in which the philosopher is not the one who knows and therefore does not teach or judge, but facilitates his partner to teach and judge himself.

Rogers did not derive his image of man directly from philosophical tradition or apply this to psychology and psychotherapy. In accordance with his principle 'First there is experiencing, then there is a theory' (Rogers and Wood, 1974: 216), he started out from experience, drafted a therapeutic concept of procedure and it was only later that he developed the corresponding psychological and anthropological theory. Nevertheless, he is deeply rooted in Western philosophy and was mainly influenced, amongst others, by the existential philosophers who emigrated from Germany, by phenomenology and by dialogical philosophy.

Rogers did not explicitly define the term 'person' anywhere in his work; neither in his fundamental exposition of therapy theory and personality theory (1959), nor subsequently.[5] In his chapter 'A theory of therapy, personality and interpersonal relationships as developed in the client-centered framework' (1959), the meaning of the term is assumed to be self-evident – in a text in which almost every relevant expression used is painstakingly explained. Many of the titles of his articles and books contain the word 'person', and numerous chapters are thus entitled. In his writings the expression can be found over and over again; indeed from a certain moment on it is almost 'omnipresent'. In a theoretical discussion in Salzburg in 1981, Rogers answered my question about the definition of the expressions 'organism', 'self' and 'person': 'I use the term organism for the biological entity. The actualizing tendency exists in the biological human organism. I use the term self when I am referring to the concept a person has of himself, the way he views himself, his perceptions of his qualities, and so on . . . I use the term person in a more general sense to indicate each individual' (Rogers, 1981b). Therefore, in a certain sense person is a superordinate concept. Where Rogers speaks of the person, he always means the human being as a whole and he takes into account the points of view and assumptions which are relevant to person-centred anthropology, like the actualizing tendency, dependence on relationships, trustworthiness, the organismic process of evaluation and so on.

The expression, like much of Rogers's image of man and of his theory (especially in the latter stages of his life), becomes clear mainly in his descriptions which are close to experience and in his case examples. His observations of interpersonal experiencing and of the change in therapeutic processes or in personal encounters illustrate his conception of the person best. (At the same time, this inductive approach 'empirically confirms' the conception of the person, developed in philosophical history in an impressive way.)

Although this emphasis changed every now and again, the focus of Rogers's attention was always on the development of the person. *On Becoming a Person* (1961b) therefore became his most popular book title, and not without good reason. If the initial emphasis was on therapy, to be more precise on the therapeutic process, later, through his experiences with groups, his focus shifted towards the development of the person in general and, consistently, social and socio-political questions came to the fore.

In the introduction to *On Becoming a Person* Rogers describes his own view of the significance of his work and how his anthropology can be classified:

> I believe these papers belong in a trend which is having and will have its impact on psychology, psychiatry, philosophy, and other fields. I hesitate to label such a trend but in my opinion there are associated with it adjectives such as phenomenological, existential, person-centered; concepts such as self-actualization, becoming, growth. (Rogers, 1961b: viii)

When he was asked what relationship he had to theological and philosophical tradition, Rogers once said:

> There have been many, many philosophers and spiritual leaders . . . who have regarded the person as being very important. So I certainly don't claim that the term 'person-centered' is original or anything like that. I think we've tended to give it a special meaning, particularly in counseling or therapy, in that the relationship is centered in the person who is seeking help. And then gradually we've come to include the person giving help. So it is a two-way relationship. . . . And then the use of the term has also been a protest again the depersonalization, the dehumanization of education, of a lot of religion, of military life, many aspects of business. So that it's another way of saying we are person-centered and not object-centered, or not materialistic-centered. So that's some of the reasons why we use that term. (Rogers, 1981a)

From philosophy to the person-centred conception of the person: the dilemma of the individual and the personal encounter

It is certainly no coincidence that Rogers repeatedly referred to two philosophers explicitly (for example Rogers, 1961b: 199) to whom the history of the conception of the person has always accorded a position of prime importance: Kierkegaard, who considers the misery of the individual, and Buber, who points out the opportunities implied by dialogue. Even if Rogers's reference to them occurred a posteriori and – as is frequently the case with psychotherapists – rather eclectically, frequently on the basis of apposite quotations, it started a discussion of their tenets which has been persistently fertile for the continuing development of person-centred anthropology. In his typically modest way, Rogers (1973: 10) called his thinking 'a home-grown brand of existential philosophy'.

Amongst other things, his conceptions of decision and responsibility (engagement, commitment), of freedom and choice and of the linked process of evaluation are reminiscent of Kierkegaard. Rogers considers Kierkegaard a sensitive and highly perceptive friend who loosened him up and made him more willing to trust and express his own experience (Rogers, 1961b: 199f.). According to Rogers, Kierkegaard pictured the dilemma of the individual with keen psychological insight; some passages can be found in his writings that recall clients as they search for the reality of self. He pointed out that the most common despair is to be in despair in not choosing to be oneself, but the opposite is 'to will to be that self which one truly is' (Rogers, 1961b: 116f.). According to Kierkegaard (1957: 78) 'an existing individual is constantly in process of becoming', which Rogers (1961b: 172) quotes with approval.

Rogers's basic attitudes concerning a helpful relationship are equally related to Buber's conception of the I–Thou relationship and encounter, to his idea of the interpersonal (*das Zwischen[menschliche]*), to his attitudes towards dialogue, to inclusion (*Umfassung*), to becoming aware (*Innewerden*) and to confirmation.[6] According to Buber, persons are those human beings who – unlike 'Eigenwesen [egotists]' – are responsible, ready to take decisions, prepared to run risks and to act accordingly. After the remarkable dialogue with Buber in 1957 (Rogers and Buber, 1994), in which the differences became clearly apparent in spite of all the similarities, Rogers on the one hand became more differentiated in using Buber's concepts, and attached greater value to what happens *between* persons. Evidently Buber on the other hand referred in his epilogue to *Ich und Du* (Buber, 1974, first published 1923) to his conversation with Rogers. In this dialogue Buber defined 'person' as 'an individual living really with the world . . ., in real contact, in real reciprocity in all the points in which the world can meet man. . . . If I may say expressly "yes" and "no" to certain phenomena, I am against individuals and for persons' (Rogers and Buber, 1994: 51).

From the person-centred conception of the person to philosophy: the fulfilment of a claim

As has frequently happened in the history of the conception of the person, the word experienced a semantic change when it was adopted by the person-centred approach. At first, it seemed to offer an adequate way of understanding the Other and of describing most precisely what Rogers aimed at in his approach. As regards its psychological significance, however, it was radicalized by the image of man derived from therapeutic experience: here psychology not only came to assert the primacy of change through understanding in a relationship as opposed to objectifying, problem-centred interpreting and expert-centred psychotherapeutic treatment; but the conception of man and of interpersonal relationships that was gained therefrom also further developed the conception of the person. Rogers (1981a) is well aware of this: 'I think we've tended to give it a special meaning.' For what philosophy has long known and psychology has discussed for some length of time is consistently being put into practice by the person-centred approach: the human being is not observed and treated as an object; instead individuals are encountered as persons. The personal encounter which emerges from acting in a person-centred way is the fulfilment of this claim in practice. This shift in focus from the object to the person implies a change from experts considering themselves as responsible or having responsibility delegated to them to self-responsibility – a further stage on the road to 'man's escape from his minority, for which he himself is to be blamed', hence work of enlightenment. In the person-centred conception, the primacy of experience in the construction of theories and in research leads consequently to the primacy of empathy, a fact which is also of great significance in philosophy, in particular in epistemology. In theory and in practice, the person-centred approach has performed a shift of paradigms from the object to the person, from observation to encounter, and from interpretation to empathy. Wherever this new conception is realized in a concrete attitude or action, this can be seen as the fruitful and the immediate practical effect of philosophy on human life.

'Become who you are' (Pindar)

The tension which must be endured between the two conceptions of the person is undoubtedly characteristic of the person-centred conception of the person. This tension can also be found in therapy; where the client aims at becoming himself or herself through the relationship, understanding what he or she has always been and can become. Here the therapist remains authentically him/herself, yet related to the other person, empathically and offering positive regard. There is this tension in every helpful relationship: inasmuch as the offer of a relationship made by one person actually leads to such a relationship, evoking and revealing what was already present in the other person, but requiring the relationship to awaken it and to stimulate its (further) growth. This tension can be found in every person-centred relationship: inasmuch as the authenticity of each partner can be achieved through encounter, the tension between sovereignty *and* commitment, between self-confidence *and* devotion, between I *and* We. It is by living these differences, not by reconciling them, by continuously standing face to face in the encounter (see Chapter 7) that the actualization of the potential of the person takes place and that the personality grows.

> In the person-centred conception the person is someone who realizes his being-himself in a unique, distinctive way, by evolving more and more towards the personality he can be; by being there for others, by realizing his being most intensely in such a way that he allows room to others and loves them, because he finds himself to be someone who has been made possible and who is loved by others: as someone who was already addressed before he could even speak, and who now responds and assumes and bears responsibility – and who himself again evokes this process in others.

In his essay 'What it means to become a person', Carl Rogers (1961a: 123) explicitly asks: 'Who am I?' – the question philosophy has recognized to be about man's personhood. And he adds another one: 'How may I *become* myself?' (italics added). In these words he expresses the specifically person-centred contribution to man's personhood: the question about the person is the question about being a person *and* the question about becoming a person – linked to the question as to what sort of encounter must take place in order to bring this 'becoming' about.

Hence the approach is based on an image of man whose claims have still to be fulfilled in theory and practice if we are to be able to speak of a truly *person*-centred approach.

Notes

This chapter was translated by Elisabeth Zinschitz.

1 Of course both sexes are included in these expressions – but we must not forget that, apart from feminism, women are hardly represented in the history of philosophy. As yet there has been no detailed discussion of the relevant consequences of this for the concept of the person as such.

A more detailed description of the basic philosophical and psychological ideas outlined here can be found with references in Schmid (1995a, 1995b).

2 In its significance as an encounter-philosophical term 'the Other' is written with a capital letter. The term naturally includes men and women.

3 Approaches to person-centred ethics can be found in Schmid (1996: 521–32).

4 Theologically speaking, as a person man is the response to the word that in history was spoken by the 'God-with-us' ('Immanuel', Isaiah 7, 14), who revealed himself as Yahveh ('I am the one who is here for you', Exodus 3), of a God of relationship and experience, a God who is in dialogue with man.

5 Incidentally, it is known that in his writings Rogers does not always use his terms consistently and distinctively. As regards the term 'person', Rogers is in good company with regard to philosophical history; repeatedly, the charge is now raised that the conception of the person has been phrased too vaguely, or not broadly enough. The struggle for an exact term is not yet over; quite a few authors even say that the conception of the person cannot be defined precisely anyway.

6 Cf. Schmid (1994: 126–36, 178–80, 183–200). Also see Chapter 7 on encounter in this book.

References

Buber, Martin (1974) *Ich und Du*, 8th edn, trans. E. Zinschitz. Heidelberg: Lambert Schneider. First published as *Dialogisches Leben*. Zurich, 1923.

Buber, Martin (1982) *Das Problem des Menschen*, 5th edn. Heidelberg: Lambert Schneider. First published 1948.

Kierkegaard, Søren (1924) *Die Krankheit zum Tode*, 2nd edn. Jena 1924. First published 1849.

Kierkegaard, Søren (1957) *Abschließende unwissenschaftliche Nachschrift zu den Philosophischen Brocken*, Part 1. Düsseldorf/Cologne. First published 1846.

Kirschenbaum, Howard (1979) *On Becoming Carl Rogers*. New York: Delacorte.

Rogers, Carl R. (1957) 'The necessary and sufficient conditions of therapeutic personality change', *Journal of Consulting Psychology*, 21 (2): 95–103.

Rogers, Carl R. (1959) 'A theory of therapy, personality, and interpersonal relationships, as developed in the client-centered framework', in Sigmund Koch (ed.), *Psychology, the Study of a Science*, Vol. 3: *Formulations of the Person and the Social Context*. New York: McGraw-Hill. pp. 184–256.

Rogers, Carl R. (1961a) 'What it means to become a person', in Rogers (1961b). pp. 107–24.

Rogers, Carl R. (1961b) *On Becoming a Person. A Therapist's View of Psychotherapy*. Boston: Houghton Mifflin.

Rogers, Carl R. (1973) 'My philosophy of interpersonal relationships and how it grew', *Journal of Humanistic Psychology*, 13 (2): 3–15.

Rogers, Carl R. (1981a) *Carl Rogers in Österreich. Gespräch mit evangelischen und katholischen Theologen.* VHS, Vienna: APG (English/German video).

Rogers, Carl R. (1981b) *Carl Rogers in Österreich. Diskussion über personzentrierte Theorie mit Carl Rogers beim La Jolla Programm in Salzburg 1981.* VHS, Vienna: APG (English/German video).

Rogers, Carl R. and Buber, Martin (1994) Dialogue between Martin Buber and Carl Rogers, transcribed by Kenneth N. Cissna and Rob Anderson. First published in 1960 Martin Buber and Carl Rogers, *Psychologia. An International Journal of Psychology in the Orient* (Kyoto University) 3 (4): 208–21.

Rogers, Carl R. and Schmid, Peter F. (1995) *Person-zentriert. Grundlagen von Theorie und Praxis*, 2nd edn. Mainz: Grünewald. First published 1991.

Rogers, Carl R. and Wood, John K. (1974) 'Client-centered theory', in A. Burton (ed.), *Operational Theories of Personality*. New York: Brunner/Mazel. pp. 211–58.

Schmid, Peter F. (1994) *Personzentrierte Gruppenpsychotherapie, Vol. 1: Solidarität und Autonomie. Ein Handbuch.* Cologne: Edition Humanistische Psychologie.

Schmid, Peter F. (1995a) 'Souveränität und Engagement. Zu einem personzentrierten Verständnis von Person,' in Rogers and Schmid (1995). pp. 15–164.

Schmid, Peter F. (1995b) 'Die Person im Zentrum', in Rogers and Schmid (1995). pp. 297–305.

Schmid, Peter F. (1996) *Personzentrierte Gruppenpsychotherapie in der Praxis, Vol. 2: Die Kunst der Begegnung. Ein Handbuch.* Paderborn: Junfermann.

Schmid, Peter F. (1998) *Im Anfang ist Gemeinschaft. Personzentrierte Gruppenarbeit in Seelsorge und Praktischer Theologie, Vol. 3: Beiträge zu einer Theologie der Gruppe.* Stuttgart: Kohlhammer.

Wucherer-Huldenfeld, Augustinus (1978) 'Philosophische Anthropologie II'. Unpublished manuscript, Vienna.

5   Personality Change and the Concept of the Self

Martin van Kalmthout

Personality change in a psychotherapeutic context pertains to a process of profound or fundamental change as opposed to external behavioural or cognitive adaptation. As psychotherapy becomes more and more symptom oriented instead of person oriented, most psychotherapists (and their clients) no longer undertake this inner journey as part of their therapeutic work. For those psychotherapies which strive towards these more ambitious goals (such as the person-centred approach), the process of personality change remains a crucial subject for practical and theoretical exploration.

I consider Rogers's formulation of a theory of personality change in his 1959 publication one of the best theories of personality change available for psychotherapeutic purposes. At the same time, several points need further development and clarification. First, there is the core statement with regard to personality change formulated in the terms of Kierkegaard's: 'To be that self which one truly is'. As meaningful as this formulation might be for many people, it nevertheless raises such serious questions as: does a 'true self' exist and, if so, what are its distinctive characteristics?

Secondly, further development of Rogers's theory calls for greater attention to the conditioned nature of human beings than in the past. This includes the question of whether personality change is at all possible and just how changeable human beings may be. The question of evil also arises along with the question of the extent to which change is possible with severely disturbed clients.

A third aspect of Rogers's theory in need of further elaboration is the relative neglect of the dimension of relatedness and the one-sided emphasis on the actualization of the autonomous individual. A balanced theory of personality change should recognize both our need for autonomy and our need for belongingness. All this is not to say that absolutely no attention has been given to these issues in Rogers's theory. A comprehensive person-centred theory of personality nevertheless needs to be carefully elaborated to embrace the very complex problem of the self; one which will take the conditioned nature of human beings seriously and avoid any kind of one-sidedness with regard to autonomy versus relatedness.

The roots of the yearning for profound change

In tandem with Freud's statement that the question of life's meaning is only posed by depressed people, one can state that the longing for personality change reflects the yearning to end emotional distress being experienced by the person involved. When one finds oneself in a state of anxiety, depression, loneliness or isolation, the longing for being a completely different person readily arises. In some cases, this may lead a client to jump out of his psychological distress into the magic of alternative healing methods or impressive spiritual and religious philosophies. From a person-centred perspective, however, the process of personality change is quite different from so-called miracle cures (Miller and C'deBaca, 1994). This is not to say that sudden changes may not take place in person-centred therapy. Rather, these changes are part of a much larger process more generally characterized by struggling, fighting and discipline than by magical and instantaneous transformations. Rogers seems to have been all too aware of this when he cautions against an overly romantic view of the good life:

> I believe it will have become evident why, for me, adjectives such as happy, contented, blissful, enjoyable, do not seem quite appropriate to any general description of this process I have called the good life, even though the person in this process would experience each one of these feelings at appropriate times. But the adjectives which seem more generally fitting are adjectives such as enriching, exciting, rewarding, challenging, meaningful. This process of the good life is not, I am convinced, a life for the faint-hearted. It involves the stretching and growing of becoming more and more of one's potentialities. It involves the courage to be. It means launching oneself fully into the stream of life. (Rogers, 1961: 195–6)

For a person-centred description and analysis of personality change, the foregoing implies that we should travel very carefully, very factually and as close to the ground as possible because we are no different from our clients in our inclination to escape from our psychological roots into illusionary mythologies which promise an end to all suffering. For this reason, I will first consider the role of conditioning.

The heavy weight of human conditioning

Nothing is as impressive in clinical practice as the weight of human conditioning. Clients are frequently bowed down under a past consisting of being hurt by the emotional or physical violence of key figures in their childhood, resulting in isolation, defensiveness, uncertainty, and so on. In order to survive, they have developed specific interpersonal patterns which are usually the expression of a deeply rooted negative self-concept. Many times the psychological growth of these clients has simply stagnated because these hurts occurred at critical stages in their personality development. It is perhaps no surprise that these people can be easily described in terms of specific personality disorders with disturbances of the self at the core. It is my experience that for person-centred psychotherapy to be successful, the central underlying conflict crystallized in these intrapsychic and interpersonal patterns will sooner or later have to be addressed. It is also my experience that the task of breaking these patterns is very hard precisely because they still serve deeply rooted emotional needs and are therefore experienced as the very core of the self or personality (Benjamin, 1993). That is why clients involved in giving up these old adaptations sometimes have the feeling of giving up their old self and become anxious in response to this lack of anchorage and the unfamiliarity of the new.

In person-centred therapy, the conditioned nature of human beings is recognized and expressed in the theory of the conditions of worth (Rogers, 1959). It is simply not true that person-centred therapy denies the role of past history in the development and maintenance of psychological problems. On the contrary, the theory explains how psychological problems arise as a result of past conditioning. What crucially distinguishes person-centred therapy from more deterministic approaches is the assumption that it is possible to go beyond such conditioning. The question is not whether we are determined by the past or not, but to what degree change is possible. Psychotherapy is considered a fight against the conditioning of the past.

It should be emphasized that in person-centred theory this conditioning is phrased in interpersonal concepts not very different from those of Sullivan, Horney, Stern and other interpersonal theorists of psychopathology. In order to hold love, the child introjects the value system of his or her key figures and becomes estranged from the organismically experiencing self. A façade (which we may call the 'false self') is built to hide the 'true self'. The lack of empathic, respectful and genuine relating between the child and key figures means a loss of contact with the inner self. That is, the child is also unable to listen empathically, respectfully and honestly to himself or herself. Instead, he or she develops all kinds of interrelational patterns which serve to keep others at a distance or lead to fusion. One way to summarize this perspective on the development of psychopathology is to cast it in terms of a universal conflict between our need for separateness and our need for relatedness. The dialectic between these two needs in the developmental history of a child determines the adult personality to a high degree (Teyber, 1992).

Although person-centred therapy is rooted in an optimistic philosophy of human nature, the conditions of worth can explain the cruelties of which human beings are capable. Such cruelties are the direct result of the conditions of worth and the lack of their counterpart (empathy, respect and authenticity). Rogers wanted not to be misunderstood in this respect:

> I am quite aware that out of defensiveness and inner fear individuals can and do behave in ways which are incredibly cruel, horribly destructive, immature, regressive, antisocial, hurtful. Yet one of the most refreshing and invigorating parts of my experience is to work with such individuals and to discover the strongly positive directional tendencies which exist in them, as in all of us, at the deepest levels. (Rogers, 1961: 27)

In other words, person-centred theory does not deny the existence of evil but explains it within its own framework. In contrast to many deterministic philosophies, the actual existence of evil does not preclude the possibility for change. Person-centred theory postulates a basic constructive tendency for every person which may nevertheless be buried by layers and layers of conditioning.

Person-centred theory does not deny the difficulties of psychotherapy with severely disturbed clients. It is recognized that the challenge may be far greater and the required effort far more demanding, but the assumption is that a basic constructive tendency also exists in such people and that personality change is therefore possible, although by no means certain.

The primacy of the therapeutic relationship

As an interpersonal theory, it is logical that person-centred therapy takes the therapeutic relationship as primary. The cause of the problems is conceptualized as interpersonal, so the therapy should be interpersonal as well. That is, basically, the reason why, according to Rogers (1957: 96), the relational qualities of the therapist are necessary and sufficient for personality change to occur. Put differently, 'significant positive personality change does not occur except in a relationship'. This also means that what did not happen in the past should happen in the therapeutic relationship and is very akin to what psychodynamic therapists refer to as corrective emotional experience.

The foregoing description of person-centred theory and therapy in interpersonal concepts may almost seem to contradict its often mentioned (and criticized) emphasis on individual autonomy. We can only conclude that there is as much attention to the aim of attaining autonomy as to the aim of developing satisfying interpersonal relationships when the theory is closely examined. The emphasis on autonomy may be a cultural (largely American) and /or personal artifact (Rogers described himself as being a 'shy loner': 1972: 37). In any case, an interpersonal conceptualization of person-centred theory implies that personality change should be described in interpersonal terms as well. This means that not only individual self-actualization should be the goal of such therapy but also the establishment of harmonious interpersonal relations. A more active interpersonal presence may therefore be demanded of the person-centred therapist than often seems to be the case. It being his or her task to provide the client with the opportunity to experience new ways of relating (depending on the client's interpersonal pattern – for example, too distant or too close), the therapist should relate more intimately or in a more disengaged manner. Given the one-sided emphasis on autonomy mentioned above, person-centred therapists are more familiar with behaving intimately than distantly. Many times they seem unable to confront their clients or to set limits. They are also frequently blocked in their power to influence clients in the direction of change. The limitations of person-centred practice, particularly with so-called difficult clients, do not, however, follow from the theory itself. The interpretation of the theory has been one-sided, which means that person-centred therapists should pay greater attention to the development of congruence and avoid limiting themselves to a technical form of empathy. They should dare to be more present as persons of flesh and blood and not just as mechanically reflecting mirrors (Rogers, 1986).

The process of change

The therapeutic relationship in person-centred therapy is not a goal in itself although it seems to be in some forms of dialogical psychotherapy (Friedman, 1985). Nor is the therapeutic relationship secondary to the experiential change process of the client, as it seems to be in some forms of experiential psychotherapy (for example Mahrer, 1996). In person-centred theory, the psychotherapeutic relationship is seen as a safe environment where the client can start learning to trust his or her own experiential world and later move on. This process of the client becoming his or her own therapist is the ultimate goal of psychotherapy. The therapeutic relation-ship and the experiential change process are intrinsically linked in person-centred theory and constitute the two central pillars within this approach. Every endeavour to separate the two inevitably leads to one-sidedness. Personality change refers not only to the experiential change process but also to fundamental changes in interpersonal relationships.

In popular usage, the expression 'personality change' refers to the experience of replacing one personality ('the one I don't like') with another ('the one I like'). This is quite different from the person-centred description of personality change as 'to be that self which one truly is'. It is not unlike Jung's conception of individuation. Personality, in this context, refers to the entire complex of intrapersonal and interpersonal patterns contained within the individual and is, in fact, the end-result of our psychological conditioning. Personality change, on the other hand, refers to quite a different state of being, namely the unconditioned quality of the organism or what has been designated as authenticity and congruence in the person-centred tradition. This means becoming aware of those feelings and experiences which have previously been denied or distorted. Experiencing what you really are instead of what you would like to be (the ideal self) or what you are afraid of being (negative self-image) is the essence of the experiential process. It is assumed that experiencing oneself as one really is facilitates the process of accepting or liking oneself and thereby enables one to accept and like others as they really are. According to Rogers (1961: 187–92), this process of change can be characterized by (1) an increasing openness to experience, (2) increasingly existential living, (3) an increasing trust in the organism and (4) the process of functioning more fully. The conceptualization of personality change as 'experiencing the reality of what one is' is not very different from those old philosophical and religious traditions which have 'the search for truth' (in the experiential as opposed to ideological sense of the word) as their major aim. One such example is Buddhism (Purton, 1996).

In interpersonal terms, personality change implies relating to others in a balanced manner. This means maintaining one's autonomous self in relations with others; not being absorbed (or afraid of being absorbed) by others; and also not isolating oneself. This means the end to all kinds of pathological interpersonal patterns, including enmeshment or fusion at the one end and extreme isolation at the other end. Having accepted oneself, there is no longer the pathological need to fuse with others, to dominate them or to own them. Nor is there the urge to hide out of fear of being dominated, controlled or hurt by others.

The search for good interpersonal relationships is part of many traditions and is often designated as the domain of love. One such example is Christianity (Thorne, 1996). Just like the search for truth, the search for love has often been misunderstood. For example, love is often described in a romantic or sentimental way. Rogers's understanding of love is described through his triad of empathy, respect and congruence which he states form the cornerstone of good interpersonal relations. This meaning has nothing to do with the popular use of the word 'love' but reflects a much deeper sense. Finally, the presence of the core conditions and the experiential change process in religions and philosophical traditions reveal their universal nature. Their actual form and implementation may nevertheless be culturally determined.

The complexities of the self

Personality change in a person-centred perspective means becoming your real, true, organismic self. This self is *not* the conditioned false self or façade which is the product of the conditions of worth. Nor is it to be equated with the self-*concept*, be it idealized or negative. In fact, it is very difficult to define the self in positive terms.

In some humanistic and transpersonal circles, the word is capitalized as the Self. The underlying assumption seems to be that a divine entity is seated within us, sometimes designated as the Soul or the God within (or in the East, as the Buddha within). This can very easily lead to abstract theoretical speculations about the characteristics of the Self, and take us far from the actual experiencing of ourselves. In particular, this approach can produce a thing-like conceptualization of the self. In contrast, person-centred approaches to the self emphasize the process rather than the structure. Rogers went so far in accentuating the fluidity of the self that some critics have wondered whether change was more important to him than the sense of a coherent identity (for example Van Belle, 1980). One of the most distinguishing characteristics of the organismic self for Rogers is its flexibility, in contrast to the rigidity and fixed nature of the conditioned self: 'Life, at its best, is a flowing, changing process in which nothing is fixed' (Rogers, 1961: 27). Daring to live in the here and now of the experiential process (instead of the fixed, conditioned patterns of the past) is the essence of this true self.

To me, Rogers's emphasis on the ever-changing character of the self is a profound and original approach with implications which are still far from clear. The conditioned nature of human beings is taken seriously and a doorway to the possibility of fundamental change is opened in a concrete and down-to-earth manner. The ever-changing character of the self reminds me of the Buddhist concept of the empty self which has recently been discussed in the context of systemic thinking and family therapy by Rosenbaum and Dyckman. According to these authors, a fixed self inevitably leads to the introduction of reified physical concepts in the realm of relationships while the 'self is not a thing, but a process' (1995: 27). If we assume, in contrast, that the self has no core identity or unchanging essence, then we can see the self as 'an ongoing, ever-changing manifestation of potentiality' (1995: 28). Recognition of the potential within this emptiness can give a person a sense of relief and increased freedom because it carries the realization that as a person one can never be reduced to a certain image or personality. The dis-identification with a limited self-concept opens the door to fundamental change. What is more, it opens the door to relatedness, because as Rosenbaum and Dyckman (1995: 40) indicate: 'fundamentally, empty self is connected self . . . [as] we are all intimately connected to that well from which all experience comes'.

Insight

In the process of personality change described in this chapter, it is assumed that human beings are capable of self-knowledge. They are generally willing and able to experience their unconscious feelings and confront their intrapersonal and interpersonal patterns. In person-centred therapy, the main task of the therapist is actively to help the client to contact his or her inner source of experiencing and to mirror the client's interpersonal style of relating. It is also the task of the therapist to further the client's cognitive and, far more important, emotional awareness of the role of past conditioning in present difficulties.

All of this requires a receptive attitude on the part of the client and a willingness to be really honest in listening to oneself. In many clients this attitude is lacking (often for the same reasons which brought them to therapy). Such a receptive attitude has to be gradually developed in therapy. The heavy weight of past conditioning very often hinders the possibility of experiencing what and who one really is or could be. Essential to the process of change described here is the development of such a capacity not only as a means towards an end but as the goal of the personality change itself. This clarity of awareness has been referred to as the 'observing self' (Deikman, 1982). If a client is able to develop and maintain such an awareness, then he or she can become his or her own therapist and trust his or her own experiencing. The client may also then be able to see others as they are and relate to them in a harmonious – that is, autonomous but related – manner.

How should we characterize this clarity of mind? Is it something extra-ordinary, divine or even extrasensory? Deikman describes the observing self as follows:

> The observing self is not part of the object world formed by our thoughts and sensory perception because, literally, it has no limits; everything else does. Thus, everyday consciousness contains a transcendent element that we seldom notice because that element is the very ground of our experience. The word tran-scendent is justified because if subjective consciousness – the observing self – cannot itself be observed but remains forever apart from the contents of con-sciousness, it is likely to be of a different order from everything else. Its fundamentally different nature becomes evident when we realize that the observing self is featureless; it cannot be affected by the world any more than a mirror can be affected by the images it reflects. (Deikman, 1982: 95)

Insight, as conceptualized here, is a state of being in which our con-ditioning is transcended and a real transformation takes place. In the person-centred tradition, this state of mind has been variously referred to as authenticity, congruence or 'being that self which one truly is'. Insight pertains to that inner source which is characterized by changingness, spontaneity, originality and vitality. It might well be that old religious traditions describe the same quality when they talk of 'that which is not touched by thought' and referred to as 'the holy' (see Otto, 1950). 'The wholly other', as Otto observes, is of a totally different order than our conditioned intra- and interpersonal patterns (or façade), and it can only come about and flourish in a relational climate of love and compassion.

Conclusion

The process of personality change is one of the most distinctive features of psychotherapy. This process is nevertheless complicated and should therefore be approached with the utmost care. Central to a person-centred conceptualization of personality change is the concept of the self, which represents an equally complex phenomenon. To be that self which one truly is means a self which is flexible, not fixed. The person is always more than his or her conditioned intrapersonal and interpersonal patterns and should never be identified with these or any other label or categorization. Freedom in this context arises from awareness and emotional insight into conditioned patterns. Change does not mean the substitution of one complex of patterns for another (which is often the goal of behavioural and cognitive therapies). Change means becoming that organismic self which one has always been, and this is the essence of congruence or authenticity in the person-centred tradition.

References

Benjamin, L.S. (1993) *Interpersonal Diagnosis and Treatment of Personality Disorders.* New York: Guilford.

Deikman, A. (1982) *The Observing Self: Mysticism and Psychotherapy.* Boston: Beacon.

Friedman, M. (1985) *The Healing Dialogue in Psychotherapy.* New York: Jason Aronson.

Mahrer, A. (1996) *The Complete Guide to Experiential Psychotherapy.* New York: Wiley.

Miller, W. and C'deBaca, J. (1994) 'Quantum change: toward a psychology of transformation', in T. Heatherton and J. Weinberger (eds), *Can Personality Change?* Washington: American Psychological Association. pp. 253–80.

Otto, R. (1950) *The Idea of the Holy.* London: Oxford University Press. First published 1917.

Purton, C. (1996) 'The deep structure of the core conditions: a Buddhist perspective', in R. Hutterer, G. Pawlowsky, P. Schmid and R. Stipsits (eds), *Client-centered and Experiential Psychotherapy: A Paradigm in Motion.* Frankfurt-on-Main: Peter Lang. pp. 455–67.

Rogers, C. (1957) 'The necessary and sufficient conditions of therapeutic personality change', *Journal of Consulting Psychology*, 21: 95–103.

Rogers, C. (1959) 'A theory of therapy, personality, and interpersonal relationships, as developed in the client-centered framework', in S. Koch (ed.), *Psychology: A Study of a Science, Vol. III. Formulations of the Person and the Social Context.* New York: McGraw-Hill. pp. 184–256.

Rogers, C. (1961) *On Becoming a Person.* London: Constable.

Rogers, C. (1972) *Becoming Partners: Marriage and its Alternatives.* New York: Delacorte.

Rogers, C. (1986) 'Reflection of feelings', *Person-Centered Review*, 1: 375–7.

Rosenbaum, R. and Dyckman, J. (1995) 'Integrating self and system: an empty intersection', *Family Process*, 34: 21–44.

Teyber, E. (1992) *Interpersonal Process in Psychotherapy*, 2nd edn. Pacific Grove, CA: Brooks/Cole.

Thorne, B. (1996) 'Person-centred therapy: the path to holiness', in R. Hutterer, G. Pawlowsky, P. Schmid and R. Stipsits (eds), *Client-centered and Experiential Psychotherapy: A Paradigm in Motion.* Frankfurt-on-Main: Peter Lang. pp. 107–16.

Van Belle, H. (1980) *Basic Intent and Therapeutic Approach of Carl R. Rogers.* Toronto: Wedge.

6   From Non-Directive to Experiential: A Paradigm Unfolding

Germain Lietaer

Fifty-seven years ago client-centred therapy was born under the star of non-directivity. This key aspect of its identity has been an issue of debate ever since and even to this day the battle about its importance and precise meaning occasionally flares up (Brodley, 1990, 1997). In this chapter we hope to contribute to the clarification and perhaps partial mitigation of the controversy surrounding the concept of non-directivity. We will in turn:

- define the concept of directivity clearly (it is often given divergent meanings);
- describe how client-centred therapy practice has evolved from 'non-directive' to 'experience-oriented' (indeed, discussions reveal that, even among practitioners of the approach, this evolution is often unknown);
- explore further the process of selective reinforcement in client-centred therapy (about which simplistic opinions are sometimes offered).

Directivity versus manipulation

We will start our attempt at defining the concept of directivity by pointing out what it should *not* be confused with. Systems thinkers have drawn our attention to the fact that it is impossible to 'not-influence' and that non-directive therapy cannot therefore exist. Hence, 'a minimal structure' influences the actual process sequence just as much as a clearly structured approach. We are bound to influence and, after all, that is what we want: as therapists we hope to have an impact on the client's process. Next, the concept of directivity is sometimes related to the difference between self-treatment and 'being in treatment'. But then, isn't all psychotherapy in essence self-treatment? Thus behaviour therapy constantly appeals to the client's own activity: although a specific method may be prescribed, it remains up to the client to follow the proposed procedures and do his or her own 'homework'. Finally, directivity is often associated with the contrast between entering a relationship as an expert and entering it as an equal. We believe that, in this instance, equality is being confused with being equally valuable. Client and therapist may then be equally valuable but they do not enter the relationship as equals. There is an allocation of roles whereby it is the therapist's task to facilitate the client's process of change and not the other way round. This decreases the mutuality in a professional therapeutic relationship and makes for structural inequality. Some client-centred therapists rather abhor the notion of 'expert'. But is it not the case that they get intensive training, hoping to become experts in offering the 'therapeutic conditions'? A training in which they learn to steep themselves as process-experts in the client's experiential world, to bring in their own experiences and impressions in a constructive way, and to use clinical concepts and experience-unfolding techniques in an expert way!

Seen in its positive aspects, we believe directivity to refer to the therapist's task-oriented responses and interventions. Theory and research into the therapist's contribution (Bierman, 1969) generally come up with two basic dimensions which are in reality very much interlinked. The horizontal dimension refers to the quality of the contact. This dimension's positive pole is characterized by relationship-enhancing attitudes and behaviours such as: dedication, respect, affirmation, acceptance, integrity, warmth and empathy. There is also a vertical dimension which refers to the therapist's instrumental, task-oriented responses and interventions and, more generally, to the way in which he or she shapes the therapeutic process. This vertical dimension consists of a great many activities, interventions and procedures which may, or may not, or may only to a certain extent – depending on the therapist's therapeutic orientation and personality and on the client's problems – be part of the therapist's input. Thus we see substantial differences in the intake procedures, in the presence or absence of concretely formulated goals, in the frequency and length of the responses, in the use of specific procedures, in the frequency and content of interpretations, in the use of confrontations and feedback, in the reflection and evocation of feelings, in the explicit giving of information and advice. . . . Directivity is thus a multidimensional concept and so it makes little sense to wonder whether a therapist is directive or not. It only makes sense to see *in what way* he or she is directive or task-oriented. There is no negative colouring to this many-sided vertical dimension: it does not stand in the way of an optimal relationship (as factor-analytic studies show: Gurman, 1977; Lietaer, 1989). What may vary greatly is the therapist's degree of expertise and the degree to which the method employed corresponds to the client's expectations of what will be helpful.

Yet it was with good reason that Rogers – and others with him – warned so strongly against manipulation and stressed clients' personal responsibility, their 'personal power' and their right to live according to their own views (Rogers, 1977). This is, however, a new factor – the danger of external control – which Rogers always distinguished from influencing (Rogers and Skinner, 1956). Indeed, control and manipulation refer to a formal-ethical aspect which is inherent in our actions. Almost all task-oriented interventions may be carried out with respect for the client's freedom and autonomy. They may also be forced upon the client or the therapist may slip into unwanted or unnoticed manipulation (see also Coghlan and McIlduff, 1990). The same may be said of the horizontal dimension: empathy can be misused and the therapist's 'warmth' can become disastrous to the client when it is offered out of the therapist's personal need or because of personal problems. Personal therapy, supervision and the client-centred basic rule of keeping in touch with the client's 'felt sense' in everything we offer as therapists hopefully will protect against such forms of manipulation. In any case, they increase the chances of the influencing process, which therapy happens to be, being owned and endorsed by the client.

From non-directivity to being experience-oriented

Initial phase: emphasis on the non-directive

What was Rogers initially after with the non-directive character of his therapeutic method? It was a reaction against the directive counselling of his time, which used such 'authoritarian' methods as forbidding, ordering, advising, interpreting, suggesting, reassuring and persuading (Rogers, 1942: 130–45). He was also sceptical about psychoanalysis (or at least certain of its excesses): he found psychoanalysts sometimes too fascinated by their own theories and hence listening more to themselves than to their clients. Gradually his practical experience at Rochester Guidance Clinic led him to abandon the 'diagnostic-prescriptive' model of his time. He describes the following incident which led to what may perhaps be viewed as the first client-centred therapy session:

> An intelligent mother brought her very seriously misbehaving boy to the clinic. I took the history from her myself. Another psychologist tested the boy. We decided in conference that the central problem was the mother's rejection of her son. I would work with her on this problem. The other psychologist would take the boy on for play therapy. In interview after interview I tried – much more softly and gently now, as a result of experience – to help the mother see the pattern of her rejection and its results in the boy. All to no avail. After about a dozen interviews I told her I thought we both had tried but were getting nowhere, and we should probably call it quits. She agreed. Then, as she was leaving the room, she turned and asked, 'Do you ever take adults for counseling here?' Puzzled, I replied that sometimes we did. Whereupon she returned to the chair she had just left and began to pour out a story of the deep difficulties between herself and her husband and her great desire for some kind of help. I was bowled over. What she was telling me bore no resemblance to the neat history I had drawn from her. I scarcely knew what to do, but mostly I listened. Eventually, after many more interviews, not only did her marital relationship improve, but her son's problem behavior dropped away as she became a more real and free person. . . .

> This was a vital learning for me. I had followed *her* lead rather than mine. I had just *listened* instead of trying to nudge her toward a diagnostic understanding I had already reached. (Rogers, 1980: 36–7).

From this and other experiences, Rogers learned an important lesson: in order to provide actual help, the therapist has to be in touch with the problem as the client experiences it and follow the client within the client's own frame of reference. Not the therapist but the client knows best! This instantly became a basic principle of client-centred therapy: 'the client-centered therapist aims to concentrate on the *immediate phenomenal world* of the client. For he believes that it is in confusions or contradictions within this world that the client's difficulties lie' (Rogers, 1966: 191; original emphasis). Central to this axiom is the *pervading* nature of his therapeutic mandate:

> All therapeutic approaches are of course centrally interested in the client, and in this sense might be thought of as client-centered. But the term 'client-centered' has, for our group, a technical meaning not often explicated. Many therapeutic systems consider the achievement of an empathic grasp of the client's private world only a preliminary to the real work of the therapist. For these therapists, coming to understand the client's phenomenal universe is rather like taking a history; it is a first step. Instead, the client-centered therapist aims to remain within this phenomenal universe throughout the entire course of therapy and holds that stepping outside it – to offer external interpretations, to give advice, to suggest, to judge – only retards therapeutic gain. (Rogers, 1966: 190)

Note that this basic rule was not born out of a 'preference for democracy' but out of therapeutic necessity. Initially, then, the emphasis was largely on what wasn't allowed and on a number of non-directive prescriptions meant to prevent the therapist from intervening on the basis of his own frame of reference. Gendlin quotes some of them (1970: 547–9): 'Don't interpret . . . don't answer the client's questions . . . don't express your own opinion . . . if you are puzzled about something, don't mention it . . . if you have a strong liking and appreciation for the client, don't mention it. . . . If there is something you think he ought to talk about, forget it . . . if he is silent, you must remain silent also, indefinitely . . .'. These prescriptions were always aimed at not leading the client away from his own experiential track and not making him dependent on the therapist. Here is, for example, how Tomlinson and Whitney describe why 'supporting-comforting' interventions don't help:

> Support is probably the best intentioned of the nongrowth responses. The giving of support usually follows some utterance of pain by the client to which the therapist attempts to indicate his understanding or sympathy by statements such as these: 'It's all right, I've felt the same way in the past', or 'gee, you shouldn't feel that way, I think you're nice,' or 'don't feel badly, that happens to a lot of people.' The aim of all these statements is to relieve pain by reducing the

seriousness or uniqueness of the complaint. However, the motive of the pain-reliever is not so altruistic as it would seem, and in the long run he may do more damage than help with his support.

The unstated meaning conveyed in a message of support is that the communicator is made so anxious by the client's painful sounds that he or she cannot tolerate its expression, and must somehow reduce it, that is, the therapist is made so uncomfortable by the perception of pain in his client that he or she is moved to relieve it by supporting a view *contrary* to the client's. Thus the motive for support is not so much to do the other good as it is to reduce one's own anxiety generated by the other's pain.

An additional assumption is that the person is either too weak to bear the pain without help or that he is weak for having the pain. Support frequently carries and communicates the implicit message that the other's experience is of lesser or little importance since 'I've had one like it, or worse.' When the response to painful feelings is 'you shouldn't feel that way . . .,' the message again is that your feelings are either wrong or unimportant.

Whatever the outcome of the support statement, the important result, and the debilitating one, is that the client is never allowed to express, fully explore, and own the pain. (Tomlinson and Whitney, 1970: 461)

Being experience-oriented

Even though much truth is (still) contained in these non-directive rules, their dogmatic wording nevertheless hampered therapists' 'freedom of action' unnecessarily and reduced them all too often to adopting a waiting-receptive stance. Non-directivity has sometimes been confused with inactivity and active-steering interventions originating in the therapist's own frame of reference were all too readily seen as manipulations. This was, however, to change between 1955 and 1962 (see Lietaer, 1993: 32–4; Van Balen, 1990). Their work with schizophrenics as well as their contact with the existential branch in American psychotherapy (Truax and Carkhuff, 1967) incited client-centred therapists gradually to define the therapist's contribution in positive terms; the forbidden was to disappear into the background and what really mattered came into focus: 'maximizing the client's experiential process, using our own to do so' (Gendlin, 1970: 549). Thus, client-centred therapy evolved from 'non-directive' to 'experiential' (Gendlin, 1968) and the steering interventions originating in the therapist's own frame of reference were no longer regarded as fundamentally wrong.

As a result (most) client-centred therapists have lost their directivity phobia; they no longer feel uneasy about describing their work as an active influencing process in which task-oriented responses and interventions are used to stimulate or even give an impetus to the unfolding of the client's experiential process. They have learned to take the initiative in an active way as process-experts, without slipping into manipulation and author-itarian control. This is done according to the basic principle of keeping the client's experiencing as a continuous reference point for all therapist responses and interventions: the therapist may then use his or her own frame of reference as a starting point as long as he or she keeps returning to the client's experiential track, remaining receptively in touch with the client's response to interventions and bringing responses to bear on that response. The former non-directive rules may, in this way, be transgressed in an experiential manner. Two examples:

> We used to tell therapists '*don't express your own opinion*'. Now if I am asked for it, I almost always do express my opinion, rather briefly, but showing exactly the steps of thought I go through. Then I say, 'but it isn't likely that that would fit you, because you're a different person, and besides, you probably thought of that already anyway and it doesn't work.' And I return him to his own track. (Of course he might have all sorts of feelings about the fact that I have the opinion I have, but these too we can explore, if he expresses or lets me sense these reactions in him. That too will again be his process, and we will try to respond to each other honestly in reference to his process and his concretely felt steps.) (Gendlin, 1970: 548; original emphasis)

> Our clients are not likely to experience any manipulative or controlling intent on our part if whatever we offer (e.g., exercises, strategies, tools and techniques, information, structures) derives from our understanding of their individual needs and is done in a manner that clearly communicates that 'this is an *option* you may wish to consider.' (Cain, 1989: 131; original emphasis)

Although full rights have now been accorded to steering interventions alongside the 'following' ones, our client-centred therapeutic orientation has nevertheless kept a non-directive hue. Or shall we say: a homeopathic hue (Riebel, 1984; Schott and Schott, 1990)? By this we mean that client-centred therapists view the human being as proactive and intent on self-realization and that they wish to leave this actualizing tendency as much room as possible. Theoretical critics notwithstanding (Eisenga and Wijngaarden, 1991) and despite substantial differences among client-centred therapists, the client-centred therapeutic method seems to remain more one of following than of steering and seems to show great respect for what can develop *from within* (Gendlin, 1990). Rogers had always viewed psycho-therapy as removing obstacles and thus allowing the person's own dynamic force to come to the fore again. His basic idea has always been that the main task of the therapist consists of creating a safe climate in which the client can get in touch with his or her inner experience. This reduced interpersonal fear and increased inner concentration (Rice, 1974: 302) is allowing the client to go deeper into his or her own experience. A 'self-propelling process' is started that leads to self-confrontation and reorganization.

In actual practice, this homeopathic attitude manifests itself in a minimal structuring of the therapeutic process and in a constant search to connect with the client's inner compass: his or her organismic experience. Client-centred therapists do not take on the role of director and certainly not that of guru. Their trust in the process makes them very receptive to what comes from within and makes them opt for open self-exploration in which form and direction largely (but, in my opinion, not exclusively) originate in the client. Rogers liked to quote Lao-Tzu's 25-centuries-old description of a good leader:

> But of a good leader, who talks little, when his work is done, his aim fulfilled, they will all say, 'We did this ourselves'. (Rogers, 1980: 42)

Experiential focus: a merely formal selective reinforcement?

Being experience-*oriented* implies selective reinforcement. Rogers and other client-centred therapists, too, freely admit it. Not every statement of the client receives equal attention. We always try to move from the narrative to the feelings, from the theoretical-abstract level to what is actually experienced. Rogers writes in this way about his interventions in an encounter group:

> There is no doubt that I am selective in my listening, hence 'directive' if people wish to accuse me of this. I am centered in the group member who is speaking, and am unquestionably much less interested in the details of his quarrel with his wife, or of his difficulties on the job, or his disagreement with what has just been said, than in the *meaning* these experiences have for him now and the *feelings* they arouse in him. It is to these meanings and feelings that I try to respond. (1970: 47; original emphasis)

Consequently there is a formal kind of process directivity, which amounts to a reinforcement of the client's experience. In addition, we support our clients as they evolve towards a more experience-oriented way of living, hold on less tightly to external norms, undertake actions towards more autonomy, dare to risk themselves more personally in relationships – in short, when they change in the direction of our concept of the 'fully functioning person' (Rogers, 1963).

The question remains, however, whether we also reinforce selectively *within* experience itself, whether our directivity is also content-oriented. Rogers hopes it is not. He believes that he is at his best as a therapist when every feeling of the client is welcome, when the client is 'rewarded' through therapy for each expression of self, whatever the content of the feeling (Rogers, 1967: 519). Also, when a client withdraws for instance, or decides to quit therapy because of fear of what it might entail, or relapses into former ways of behaviour, and so on: in such moments we can help our clients best of all by accepting where they find themselves now, by focusing on and exploring more in depth what they experience now. Another aspect of this non-directivity with regard to experiential content lies in the fact that in client-centred therapy there is no preliminary strategy or planning for therapy. Therapy is considered to be an adventure from moment to moment, in which it is not necessary that the therapist understand in advance the heart of the client's problem (Rogers et al., 1967: 509). On the contrary, we rely on the assumption that what is really important to the client will come up in therapy. The only instruction we give ourselves is to follow as receptively as possible the experiential flow of our client. Neither the therapist nor the client knows in advance where this will lead. Thus we have not 'mapped out' anything, nor have we decided in advance that certain contents *must* be explored.

Very much in line with this non-directivity and receptivity with regard to content, Rogers emphasizes his 'gullibility' (Rogers and Wood, 1974: 232): he does not listen to the client's tale with suspicion, wondering if the client is trying to conceal something. He is well aware that the client does not always speak 'all of the truth' but he finds that taking seriously what the client is able to say *now* is the best way of inviting her to become more authentic. On the other hand, he does not try to avoid painful experiences. He has the basic confidence that all will eventually be well and declares himself prepared 'to plunge to the depths of fear with this client and trust that they return. I face the unknown in my client and in myself without a complete assurance of, but a trust in, a positive outcome' (Rogers and Wood, 1974: 231). This 'unconditional confidence' (Harman, 1990) goes to show that client-centred therapy is not into covering up: what lives in the client, however painful and anxiety-provoking it may be, is not avoided. 'No unmentionables', as Gendlin puts it:

> I have the choice only whether to leave him alone with it, or keep him interactive company with it. . . . Often the patient refers to something which is unmentionable because it 'dare not be,' cannot be tolerated – for example, 'that they don't care for me,' or 'that I am crazy,' or 'that the therapist doesn't care for me,' or 'that I am ugly.' It helps if I speak these out loud. The patient is still here. He has not been shattered. I phrase it with a 'maybe' so we can back out if need be. I say, almost lightly, 'Maybe you're awful scared you really *are* crazy.' Or, 'Maybe I don't care for you at all,' or, 'Maybe you're too ugly for anybody to like.' The result is usually relief. I respect the patient, not the trap he is caught in. (Gendlin 1967: 397)

When we talk about selective reinforcement, we clearly distinguish between formal process and content. This distinction allows us to comment in a more nuanced manner on Murray's (1956) and Truax's (1966) studies of the degree to which Rogers 'conditions verbally' (see also Lieberman, 1969a, 1969b; Truax, 1969; Wachtel, 1979). Our own analysis of their findings (Lietaer, 1984: 52–3) indicated that the selectivity used here is essentially a formal one, in favour of experience, and that receptivity to specific experiential content remains high. Thus, Rogers does not appear to react more empathically or acceptantly the more the client brings, for example, positive or low-anxiety content, but he does show more empathy and acceptance when the self-exploratory process demonstrates a high level of commitment. However, this content-receptivity remains forever a counsel of perfection.

Our own personalities and blind spots may at times prevent us from noticing certain types of experiential content in our clients or require that we leave them untouched because we do not really dare to confront them. Furthermore, our training within a certain therapeutic orientation may sharpen or blunt our sensitivity to certain types of experiential content. This shows, for example, in the reactions of some psychoanalytically oriented and existential therapists to fragments of three client-centred therapies with schizophrenics. Truax and Carkhuff summarize their comments as follows:

> Particularly striking was the observation by almost all the theorists that the client-centered process of therapy somehow avoids the expected and usual patient expressions of negative, hostile, or aggressive feelings. The clear implication is that the client-centered therapist for some reason seems less open to receiving negative, hostile, or aggressive feelings. Is it that the therapists have little respect for, or understanding of their own negative, hostile, or aggressive feelings, and are thus unable to receive those feelings from the patient? Do they simply 'not believe' in the importance of the negative feelings? (Truax and Carkhuff, 1967: 503)

In addition, our concept of optimal psychic functioning and our concept of man will inevitably influence our responses and interventions. And here, formal and content selectivity almost coincide. We notice, for example, how Rogers gradually arrived at a very concrete concept of 'the person of tomorrow, spearhead of a quiet revolution' (1977: 255–82; 1980: 348–52). In this concept, independence and individual self-realization obviously count for more than interdependence and solidarity. Some client-centred therapists point out the value judgement in, and the culture-bound character of this concept (Eisenga and Wijngaarden, 1991; Holdstock, 1990; Pfeiffer, 1989) and Rogers was aware of it himself (1979). In any case, therapists do have their 'ideals'. However, we surmise that the *way in which* therapists use their influence is more important in this context than the distinction between formal and content selectivity; the *non-imposing* character of whatever the therapist does is the crucial thing. A therapist of sufficient integrity who is capable of putting his or her own values aside during therapy, a therapist who checks continuously his or her (steering and following) responses and interventions against the client's experience, will not venture into blind conditioning in the manipulative sense of the word but will stay firmly located within a mutually desired process of influencing that takes place as consciously as possible and in which the client always has the last word.

Conclusion

From the above it should be clear that directivity cannot be equated with external control or 'surrender to authority'. It is possible for a therapist to be process-directive in a truly dialogic and democratic way. Offering the 'Rogerian' attitudes and focusing on the experiential world of the client – to me the core aspects of the experiential paradigm – merge into a highly influential process, as so much research has shown (for example Greenberg et al., 1994; Orlinsky et al., 1994); yet at its best it is always a process in which the organismic awareness of the person functions as the ultimate guide. Therefore I hope that 'the impossible concept of non-directivity' – which Rogers already dropped in 1951! – will disappear as a 'hot issue' within our paradigm and that an attitude of tolerance and even of welcome will become prevalent as to variation in degree and type of process directivity. With Warner (1993) I am convinced that different levels of intrusiveness are acceptable and possible within an interactive and non-imposing way of experiential psychotherapy. The level of choice depends on many variables, such as the personality and 'training history' of the therapist, the phase of therapy, the type of client problem, the specificity of the ongoing process. Using diagnostic knowledge or proposing certain procedures can be part of our working differentially with clients as long as we stay in touch with their experiential track (Gendlin, 1996; Greenberg et al., 1993), as long as we use these procedures or knowledge only as tools, only as 'fishing lines, not fish' (Gendlin, 1974: 243).

References

Bierman, R. (1969) 'Dimensions of interpersonal facilitation in psychotherapy and child development', *Psychological Bulletin*, 72: 338–52.

Brodley, B.T. (1990) 'Client-centered and experiential: two different therapies?', in G. Lietaer, J. Rombauts and R. Van Balen (eds), *Client-centered and Experiential Psychotherapy in the Nineties.* Leuven: Leuven University Press. pp. 87–107.

Brodley, B.T. (1995) 'Meanings and implications of the nondirective attitude in client-centered therapy'. Unpublished manuscript, Illinois School of Professional Psychology, Chicago.

Brodley, B.T. (1997) 'The nondirective attitude in client-centered therapy', *The Person-centered Journal*, 4 (1): 18–30.

Cain, D. (1989) 'The paradox of nondirectiveness in the person-centered approach', *Person-Centered Review*, 4: 123–31.

Coghlan, D. and McIlduff, E. (1990) 'Structuring and nondirectiveness in group facilitation', *Person-Centered Review*, 5: 13–29.

Eisenga, R. and Wijngaarden, H. (1991) 'Het mensbeeld van de cliëntgerichte therapie', in H. Swildens, O. de Haas, G. Lietaer and R. Van Balen (eds), *Leerboek gesprekstherapie.* Amersfoort/Leuven: Acco. pp. 251–64.

Gendlin, E.T. (1967) 'Therapeutic procedures in dealing with schizophrenics', in C.R. Rogers, E.T. Gendlin, D.J. Kiesler and C.B. Truax (eds), *The Therapeutic Relationship and its Impact: A Study of Psychotherapy with Schizophrenics.* Madison, WI: University of Wisconsin Press. pp. 369–400.

Gendlin, E.T. (1968) 'The experiential response', in E.F. Hammer (ed.), *Use of Interpretation in Therapy: Technique and Art.* New York: Grune & Stratton. pp. 208–27.

Gendlin, E.T. (1970) 'A short summary and some long predictions', in J.T. Hart and T.M. Tomlinson (eds), *New Directions in Client-centered Therapy*. Boston: Houghton Mifflin. pp. 544–62.

Gendlin, E.T. (1974) 'Client-centered and experiential psychotherapy', in D.A. Wexler and L.N. Rice (eds), *Innovations in Client-centered Therapy*. New York: Wiley. pp. 211–46.

Gendlin, E.T. (1990) 'The small steps of the therapy process: how they come and how to help them come,' in G. Lietaer, J. Rombauts and R. Van Balen (eds), *Client-centered and Experiential Psychotherapy in the Nineties*. Leuven: Leuven University Press. pp. 205–50.

Gendlin, E.T. (1996) 'Integrating other therapeutic methods,' in *Focusing-oriented Psychotherapy: A Manual of the Experiential Method*. New York: Guilford. pp. 169–304.

Greenberg, L.R., Rice, L.N. and Elliott, R. (1993) *Facilitating Emotional Change: The moment-by-moment Process*. New York: Guilford.

Greenberg, L.S., Elliott, R. and Lietaer, G. (1994) 'Research on experiential psychotherapies', in A.E. Bergin and S.L. Garfield (eds), *Handbook of Psychotherapy and Behavior Change*. New York: Wiley. pp. 509–39.

Gurman, A. (1977) 'The patient's perception of the therapeutic relationship', in A. Gurman and A. Razin (eds), *Effective Psychotherapy: A Handbook of Research*. New York: Pergamon Press. pp. 503–43.

Harman, J.J. (1990) 'Unconditional confidence as a facilitative precondition', in G. Lietaer, J. Rombauts and R. Van Balen (eds), *Client-centered and Experiential Psychotherapy in the Nineties*. Leuven: Leuven University Press. pp. 251–68.

Holdstock, L. (1990) 'Can client-centered therapy transcend its monocultural roots?', in G. Lietaer, J. Rombauts and R. Van Balen (eds), *Client-centered and Experiential Psychotherapy in the Nineties*. Leuven: Leuven University Press. pp. 109–21.

Lieberman, L.R. (1969a) 'Reinforcement and non-reinforcement in Rogerian psychotherapy: a critique', *Perceptual and Motor Skills*, 28: 559–65.

Lieberman, L.R. (1969b) 'Reinforcement in Rogerian psychotherapy: rejoinder', *Perceptual and Motor Skills*, 29: 861–2.

Lietaer, G. (1984) 'Unconditional positive regard: a controversial basic attitude in client-centered therapy', in R. F. Levant and J.M. Shlien (eds), *Client-centered Therapy and the Person-centered Approach: New Directions in Theory, Research and Practice*. New York: Praeger. pp. 41–58.

Lietaer, G. (1989) 'De werkrelatie in client-centered psychotherapie: bedenkingen bij bevindingen uit een vragenlijstonderzoek', in H. Vertommen, G. Cluckers and G. Lietaer (eds), *De relatie in therapie*. Leuven: Leuven University Press. pp. 207–35.

Lietaer, G. (1993) 'Authenticity, congruence and transparency', in D. Brazier (ed.), *Beyond Carl Rogers: Towards a Psychotherapy for the Twenty-first Century*. London: Constable. pp. 17–47.

Murray, E.J. (1956) 'A content-analysis method for studying psychotherapy,' *Psychological Monographs*, 70 (whole no. 420).

Orlinsky, D., Grawe, K. and Parks, B.K. (1994) 'Process and outcome in psychotherapy – noch einmal', in A.E. Bergin and S.L. Garfield (eds), *Handbook of Psychotherapy and Behavior Change*. New York: Wiley. pp. 270–376.

Pfeiffer, W.M. (1989) 'Klientenzentrierte Therapie im kulturellen Zusammengang', in M. Behr, F. Petermann, W.M. Pfeiffer and C. Seewald (eds), *Jahrbuch für personenzentrierte Psychologie und Psychotherapie*. Vol. 1. Salzburg: Otto Müller. pp. 60–79.

Rice, L.N. (1974) 'The evocative function of the therapist', in D.A. Wexler and L.N. Rice (eds), *Innovations in Client-centered Therapy*. New York: Wiley. pp. 289–311.

Riebel, L. (1984) 'A homeopathic model of psychotherapy', *Journal of Humanistic Psychology*, 24 (1): 9–48.

Rogers, C.R. (1942) *Counseling and Psychotherapy*. Boston: Houghton Mifflin.

Rogers, C.R. (1963) 'The concept of the fully functioning person', *Psychotherapy: Theory, Research and Practice*, 1: 17–26.

Rogers, C.R. (1966) 'Client-centered therapy', in S. Arieti (ed.), *American Handbook of Psychiatry*, Vol. 3. New York: Basic Books. pp. 183–200.

Rogers, C.R. (1967) 'A silent young man', in C.R. Rogers, E.T. Gendlin, D.J. Kiesler and C.B. Truax (eds), *The Therapeutic Relationship and its Impact: A Study of Psychotherapy with Schizophrenics*. Madison: University of Wisconsin Press. pp. 401–16.

Rogers, C.R. (1970) *On Encounter Groups*. New York: Harper & Row.

Rogers, C.R. (1977) *Carl Rogers on Personal Power*. New York: Delacorte Press.

Rogers, C.R. (1979) 'Groups in two cultures', *Personnel and Guidance Journal*, 38 (1): 11–15.

Rogers, C.R. (1980) *A Way of Being*. Boston: Houghton Mifflin.

Rogers, C.R. and Skinner, B.F. (1956) 'Some issues concerning the control of human behavior', *Science*, 124: 1056–66.

Rogers, C.R. and Wood, J.K. (1974) 'Client-centered theory: Carl R. Rogers', in A. Burton (ed.), *Operational Theories of Personality*. New York: Brunner/Mazel. pp. 211–54.

Rogers, C.R., Gendlin, E.T., Kiesler, D.J. and Truax, C.B. (1967) 'A dialogue between therapists', in C.R. Rogers, E.T. Gendlin, D.J. Kiesler and C.B. Truax (eds), *The Therapeutic Relationship and its Impact: A Study of Psychotherapy with Schizophrenics*. Madison: University of Wisconsin Press. pp. 507–20.

Schott, E. and Schott, U. (1990) 'Homöopathie und personzentrierte Psychotherapie: Ihre Gemeinsamkeiten, ihr Zusammenspiel – dargestellt an einem klinischen Fall', *GwG Zeitschrift*, 21 (78): 36–41.

Tomlinson, T.M. and Whitney, R.E. (1970) 'Values and strategy in client-centered therapy: a means to an end', in J.T. Hart and T.M. Tomlinson (eds), *New Directions in Client-centered Therapy*. Boston: Houghton Mifflin. pp. 453–67.

Truax, C.B. (1966) 'Reinforcement and nonreinforcement in Rogerian psychotherapy', *Journal of Abnormal Psychology*, 71: 1–9.

Truax, C.B. (1969) 'Reinforcement and nonreinforcement in Rogerian psychotherapy: a reply', *Perception and Motor Skills*, 29: 701–2.

Truax, C.B. and Carkhuff, R.R. (1967) 'The client-centered process as viewed by other therapists', in C.R. Rogers, E.T. Gendlin, D.J. Kiesler and C.B. Truax (eds), *The Therapeutic Relationship and its Impact: A Study of Psychotherapy with Schizophrenics*. Madison: University of Wisconsin Press. pp. 419–505.

Van Balen, R. (1990) 'The therapeutic relationship according to Carl Rogers: a climate? A dialogue? Or both?', in G. Lietaer, J. Rombauts and R. Van Balen (eds), *Client-centered and Experiential Psychotherapy in the Nineties*. Leuven: Leuven University Press. pp. 65–85.

Wachtel, P.L. (1979) 'Contingent and non-contingent therapist response', *Psychotherapy: Theory, Research and Practice*, 16: 30–5.

Warner, M.S. (1993) 'Levels of intrusiveness: A framework for considering the integration and differentiation of styles of psychotherapy'. Unpublished manuscript, Illinois School of Professional Psychology, Chicago.

7 'Face to Face' – The Art of Encounter

Peter F. Schmid

All real life is encounter
Martin Buber (1974: 18)

Encounter as a personal form of relationship

If in a helping relationship the other human being is considered as a person and not as an object which has to be treated or guided, then as a matter of principle there can be no way of instrumentalizing him or her. The 'helper' enters into a process of change while letting himself or herself become involved in a relationship on a personal level and as such leaves the protection traditionally provided by the role of expert. Therefore, according to the person-centred approach, psychotherapy as much as other socio-psychological activities is a form of interpersonal relationship which takes into account this fundamental equality. Accordingly the ultimate aim is a 'personal encounter' – which is the form of relationship that shows this personal quality, in which there is an immediate communication, person to person. The term 'encounter' as an expression of this quality has finally become established not only in theology and philosophy, but also in psychology and psychotherapy. One of the constituent characteristics of what we understand nowadays by 'person' is the encounter with other persons. It is only in the 'community of personal encounter' that persons can grow (Tillich, 1956: 208).

Rogers himself describes therapy as an encounter – emphasizing the relationship and the genuineness of the therapist ('therapy as relationship encounter', 1962b: 185) which, according to him, take precedence over techniques, theory and ideology. Consequently the person-centred approach makes a high claim: 'Every form of therapy more or less lives on the encounter between therapist and client and, in group and family therapy, on the communication between clients. But there are not many theories which understand encounter . . . as the central source of healing and not as a subordinate one' (Friedman, 1987: 11). At any rate, in the person-centred approach the interpersonal encounter is the basis, the process and the goal of therapy, in the relationship of two persons as well as in the group.

With this short outline of a phenomenology of encounter I here intend to counterbalance the view that Rogers's approach is one-sidedly individualistic.[1] It has to be admitted that the relational aspect was only developed by him at a later stage and was not presented in such a systematically theoretical way as his earlier, more individualistic expositions of theory. (Most of Rogers's theoretical statements concerning the person-centred approach date from his early years, while later on he added significantly to the approach, in particular the relationship dimension, but did not conceptualize it theoretically to the same extent. This makes it necessary to reconceptualize person-centred theory in line with these developments.) Person-centred group work especially has made the immediately present interpersonal relationship central to the image of man and thus has made a crucial contribution to the understanding of what it means to be a person. With the expression 'encounter group' it points to an anthropology of relationality which affirms that the fundamental fact that humans live in groups is integral to the nature of the human being.

'En-counter' – etymology and semantics

Etymology shows that the English word 'encounter' as well as the French word *rencontre* contains the root *contra*, the Latin word for 'against', in the same way as the German word *Begegnung* is formed from the root *gegen* (against).

The word meaning points to the 'against', indicating *vis-à-vis* as well as resistance. 'Encounter' in the sense of 'meeting face to face' at first frequently meant a hostile encounter, but later also a friendly, even loving one.[2] (In German we find a parallel, where *begegnen* is also used when one speaks for instance of being confronted with difficulties or with an enemy.) One can encounter an object (a landscape for instance or a piece of art: 'reality encounter') or a person ('Thou-encounter', 'interpersonal encounter'). While in everyday life this word is used without any special interpretation (for instance in the sense of meeting coincidentally), in personalistic philosophy, which in this context has also been called 'encounter philosophy', it acquires an existential meaning.

How are relationship and encounter connected? Relationship can precede encounter, but also emerge from it or add a new quality to it. Relationship can be a consequence of encounter as well as disposition to a new encounter. Relationship implies the attitude; encounter implies the uniqueness of the experience. Relationship, it follows, can be understood as facilitating encounter as well as resulting from encounter.

'The Other' – encounter philosophy

As was indicated in Chapter 4 about the conception of the person, the philosophical notion of the human being as a fellow man, as a Thou, as an

Other, as an 'encountered one', only found acceptance in the twentieth century. This shift of philosophical paradigm not only produced encounter philosophy, but consequently also brought about an enormous change in the human sciences.

One of the important roots lies in the Jewish-Christian tradition: the Jewish precept of charity, which Jesus expanded beyond clan members or compatriots into the love for every human being, including the most distant ones, considers the Other (through love) to be a brother. This concept becomes particularly clear in the parable of the Good Samaritan (Luke 10: 29–37). The reason for biblical brotherly love is the universal love of God in whose sight all are equal. God, who identifies himself with 'the least', is loved if man loves his brother; man encounters God in concrete brotherly love, as is expressed in the parable of the Last Judgement (Matthew 25: 31–46): 'What you did to the least of my brothers, you have done to me' (Matthew 25: 40).

Apart from certain exceptions (for instance, Augustine and his primacy of love) this radical approach was for a long period of time hardly accepted in Christian philosophy because of the influence of Greek thinking and the primacy of cognition, on which Thomas Aquinas insisted. Without doubt Kant's understanding of the other one as a moral imperative, Hegel's dialectic, the empathy theoreticians (*Einfühlungstheoretiker*) and the phenomenologists (e.g. Wilhelm Dilthey, Edmund Husserl) as well as the existentialists (Søren Kierkegaard, Martin Heidegger, Karl Jaspers) are to be seen as paving the way for a philosophy which considered the Other. But they all more or less took the I as their starting point. Martin Buber, Ferdinand Ebner and Franz Rosenzweig, the principal founders of encounter philosophy (also called 'dialogism' or 'personalism') are justified in calling it the 'new dialogical thinking'. The reasons for this are complex: it can be considered as a counter-movement to rationalism and to the system philosophy of German idealism, but also as a reaction to the depressing experience of the isolation of the I, of loneliness, of objectification, alienation and functionalization in modern life, the reaction to the mechanistic worldview of the natural sciences, and a consequence of growing understanding of social mechanisms and the increasing absence of religion.

Approaches of dialogical anthropology

Romano Guardini (1885–1968) understands encounter as an amazing meeting with the reality of the Other. According to him, encounter means that one is touched by the essence of the opposite (Guardini, 1955). To let this happen, a non-purpose-oriented openness, a distance which leads to amazement and the initiative of man in freedom are indispensable conditions: encounter cannot be created, it is, at one and the same time, both being touched and touching. In interpersonal encounter affinity and alienation can be experienced at the same time. Encounter is an adventure which contains a creative seed, a breakthrough to something new. Relationship 'centres in the Other'. It is in the risk of letting oneself go towards the Other, to leave oneself behind 'going forward' and in such an experience to meet oneself again coming from somewhere else, that the dialectic character of encounter lies: only the one who will let his self go will find it anew – that is how self-actualization works.

According to Paul Tillich (1886–1965), with whom Rogers entered into an open dialogue as he did with Buber (Rogers and Tillich, 1966), the person emerges from the resistance in the encounter of the Other: if the person

> were not to encounter the resistance of other selves, then every self would try to take itself as absolute. . . . An individual can conquer the entire world of objects, but he cannot conquer another person without destroying him as a person. The individual discovers himself through this resistance. If he does not want to destroy the other person, then he has to enter into a community with him. It is through the resistance of the other person that the person is born. (Tillich, 1956: 208)

Bernhard Welte (1906–83) sees the 'art of encounter' as a loving struggle between words and counter-words, as a creative act in which it matters to bring oneself into it in dialectic awakening 'in the flash of the contact', to open up and to expose oneself, but on the other hand to 'let yourself be you' (Welte, 1966).

Gabriel Marcel (1889–1973) emphasizes that the Other has always been there in advance (1928, 1935). It is only in (bodily) communication with the Other that I am. *He* (the object which I talk to you about) is not capable of responding, but *you* respond – to you I am responsible. What we talk about is the object. You are never an object, but rather invocation and presence. I can judge objects; in you I have to believe. You are only accessible through love. In particular, Marcel protests against the objectification of the body.

According to Frederik J.J. Buytendijk (1887–1974), both game and encounter are characterized by the oscillation between closeness and distance, opening up and closing up (Buytendijk, 1951). He emphasizes that the loving encounter with the person opposite in acting and in devotion needs reciprocity and equality, even if this is hardly ever completely realized.

Buber: 'I–Thou' – encounter happens where one becomes presence to the Other

To Martin Buber (1878–1965) being a person consists in the event of encounter or dialogue, of communicating oneself. According to his well-known statement: 'All real life is encounter' (Buber, 1974: 18) the I is actually constituted only in the encounter with the Thou: 'The I becomes through the Thou; becoming an I, I say Thou' (ibid.). He describes encounter as an event in which one becomes presence to the Other. It is characterized by authenticity (of being instead of the breaking-in of seeming), through acceptance (saying yes to the Other as a person, that is accepting and confirming him or her, not only being aware of them), through inclusion (as experiencing the Other, 'tuning in on the Other') and through becoming aware (as a personal realization, that is being open for the Other in his or her concrete, typical, unique way of being, in contrast with observing the other person as an object).

This I–Thou relationship does not take place in the one or in the Other or in a neutral world including both, but in a dimension which is only accessible to the persons involved, 'on the other side of subjective, on this side of the objective, on the narrow ridge where I and Thou meet' (Buber, 1982: 167). Buber calls this sphere 'the inter(personal) [das Zwischen(menschliche)]'. The reality of dialogue is more than every individual person involved, and more than the sum of the individuals; both aspects are part of a larger area, that is the 'Zwischen' which Buber describes as a 'physical interplay [leibhaftes Zusammenspiel]' between the persons involved. Buber calls the unfolding of the 'Zwischenmenschliches' (1982: 275f.) dialogical, which he contrasts to the psychological. The 'real dialogue', an exchange which aims to be mutual, according to Buber comes from the existential centre of the person; this is not a question of information transfer, but of participating in and sharing the being of the Other. In order to let communication turn into dialogue, it needs mutual reflection, the metacommunicative element in conversation. That was the way Buber himself understood what he did: 'I have no doctrine, but I'm in a dialogue' (1963: 593).

In Buber's philosophy we find many more strands than the parallels Rogers himself acknowledged, which are well known and traditionally quoted again and again, statements which are not yet thoroughly explored, and which put serious questions to the person-centred conception of the person and of relationship, questions which were already clearly voiced in the dialogue between the two in 1957. Unfortunately there is more often a superficial and rash harmonization of ideas to be detected where Rogers's notions are simply equated with Buber's. Even if much of what Buber says recalls the conditions which are necessary for personal development, there is no simple comparison between the two. Instead of rashly equating them following the model 'Rogers = Buber put into practice', it makes more sense to examine Rogers's stances critically, comparing them with Buber's philosophy and with other encounter philosophers, and to develop them further, taking particularly into account the fact that Buber focuses on the asymmetrical nature of the therapeutic relationship.

Lévinas: 'Thou–I' – encounter as a common transcending of the presence in personal trinity

Emmanuel Lévinas's (1905–95) anthropological premise is, in a much more radical way than Buber's, the 'absolute being-different' of the Other. While

Buber understands his approach in a metapsychological sense, Lévinas (1978, 1980, 1992) understands his in a metaontological sense: it leads from the encounter experience towards ethics as a foundation for all science. First of all comes the responsibility which springs from contact with the Other. The awakening from the totality of the being-caught-in-oneself does not happen through 'being independent' (whatever made one dependent). Rather, the Other is the power which liberates the I from oneself. Thus, the Other is not in my view, but I am in the view of the Other. The movement goes from the Thou to the I. This Other is an appeal and a provocation, and the relationship to him or her *in principle* is asymmetrical: out of the being addressed by the Other (which is a demand) grows a fundamental responsibility (*diakonia*). By responding I only fulfil my duty. But what people do owe each other is love. Thus, encounter in dialogue turns out to be a condition for self-consciousness, to be a common transcendence of the (totalitarian) status quo, to be a start without return: Abraham, who starts his journey to an unknown country without return, and not Ulysses, who at the end returns to his starting point, is to be seen as the symbolic character.

While Buber starts to explore the question of what man is by understanding him as the dialogical nature of being-two and thus relatively contained, Lévinas pushes on: from the Other to the Others. I and the Other, my fellow man, are not an isolated entity, there is also 'the Third One', who himself is a fellow man; there are the Others. Therefore how to act is no longer obvious, and among Others the question of justice and the necessity of judgement arise. A new understanding of We emerges: no longer the We of the two of us, but rather of the three of us – where two lovingly include a third one in their community. In such a way the tri-unity turns out to be the foundation of interpersonality. Duality does not, therefore, exclude the Third One, but rather includes him or her, because it is predisposed to transcend itself towards the group.

'Personality development through encounter' – encounter according to Rogers and other person-centred authors

It is true that, from the very beginning, relationship played a significant role in the client-centred approach,[3] but the development from the notion of the therapist as a 'depersonalized' (Rogers, 1951: 208) *alter ego* to the notion of the therapist as partner in the encounter happened only gradually. The discussions with Buber and existentialism contributed to this as much as Rogers's working with the severely disturbed clients of the 'Wisconsin project' (Rogers et al., 1967) and his experience in the non-therapeutic setting of encounter groups. Consequently, Rogers increasingly used the term 'encounter', which had already been used by Otto Rank.[4]

In 1955 he is already writing about the therapeutic relationship: 'I risk myself . . . I let myself go into the immediacy of the relationship. . . . In these moments there is, to borrow Buber's phrase, a real "I–Thou" relationship, a timeless living in the experience which is *between* the client and me. It is at the opposite pole from seeing the client, or myself, as an object' (1955: 268f.; original emphasis). In 1961, in his account of the case of Ellen West, Rogers describes healing through encounter in Buber's sense as the centre of therapy (Rogers, 1961b: 175). In his 1962 article: 'The interpersonal relationship: the core of guidance' he describes the relationship (as from then on he does more and more frequently) with reference to the congruence of the therapist as a 'direct personal encounter with his client, meeting him on a person-to-person basis' (1962a: 90).

In 1957, in dialogue at the University of Michigan, Rogers asked Buber directly if his concept of I–Thou corresponds to what he considers to be the most effective element in a therapeutic relationship. Buber pointed to the most essential difference in the roles of the therapist and the client: 'He comes for help to you. You do not come for help to him' (Rogers and Buber, 1994: 15). Therapist and client, according to Rogers, encounter each other mutually in the experiential world of the client. To Buber this is a one-sided encounter, offered only by the therapist. Buber described the 'decisive difference' between both conceptions as different 'by the whole heaven, but I would rather prefer to say by the whole hell' (ibid.: 29f.). In contrast to this, Rogers emphasized that in these moments helping is almost a by-product; according to him, what is the most important is that 'I want to understand you. What person are you . . . behind all these masks that you are wearing in real life? Who are you?' In this there is the 'desire to meet a *person*', not the wish to help. 'I've learned through my experience that when we can meet, then help does occur, but that's a by-product' (ibid.: 30f.).

In the beginning, Rogers quite simply equated the therapeutic relationship with Buber's I–Thou relationship; later he usually expressed himself more carefully and spoke of a similarity (e.g. Rogers and Polanyi, 1966: 197). He himself describes the development as follows: The 'recognition of the significance of what Buber terms the I–thou relationship is the reason why, in client-centered therapy, there has come to be a greater use of the self of the therapist, of the therapist's feelings, a greater stress on genuineness, but all of this without imposing the views, values, or interpretations of the therapist on the client' (Rogers, 1974: 11). The more Rogers states that the goal is to become more open for others, that congruence begets congruence, the closer he is getting to an encounter-oriented concept of therapy.

In his description of the process of an encounter group Rogers does not define directly the 'basic encounter' – 'this appears to be one of the most central, intense, and change-producing aspects of group experience' (Rogers, 1970: 33) – but gives examples of intense interpersonal relationships which he interprets as a much closer and more direct form of contact than is usual in everyday life: encounter now implies an immediate and direct mutual relationship: 'I like my functioning best in a group when my "owned feelings" – positive or negative – are in immediate interaction with the feelings of a participant. To me this means that we are communicating on a deep level of personal meaning. It is the closest I get to an I–thou relationship' (Rogers, 1971a: 278).

Other person-centred authors also point out the connection with encounter philosophy: Jim Bebout in a paper about 'encounter as contact' (1974: 372–4) emphasizes precisely this point: encounter is touching and being touched. Alienation, which is the opposite, consists in distance, in the incapability of establishing this contact of 'direct intimacy'. In this context, Bebout points to Sartre, Plessner, Polanyi and Strasser. He also proposed the expression 'encounter therapy' for person-centred psychotherapy (Bebout 1974: 372f.). Bill Coulson (1973: 205) translated encounter as 'to come across the unexpected'. Hans Swildens (1991: 53) considers encounter to be 'more than contact . . ., i.e. sharing my existential situation with you. . . . It is a question of experiencing in community, a We-experience, where I and you do not exchange anymore, but which together I and you experience as We.' In German-speaking countries, amongst others, it is Arnold Mente (1990) and Wolfgang Pfeiffer (1989, 1991, 1993, 1995), who emphasize personal encounter. Reinhard Tausch and Anne-Marie Tausch (1990: 16) also use the expression 'Begegnungsgruppe'.

Here we can only mention that not only for Jacob Levi Moreno, the founder of psychodrama, but also in personalistic movements in depth psychology (Binswanger, von Weizsäcker, Trüb) and in dialogical therapy (Hycner, Friedman, Fuhr) does the encounter concept play a central role.

'Authentic game of love in presence' – a person-centred understanding of encounter

Now, how are we to understand the quality of this encounter from a person-centred perspective?

Each encounter involves *meeting reality* and *being touched* by the essence of the *opposite*. It always has the character of the unexpected, of surprise; it cannot be manufactured, it cannot be used; it is a gift. Its starting point is separateness, distance. In the opposite resistance is met: there is no encounter without confrontation as the word 'en-counter' suggests.

The opposite in the *personal* encounter is *the Other*. He is no alter ego, no close friend a priori, no identifiable person, but 'a continuous enigma which keeps us awake' (Lévinas, 1959: 120). The Other, however, does not come up to me as an anonymous stranger, but as a *Thou*. As a person the Other breaks the limits of our knowledge, but, in reflection, he can still be generalized, as if he were a thing. For 'the Thou' – now it is more correct to say 'for you' – this is entirely impossible. You have essentially nothing in common with a thing any more. Instead of (factual) knowledge, *acknowledgement* is required. (In the old meaning of the word 'to know' in the sense of sexual contact, this meaning of 'acknowledging' is still implied.) Encounter does not aim at the certainty of knowledge; it is a belief: acknowledgement equals love in which I and Thou are one, but where we mutually experience each other as Other. Hence, with oneness otherness also grows, and independence grows with being Thou-related. The person opposite initiates the individual into becoming a person and initiates community.

The most adequate form of communication is *dialogue* in the sense of having (at least a kind of) exchange which aims at reciprocity, as an 'understanding confrontation'. Hence, encounter initiates connection but also separation, community and loneliness. The result is a 'dialogical tension'. It is always a new challenge, however, to resist the temptation to dissolve this tension between opposite and community or to play it down instead of enduring it. It is in the dialogical tension of being-entirely-oriented-to-the-Other (solidarity) and also being-entirely-oneself (auto-nomy) where self-actualization happens. The movement always originates from the Thou, and from a developmental perspective: it is the call, the addressing of another human being, which evokes a response, confronts us with freedom and risk. Encounter happens long before one can aim at obtaining such an experience, although only to some extent.[5] Therefore, in the encounter there always lies the *response to a call*. And from the response follows respons-ability which is grounded in the fact that nobody else can respond instead of me. Thus, the ethical dimension of encounter is denoted.

The 'moment-to-moment encounter of psychotherapy' (Rogers, 1980: 2155) happens in the immediate present. To this corresponds the existential attitude of 'presence' (*Gegenwärtigkeit*), confidently taking part in the present moment of life (which means a lot more than the slogan of here-and-now). Rogers mentioned it several times towards the end of his life (for example in 1986) and in particular described it as a slightly altered state of consciousness, as a medium for personal growth and as a self-transcending aspect of therapy. Brian Thorne (1985), independently, uses the word 'tenderness' in this context. Some consider this as the fourth basic attitude. In the encounter philosophical perspective, presence is the auth-entic attitude *to be*, to fully live in the presence: unconditionally accepting the Other, empathically becoming involved in his or her presence, without any prior intention, that is with an openness and a wonder towards experience.[6]

The *im-media-cy* is born through the fact that all means, that separate us, 'decay' (Buber), become unnecessary, surplus. For this it is important first of all to dispense with all techniques and methods, all means, that serve as a protection to defend against what comes across, what is encountered. For encounter lies beyond all methods. It is involvement in the immediacy of the experience of relationship.

Another constitutive element of personal encounter is *bodily contact*. A necessary condition for encounter is bodily presence, touching, sensing and being sensed, 'physical interplay [leibhaftes Zusammenspiel]' (Buber). It is an intimate, sensual event. Encounter by its nature is a game – a game without rules, authentic, playful, not fanciful – action without intention. In encounter, man is an inter-actor (Moreno); encounter is spontaneous and creative action and activity, but also devotion. Encounter is action and passivity, taking and letting go. Encounter happens in the authentic 'game of love' without rules (Thomas, 1969). Through encounter the being-with as an essential quality of man as a fellow man becomes clear. Encounter is to be in the sense of being-with, to live in the sense of living-with-the-Others. It is, as Rogers expresses it, not only a 'way of being', but also a '*way of being with*'.[7] 'To be with', however, also means 'to be for'; to be with is to be in solidarity. Therapy or counselling is an expression of this fundamental fact.

So in encounter, only *love* is the adequate communication. But it is especially in love that encounter transcends the duality, the couple, and opens up for a Third One; first we do not live in the world of *the* human being, but in the world of human beings. Encounter transcends the synchronicity of the I–Thou, the one-sidedness of orientation, the unquestionability of this closeness, and moves towards diachronism in the relationship (Lévinas). Self-experiencing as self-transcendence is also transcendence of the dual-unity. Hence, plural is essential for encounter: it transcends the duality and is open for a Third One, for the *group*, for the community which itself offers space for encounter. The full together lies beyond the relative closedness of the I–Thou; it lies in the We, in being-together. That is where the source of freedom lies; that is what leads to the necessity for decision, for justice; that is what makes love become *love-with* (*condilectio*) in which nobody is an instrument, a means, but everybody is a setting-out and a goal: vivid plurality, which conquers the dialectic of difference and identity, of alienation and loneliness.

Encounter in therapy and in the group

To encounter a human being means to give him space and freedom to develop himself according to his own possibilities, to become and entirely to be the one he is able to become. On the one hand this is opposed to any use as a means to a particular end or any 'intention'; on the other hand it is opposed, too, to interaction based on a role or a function. Encounter means risk and daring. But it also provides the chance to receive the gift of personal contact and the possibility of full personhood.

Person-centred therapy is not simply a personal encounter at the outset. But it aims to be this. 'Therapeutic encounter' then is reciprocal or at least open to reciprocity, even if asymmetric. It is a relationship which is equal in value, even if it is not equal in intensity. In the beginning it may be only the therapist who offers a personal encounter, in the sense that what is encounter for the therapist cannot yet be reciprocated by the client. The goal of the therapeutic process, however, is still the full – and thus mutual and symmetrical – personal encounter, in which both persons face each other as persons freely and in full awareness of their responsibility, and thus, becoming one yet acknowledging each as the Other, being present as persons to each other. Therefore the final goal of therapy is to be surpassed and done away with, to make space for mutual personal encounters (cf. Schmid, 1996a). By its nature the group tends to overcome one-sided forms of encounter, because the strict separation between therapist and client does not exist.

The person-centred approach as an encounter approach

I'd like to draw some consequences for the person-centred approach from this understanding of encounter and put them in the form of propositions.

It is a fundamental element of this approach not to dissolve the tension between opposition and unity ('We') one-sidedly. It is only through the maintenance of individuality that encounter becomes possible. Hence, encounter (like person) contains a continuous and fertile tension of unity without fusion, yet also an otherness without a bridgeless difference. This tension is to be endured. Thou and I are looking at each other, face to face, just as they are looking into the same direction (and turn their face to a Third One, whether a person or an object). There is plurality and diversity *and* there is community and unity.

The task is to accept the Other in a relationship actually as the Other. Rogers took this very seriously by refraining completely from diagnosis and interpretation, from hierarchical relationship structure and deliberate influencing. For individual therapy this leads to the conclusion that the therapist should give up playing the one-sided role of an *alter ego* and really enter into a personal relationship, over against the client.

In the understanding of relationship and encounter reciprocity has to be put into practice. One can say that by taking presence seriously the reciprocal I–Thou relationship, which in the end is the goal of every personal encounter, has been put into a person-centred concreteness. Rogers's idea was always one of mutual encounter; he also meant that one could go to another for mutual therapy. In spite of the asymmetry which is a conse-quence of the different positions, it is basically dialogue. For person-centred practice this does not only mean saying goodbye to the principle of fundamental therapist abstinence (which is often regarded as non-directivity), it also demands concrete readiness to being open as a person – an openness to the actual (and not only theoretically implied) risk of engagement as a person.

In the development of the person-centred understanding of the person the relationship orientation has to be conceptualized as an axiom. In Chapter 4 on the concept of the person it became clear that an adequate under-standing of the person needs a dialectic interaction of autonomy and interconnectedness. This also holds for the concept of motivation. From this understanding of encounter the person-centred conception of the person can be put into concrete terms and developed anew: it certainly can be said that there is not only *one* axiom (i.e. the actualizing tendency) in the anthropology of the person-centred approach, as Rogers (1959: 196) postulated, but that man's potential for encounter and his dependence on relationship have also to be considered as an unquestionable basic assumption of the person-centred image of man (relationship axiom). If Rogers says that man is 'incurably social' (Rogers, 1965: 20; Rogers and Tillich, 1966), a 'social animal' (Rogers, 1953: 103) who has an innate need for love and affection (Rogers, 1971b), then he is actually presupposing it even if he does not phrase it explicitly as an axiom. What moves man, lets him grow, changes him, comes from an actualizing tendency to 'self-transcendence' (Pfeiffer, 1993: 36) *and* from the 'being-addressed', from the challenge by the Other.

Rogers's 'presence' is the existential foundation of the basic attitudes. The phenomenon of presence which Rogers described is not a fourth core condition, an added one; it comprehensively describes the basic attitudes of authenticity, unconditional positive regard and empathy, in an existential way and on a deeper, dialogical-personal level. What Rogers calls 'presence' corresponds with presence (*Gegenwärtigkeit*) in the sense of encounter philosophy. The person-centred attitude is also appositely described as the person-centred 'triad variable' (stressing the inner connectedness of the three 'variables'). It can thus be regarded, in a dialectical sense, as what Hegel calls an 'Aufhebung' of the basic attitudes. The German word *aufheben* means (1) to preserve, (2) to abolish and dissolve and (3) to supersede, transcend and revalorize. If one takes these meanings together at one and the same time, 'presence' can be understood as an *Aufhebung* of the basic attitudes: they are preserved as well as dissolved by being superseded and transcended. Hence, encounter is 'more than the variables'; what is essential in the person-centred relationship in this sense transcends the realization of the single basic attitudes towards a fundamental and extensive full way of *being* with each other: the source and the goal of person-centred action is personal encounter. Then, presence is not only to be regarded as an altered, transcending state of consciousness, as Rogers (1986) writes, but as a way of being, as 'being in encounter'. Hence, presence is an expression of genuineness, as it is related to the immediately present flow of experiencing (and as presence makes clear congruence *and* difference between my experiencing and my symbolization and between my symbolization and my communication). Presence is an expression of empathy, because it is, in existential wonderment, related to what the Other is experiencing. And presence is an expression of positive regard, as acceptance of myself and personal acknowledgement of the Other, of whatever immediately present feelings he or she is experiencing. The basic attitudes can thus be understood as encounter conditions.

Presence is the starting point for the conception of historicity. The criticism, sometimes made by adherents of psychodynamic schools, that the person-centred approach is not sufficiently aware of history and is therefore superficial instead of depth-psychological, can thus be refuted. Presence includes the 'having-become' just as much as the concept of future, i.e. the possibility of becoming. The question now has to be phrased: how does a relationship have to be in order to enable the client as well as the therapist to conceptualize their own future in a creative way, with due regard to their past, yet always in the immediacy of the present moment? If we understand this moment as *kairos* (the name of the Greek god of the omnipotential moment which had to be seized), as the essential fertile point in time, a 'person-centred kairology' (Schmid, 1992–3) can examine the meaning of the fulfilled presence and of those conditions which, in group work and therapy, facilitate the right decision at the right moment, and which facilitate grasping the right moment that cannot be forced but can be either fostered or missed.

The understanding of person-centred action as diakonia (service) can be the basis of person-centred ethics. It is in the experience of encounter that the origin of finding a meaning and of determining values lies. Here man experiences the fact that he cannot create encounter, but instead finds himself to be one who encounters. And here also lies the source of his autonomy as one who chooses his values, determining them and recognizing them as his own. On the basis of this 'inner' validating which nonetheless is evoked by 'external' experiences, a person-centred ethics can be developed (cf. Schmid, 1996b: 521–32). It can have its foundation in the understanding of action as *diakonia*: in responsibility and in the knowledge that man in principle is dependent on the Other and his 'priority' in the sense of Lévinas. Here, the old Jewish principle 'Love thy neighbour as thyself' (that is not 'more than thyself' or 'instead of thyself', but 'as thyself', that is 'just as much as you love yourself', but also 'in loving yourself'), which was adopted by Christianity, is unparalleled as a person-centred one. According to this view, psychotherapy makes personal encounter possible; the therapist is someone who gives an answer to the misery of the client. Psychotherapy is a service of engagement and solidarity rooted in an ethical commitment.

The physical dimension has to be included in the concept of the approach, along with the psychological dimension. Apart from Gendlin and his adherents, little attention has so far been given explicitly to physical processes. As a consequence we have been working with an incomplete model of personhood, because corporeality is an indispensable part of it. This does not just mean that we need to be aware of physical correlates of psychological experiencing and to observe them in our practice; it signifies the need to do justice to man as a 'body-psyche-mind-unity' (cf. Schmid, 1993; 1994a: 425–502; 1996b: 425–48; 1996c).

The group is the primary locus of person-centred experiences. If we take seriously the *conditio humana* that man is a being who generally from the beginning lives in groups where he gains his experiences, the person-centred relationship, which was only designed to facilitate development and growth of individuals, is clearly seen as a relationship which inevitably follows these initial experiences. The primary locus of encounter in the person-centred context, therefore, is the group. In it couples (as special forms of a group) are embedded (cf. Schmid, 1996d). In particular the (encounter)group provides an excellent opportunity to learn presence. It is not coincidence that Rogers found himself most particularly confronted with the phenomenon of presence in groups. The constellation of the group allows the facilitator from the beginning to be involved more as a person than in individual therapy. Unlike the very protected setting of the therapeutic relationship of two persons, the group from the very beginning offers the possibility for all the participants to be involved in manifold experiences of encounter. In the group, help is not just offered by a single person towards whom all expectations are directed. Participants very quickly learn to support each other mutually. Group work is not just more efficient in the economic sense, a kind of stopgap where there is a lack of space or money or both. It is the appropriate place for persons to learn, an interface of person and society and, in this sense, the 'primary locus of therapy'.[8]

Notes

This chapter was translated by Elisabeth Zinschitz.

1 A detailed description can be found in Schmid (1994a: 103–295, with many references); cf. Schmid (1991: 105–212; 1994b).

2 Shakespeare used it as early as 1599 in the sense of a loving encounter.

3 As early as 1940 Rogers states, in his speech on the occasion of the 'birthday' of the approach: 'For the first time, this approach lays stress upon the therapeutic relationship itself as a growth experience. In all the other approaches . . . the individual is expected to grow and change and make better decisions after he leaves the interview hour. Here the therapeutic contact is itself growth experience. . . . In some respects I am inclined to feel that this is the most important aspect of the approach.'

4 Further references in Schmid (1994a: 173–80).

5 For the sake of the clarity of terms, one has to distinguish between the 'Thou-encounter in the beginning', as experienced by an unaffected child, and the 'personal encounter' (a mutual encounter in which one responds to the call of the Other) which only becomes possible through reflection (and the implied differentiation and objectification of the I, the world and 'the Thou' as a basis for freedom and responsibility). If one takes the mother–child relationship as a paradigm for the encounter in the beginning, then the paradigm for personal encounter is the love between a man and a woman.

6 A more extensive phenomenology of the presence and an exploration of its meaning for the development of the person-centred approach can be found in Schmid (1994a: 201–78).

7 Cf. Rogers (1975: 4) or Gendlin (1970: 82): 'Human beings are always a "being-with"'.

8 The person-centred approach is traditionally considered as (a method of) individual therapy which in the course of time has been applied to many other areas, among them group work. However, from historical and content arguments and especially in the European intellectual historical context, it can be shown that the person-centred approach is by its very nature a social approach and therefore also basically a group approach (Schmid, 1996b, 1996d).

References

Bebout, Jim (1974) 'It takes one to know one. Existential-Rogerian concepts in encounter groups', in Wexler and Rice (1974). pp. 367–420.

Buber, Martin (1963) 'Antwort', in P.A. Schilpp and Maurice D. Friedman, *Martin Buber: Philosophen des 20 Jahrhunderts*, trans. E. Zinschitz. Stuttgart: Kohlhammer. pp. 589–640.

Buber, Martin (1974) *Ich und Du*, 8th edn, trans. E. Zinschitz. Heidelberg: Lambert Schneider. First published as *Dialogisches Leben*. Zurich, 1923.

Buber, Martin (1982) *Das Problem des Menschen*, 5th edn, trans. E. Zinschitz. Heidelberg: Lambert Schneider. First published 1948.

Buytendijk, Frederik J.H. (1951) 'Zur Phänomenologie der Begegnung', *Eranos Jahrbuch*, 19 (Zurich): 429–86.

Coulson, William R. (1973) *A Sense of Community*. Columbus, OH: Merrill.

Friedman, Maurice D. (1987) *Der heilende Dialog in der Psychotherapie*, trans. E. Zinschitz. Cologne: Edition Humanistische Psychologie. First published as *The Healing Dialogue in Psychotherapy*. New York: Jason Aronson, 1985.

Gendlin, Eugene T. (1970) 'Existentialism and experiential psychotherapy', in J.T. Hart and T.M. Tomlinson (eds), *New Directions in Client-Centered Therapy*. Boston: Houghton Mifflin. pp. 70–94. First published 1966.

Guardini, Romano (1955) 'Die Begegnung: ein Beitrag zur Struktur des Daseins', *Hochland*, 47 (3): 224–34.

Hutterer, Robert, Pawlowsky, Gerhard, Schmid, Peter F. and Stipsits, Reinhold (eds) (1996) *Client-Centred and Experiential Psychotherapy: A Paradigm in Motion*. Frankfurt-on-Main: Peter Lang.

Lévinas, Emmanuel (1959) 'Der Untergang der Vorstellung', in Lévinas (1992). pp. 120–39. First published in *Husserl 1859–1959: Recueil commémoratif publié à l'occasion du centenaire du philosophe (Phaenomenologica VI)*. Den Haag: Nijhoff.

Lévinas, Emmanuel (1978) *Autrement qu'être ou au delà de l'essence*, 2nd edn. Den Haag: Nijhoff. First published 1974.

Lévinas, Emmanuel (1980) *Totalité et infini: essai sur l'extériorité*, 7th edn. Den Haag: Nijhoff. First published 1961.

Lévinas, Emmanuel (1992) *Die Spur des Anderen: Untersuchungen zur Phänomenologie und Sozialphilosophie*, 3rd edn. Freiburg: Alber. First published 1983.

Marcel, Gabriel (1928) *Journal metaphysique*. Paris: Gallimard.

Marcel, Gabriel (1935) *Être et avoir*. Paris: Aubier.

Mente, Arnold (1990) 'Improving Rogers' theory: toward a more completely client-centered psychotherapy', in Germain Lietaer, Jan Rombauts and Richard van Balen (eds), *Client-Centered and Experiential Psychotherapy in the Nineties*. Leuven: Leuven University Press. pp. 771–8.

Pfeiffer, Wolfgang M. (1989) 'Psychotherapie als dialogischer Prozeß', *Brennpunkt*, 41: 18–25.

Pfeiffer, Wolfgang M. (1991) 'Krankheit und zwischenmenschliche Beziehung', in

Jobst Finke and Ludwig Teusch (eds), *Gesprächspsychotherapie bei Neurosen und psychosomatischen Erkrankungen: Neue Entwicklungen in Theorie und Praxis.* Heidelberg: Asanger. pp. 25–43.

Pfeiffer, Wolfgang M. (1993) 'Die Bedeutung der Beziehung bei der Entstehung und der Therapie psychischer Störungen', in Ludwig Teusch and Jobst Finke (eds), *Krankheitslehre der Gesprächspsychotherapie: Neue Beiträge zur theoretischen Fundierung.* Heidelberg: Asanger. pp. 19–39.

Pfeiffer, Wolfgang M. (1995) 'Die Beziehung – der zentrale Wirkfaktor in der Gesprächspsychotherapie', *GwG Zeitschrift*, 97: 27–32.

Rogers, Carl R. (1951) *Client-Centered Therapy. Its Current Practice, Implications, and Theory.* Boston: Houghton Mifflin.

Rogers, Carl R. (1953) 'Some directions and end points in therapy', in O.H. Mowrer (ed.), *Psychotherapy: Theory and Research.* New York: Ronald. pp. 44–68; also in Rogers (1961a). pp. 73–106.

Rogers, Carl R. (1955) 'Persons or science? A philosophical question', *American Psychologist*, 10 (7): 267–78; also in Rogers (1961a). pp. 199–224.

Rogers, Carl R. (1959) 'A theory of therapy, personality, and interpersonal relationships, as developed in the client-centered framework', in Sigmund Koch (ed.), *Psychology: A Study of Science.* Vol. 3: *Formulations of the Person and the Social Context.* New York: McGraw-Hill. pp. 184–256.

Rogers, Carl R. (1961a) *On Becoming a Person: A Therapist's View of Psychotherapy.* Boston: Houghton Mifflin.

Rogers, Carl R. (1961b) 'The loneliness of contemporary man, as seen in "The case of Ellen West"', *Review of Existential Psychology and Psychiatry*, 1 (2): 94–101; expanded version in *A Way of Being.* Boston: Houghton Mifflin. pp. 164–80.

Rogers, Carl R. (1962a) 'The interpersonal relationship: the core of guidance', *Harvard Educational Review*, 4 (32): 416–29; also in Rogers and Stevens (1967). pp. 89–104.

Rogers, Carl R. (1962b) 'Some learnings from a study of psychotherapy with schizophrenics', *Pennsylvania Psychiatric Quarterly*, Summer: 3–15; also in Rogers and Stevens (1967). pp. 181–92.

Rogers, Carl R. (1965) 'A humanistic conception of man', in Richard Farson (ed.), *Science and Human Affairs.* Palo Alto, CA: Science and Behavior Books. pp. 18–31.

Rogers, Carl R. (1970) *On Encounter Groups.* New York: Harper & Row.

Rogers, Carl R. (1971a) 'Facilitating encounter groups', *The American Journal of Nursing*, 71: 275–9.

Rogers, Carl R. (1971b) 'Interview with Dr Carl Rogers', in W.B. Frick (ed.), *Humanistic Psychology: Interviews with Maslow, Murphy and Rogers.* Columbus, OH: Charles E. Merrill. pp. 86–115.

Rogers, Carl R. (1974) 'Remarks on the future of client-centered therapy', in Wexler and Rice (1974). pp. 7–13.

Rogers, Carl R. (1975) 'Empathic – an unappreciated way of being', *The Counseling Psychologist*, 5 (2): 2–10.

Rogers, Carl R. (1980) 'Client-centered psychotherapy', in Harold I. Kaplan, Benjamin J. Sadock and A.M. Freedman (eds), *Comprehensive Textbook of Psychiatry*, Vol. 3. Baltimore, MD: Williams & Wilkins. pp. 2153–68.

Rogers, Carl R. (1986) 'A client-centered/person-centered approach to therapy', in Irvin L. Kutash and Alexander Wolf (eds), *Psychotherapist's Casebook: Theory and Technique in the Practice of Modern Times.* San Francisco: Jossey Bass. pp. 197–208.

Rogers, Carl R. and Buber, M. (1994) *Dialogue between Martin Buber and Carl Rogers*, transcribed by Kenneth N. Cissna and Rob Anderson, 1960. First published 1960 as 'Martin Buber and Carl Rogers', *Psychologia: An International Journal of Psychology in the Orient* (Kyoto University), 3 (4): 208–21.

Rogers, Carl R. and Polanyi, Michael (1966) *Dialogue between Michael Polanyi and Carl Rogers*. San Diego: San Diego State College and WBSI.

Rogers, Carl R. and Schmid, Peter F. (1995) *Person-zentriert: Grundlagen von Theorie und Praxis*, 2nd edn. Mainz: Grünewald. First published 1991.

Rogers, Carl R. and Stevens, Barry (1967) *Person to Person: The Problem of Being Human*. Moab, UT: Real People Press.

Rogers, Carl R. and Tillich, Paul (1966) *Dialogue between Paul Tillich and Carl Rogers: Parts I & II*. San Diego: San Diego State College.

Rogers, Carl R., Gendlin, Eugene T., Kiesler, Donald J. and Truax, Charles B. (1967) *The Therapeutic Relationship and Its Impact: A Study of Psychotherapy with Schizophrenics*. Madison, WI: University of Wisconsin Press.

Schmid, Peter F. (1991) 'Souveränität und Engagement: Zu einem personzentrierten Verständnis von "Person"', in Rogers and Schmid (1991). pp. 15–164.

Schmid, Peter F. (1992–3) 'Ansätze zu einer personzentrierten Kairologie: I. Gegenwart', *apg-kontakte*, 2 (1992): 12–22; 'II. Presence', *apg-kontakte*, 1 (1993): 15–34; 'III. Gegenwärtigkeit', *apg-kontakte*, 2 (1993): 12–37.

Schmid, Peter F. (1993) 'A new image of man? Toward male emancipation', *Theology Digest*, 3: 217–20.

Schmid, Peter F. (1994a) *Personzentrierte Gruppenpsychotherapie*, Vol. 1: *Solidarität und Autonomie: Ein Handbuch*. Cologne: Edition Humanistische Psychologie.

Schmid, Peter F. (1994b) 'Begegnung ist Verkündigung: Paradigmenwechsel in der Seelsorge', *Diakonia*, 25 (1): 15–30.

Schmid, Peter F. (1996a) 'Der Therapeut: Bescheidenheit ist eine Zier, doch weiter . . . Zum Selbstverständnis des Personzentrierten Psychotherapeuten', in Peter Frenzel, Peter F. Schmid and Marietta Winkler (eds), *Handbuch der personzentrierten Psychotherapie*, 2nd edn. Cologne: Edition Humanistische Psychologie. pp. 39–69.

Schmid, Peter F. (1996b) *Personzentrierte Gruppenpsychotherapie in der Praxis*, Vol. 2: *Die Kunst der Begegnung: Ein Handbuch*. Paderborn: Junfermann.

Schmid, Peter F. (1996c) '"Intimacy, tenderness and lust". A person-centered approach to sexuality', in Hutterer et al. (1996). pp. 85–99.

Schmid, Peter F. (1996d) '"Probably the most potent social invention of the century". Person-centered therapy is fundamentally group therapy', in Hutterer et al. (1996). pp. 611–25.

Swildens, Hans (1991) *Procesgerichte Gesprekstherapie: Inleiding tot een gedifferentieerde toepassing van de cliëntgerichte beginselen bij de behandeling van psychische stoornissen*. Leuven and Amersfoort: Acco/de Horstink.

Tausch, Reinhard and Tausch, Anne-Marie (1990) *Gesprächspsychotherapie: Hilfreiche Gruppen- und Einzelgespräche in Psychotherapie und alltäglichem Leben*, 9th edn. Göttingen: Hogrefe.

Thomas, Hobart F. (1969) 'Encounter. The game of no game', in Arthur Burton (ed.), *Encounter: The Theory and Practice of Encounter Groups*. San Francisco: Jossey Bass.

Thorne, Brian (1985) *The Quality of Tenderness*. Norwich: Norwich Centre Publications.

Tillich, Paul (1956) *Systematische Theologie*, Vol. 1, 3rd edn. Berlin: de Gruyter.

Welte, Bernhard (1966) 'Zum Begriff der Person', in Heinz Rombach (ed.), *Die Frage nach dem Menschen: Aufriß einer philosophischen Anthropologie*. Freiburg im Breisgau: Herder. pp. 11–22.

Wexler, David A. and Rice, Laura N. (eds) (1974) *Innovations in Client-Centered Therapy*. New York: Wiley.

8 Empowerment or Collusion? The Social Context of Person-Centred Therapy

Sarah Hawtin and Judy Moore

The client-centred approach appears to be utterly benign. It does not suggest that our essential natures are anti-social or destructive. Within the therapeutic context, it does not attempt to classify or define the experience of the individual, but to support self-definition and self-understanding. It aims to effect a shift of power within therapy away from the hands of the therapist, into the hands of the client. A deep, respectful and genuine presence to oneself or one's client offers a powerful catalyst for personal change. However, in considering the nature of client-centred theory and practice, we have begun to question our understanding of the relationship between 'reality' and the 'self'. This has stemmed from a feeling of discomfort with the apparent neutrality of client-centred theory towards personal experience and a sense that this neutrality could result in a failure to address, or even to be aware of, important issues.

We begin by examining Rogers's developmental theory, particularly the nature of self-awareness and the relationship of the organism to the self-concept. In order to discuss further the interrelatedness of social values, language, perception and self-awareness, this is followed by an incursion into the world of feminist discourse theory and its implications for the person-centred approach. It may help at this initial stage to outline our definition of discourse, as this will be a central theme. According to the *Oxford English Dictionary*, 'discourse' as noun can mean (sense 4) 'Communication of thought by speech'. In more recent linguistic theory 'discourse' is related to language in use as opposed to language as an abstract system. For the French philosopher Michel Foucault, 'discourses' are 'large groups of statements' within a given area (for example 'medicine', 'the family') that establish rules and conventions about how that area is discussed and by whom (Foucault, 1972: 37).

All societies have procedures whereby the production of discourses is controlled to preserve the structures and conventions of that society. The process is reinforced by our everyday use of language so that the assumptions embedded in our consciousness are repeated in our most mundane utterances. For instance, the predominant use of the male pronoun to describe universal experience is a simple but powerful example of the male cultural dominance implicit in our general shaping of the English language. It is with the effects of these embedded assumptions that we are most concerned. Towards the end of our discussion we move into the prospects for 'self-lessness' and then outline the implications of our discussions for client-centred theory and practice.

Rogers and the self

A central feature of client-centred working is the conceptualization of human beings as consisting of two parts. For Rogers, the 'organism' incorporates the totality of our functioning, while the 'self-concept' delineates those aspects which we would normally think of as our conscious self and is constructed during the process of individuation as we become self-conscious and conscious of others (Rogers, 1959: 200). It is upon this division that Rogers builds his theory of personality development with the relative congruence between self-concept and organism determining the level of an individual's psychological and emotional well-being.

Rogers writes of a basic disposition of the organism and a sub-disposition. He considers these to be the 'actualizing tendency' or 'the inherent tendency of the organism to develop all its capacities in ways which serve to maintain or enhance the organism' and the tendency towards 'self-actualization' (Rogers, 1959: 198). This latter disposition is not a separate motivational force in that 'following the development of the self-structure, this general tendency towards actualization expresses itself also in the actualization of that portion of the experience of the organism which is symbolized in the self' (Rogers, 1959: 198). However, Rogers postulates it is nevertheless possible for the actualizing tendency and the tendency toward self-actualization to find themselves working in different directions due to the need for affirmation from others. The need for positive regard from others is likely to become 'more compelling' than an individual's organismic prompting, meaning that the individual 'becomes more adient to the *positive regard* of such others than toward *experiences* which are of positive value in *actualizing* the organism' (1959: 224; original emphasis). Through a process of internalization, the individual takes on the values of others in determining the direction of conscious growth, or self-actualization, giving rise to a disorientating split between the reliable promptings of the actualizing tendency and the demands of our past and present social environments.

The overriding importance of the need for positive regard, with the necessary compliance to external conditions of worth that this involves, results in a sifting of perceptions. Experiences which are 'in accord with his [the client's] *conditions of worth* are *perceived* and *symbolized* accurately in *awareness*' whereas experiences 'which run contrary to the *conditions of worth* are perceived selectively and distortedly as if in accord with the *conditions of worth*, or are in part or whole, *denied to awareness*' (Rogers, 1959: 226; original emphasis):

> This, as we see it, is the basic estrangement in man. . . . The path of development toward psychological maturity, the path of therapy, is the undoing of this estrangement in man's functioning, the dissolving of conditions of worth, the achievement of a self which is congruent with experience, and the restoration of a unified organismic valuing process as the regulator of behaviour. (Rogers, 1959: 220–1)

The construction of self and social reality

We have come to believe that this view of our 'basic estrangement' and the subsequent path of therapy do not sufficiently acknowledge the power of discourse in shaping our introjected values. The need for positive regard suggests that relationships involve a trading of acceptance and rejection, which doubtless includes the conveyance of personal, cultural and social values. However, an emphasis on the role of language in defining our perceptions and awareness seems to be missing. The medium of language, in terms of its symbolic representation of experience, cannot simply be viewed as a neutral system available to us through which to communicate. Language comes to each of us replete with cultural and social assumptions which affect how we 'perceive' and 'symbolize'.

It could be argued that the introjection of values sufficiently includes this awareness. For the feminist writer Susan Griffin the process of internalizing social values is similar to Rogers's theory of the internalization of the values of significant others. She believes that, in our attempts to fix and control the world, ideas and values that have a personal root become impersonal and external:

> When a theory is transformed into an ideology, it begins to destroy the self and self-knowledge. Originally born of feeling, it pretends to float above and around feeling. . . . Begun as a cry against the denial of truth, now it denies any truth which does not fit into its scheme. Begun as a way to restore one's sense of reality, now it attempts to discipline real people, to remake natural beings after its own image. . . . Begun as a theory of liberation, it is threatened by new theories of liberation; slowly, it builds a prison for the mind. (Griffin, 1982: 168)

Carried in language, such values take on a power which seems to be unconnected to the values' source, meaning that external conditions of worth influence us through their appearance in language as immovable objective truths.

Yet there is a much deeper challenge to the client-centred approach. In looking at this transmutation of the personal into the impersonal, the French feminist and philosopher Luce Irigaray poses the following dilemma: 'How can women analyse their own exploitation, inscribe their own demands, within an order prescribed by the masculine?' (Sellers, 1991: 1). This would seem to translate usefully into a general observation about the position of any client coming to counselling: how do you approach a hidden or distorted truth, when the prevailing language, concepts and ideologies restrict or possibly prevent access to such truths, not just by deeming them unacceptable, but by failing to recognize their existence? For instance, in her reading of Freudian theory, Irigaray illustrates vividly its inherent suppression of the feminine (Irigaray, 1985: 68–85):

> Freud does not see *two sexes* whose differences are articulated in the act of intercourse, and more generally speaking, in the imaginary and symbolic processes that regulate the workings of a society and a culture. The 'feminine' is always described in terms of deficiency or atrophy, as the other side of the sex that alone holds a monopoly on value: the male sex. (Irigaray, 1985: 69; original emphasis)

Her critique of Freud has a central place in her reasoning because of her belief that, unintentionally, Freud revealed something previously hidden: 'the sexual indifference that underlies the truth of any science, the logic of every discourse' (Irigaray, 1985: 69). Irigaray believes this results in the unhappiness and dissatisfaction of women being explained only by reference to the individual circumstances of their development, leaving aside any consideration of social and cultural context. Therefore it is women's failure to negotiate apparently necessary developmental transitions which is seen as the source of problems, rather than the difficulty of adapting to a society which is misshapen or narrow in its conceptions of the feminine. Such an interpretation effectively negates and silences experience, causing distinct strands of knowledge, understanding and belief to become unrecognizably absorbed into more dominant discourses. As client-centred counsellors, we find ourselves working within such social contexts and our ability to empathize will be affected by this.

Wendy Hollway and Gloria

The practical consequences of internalizing commonly held beliefs is revealed through the work of feminist psychologist Wendy Hollway. Hollway has undertaken pioneering research in which she reveals social assumptions at work in the construction of gender identity. Taking Lacan's view that unconscious as well as conscious processes are involved in the formation of subjective meaning and Foucault's argument that claims about truth and knowledge can be made only from within a specific discourse, she set about recording and analysing accounts of individuals' experiences within heterosexual relationships. She broke down what her subjects revealed in dialogue and group discussion into various discourses. Her concern was not simply to discover commonality of discourse, but also to establish where individuals had positioned themselves within a particular discourse and what power they had invested in being subject (the instigator of a particular position) or object (the receiver) of the discourse. Clear gender differences began to emerge.

In relation to sexual behaviour, three discourses emerged: the 'discourse of male sexual drive'; the 'have/hold discourse' and the 'permissive discourse'. The first involves the assumption that men are 'driven by biological necessity to seek out (heterosexual) sex' (Hollway, 1989: 54), the second that sex must operate within the context of 'monogamy, partnership and family life' or at least within a committed relationship (Hollway, 1992: 243), the third that sex is 'purely physical, separate from social relations, unmediated by social significations' (Hollway, 1989: 57). There is a clear contradiction for many men in the existence of the first two discourses, which was frequently resolved by the men interviewed positioning themselves as the subject of the first discourse and object of the second. Hollway concludes that one of the ways in which men take power in our culture is by 'defining women as subjects of the have/hold discourse, thereby suppressing their own wishes to have and to hold' (Hollway, 1992: 255–6). While Hollway uses psychoanalytic theory to explain individuals' investment in taking up a particular position, her ideas can readily be translated into client-centred terminology. In effect, she is saying that it is culturally sanctioned for women to admit to wanting warmth and emotional intimacy, but that men are culturally sanctioned to deny such needs or distort them, for example by projecting them on to the woman. In this instance, distortion and denial disengage the subject from his own humanity and hence his own vulnerability.

Hollway concludes that for women, too, there will be a contradiction in most heterosexual encounters that can only be resolved by not admitting to awareness certain aspects of the self. As a result a different concept of self is activated by each discourse. It is very clear from Hollway's study that many of the women involved operated at times from a self that would be defined by the permissive discourse and at times from a self that was coming more from the have/hold position, while the common cultural requirement for the woman to be sufficiently attractive to be object of the male sexual drive underpins both other positions.

Interestingly, in her well-known filmed interview with Carl Rogers, the client, Gloria, appears to demonstrate the conflict that can arise from being caught between the 'have/hold' and 'permissive' discourses. She begins the meeting by talking about the difficulty of being honest with her daughter when she is doubtful about her behaviour, particularly with regard to sexual relationships with men. As the session unfolds she moves to focusing on the nature of her doubts:

'I have had sex for the last 11 years and I am, of course, going to want it, but I still think it is wrong unless you are really, truly in love with a man, and my body doesn't seem to agree.' (Rogers and Wood, 1974: 245)

In his written introduction to the transcript, Rogers puts Gloria's conflict in terms of personality theory:

> [T]he bifurcated nature of the actualizing tendency supports, on the one hand, the natural striving to meet her needs through sexual expression; on the other hand it tries to actualize the self – the picture she has of herself as a person with 'proper' sexual behaviour. In order to look good – to actualize the self – she lies about her actions. Now she is in a real bind since part of her self-concept is also that of a person that never lies. (Rogers and Wood, 1974: 238)

In the meeting, Gloria herself does not reach the point of feeling clear and settled about what she perceives to be the good course of action for her. Also, we believe it is not clear what the drive of the actualizing tendency is here. Is the difficulty in facing her daughter the result of feeling she has indeed gone against herself at a deep level, rather than that she finds 'her organism endeavouring to meet its consciously unacceptable desires' (Rogers and Wood, 1974: 251)? In the light of Hollway's work it is interesting to speculate whether Rogers's interpretation of Gloria's conflict may result from an understanding of heterosexuality which falls broadly within the 'male sexual drive' discourse, or that for Rogers in the 1960s the 'permissive' discourse may have been more influential than the 'have/hold' discourse. This provides us with an example of the possibility of the projection of male sexual values on to female experience, with its potential for profound misunderstanding. Clearly we do not see this as being a function only of sexism; we may all be unaware of the effect of uncon-scious assumptions, particularly when embedded in language, even when we believe we are endeavouring to be open and accepting of our clients.[1]

One self or many?

Hollway's research also offers another angle for viewing conflicts such as those presented by Gloria. Her analyses reveal that her subjects move rapidly from one position to another as they engage in dialogue with others: no position is fixed. She reveals the *process* nature of socially constructed reality and its transmission through discourses that we *each* engage in every time we seek to communicate with another human being. She suggests that the notion of operating for any length of time from *one* self is absurd. Yet it is far easier to engage with the notion of a fixed and unitary self than to admit a complexity of potentially contradictory selves into conscious awareness.

Given this view, it is fascinating that Rogers should insert a lengthy digression within his 'Theory of therapy, personality and interpersonal relationships' (1959) on his experience of the development of the construct of 'self'. While clients often entered therapy with a desire to be more of their 'real' selves, Rogers and his colleagues discovered that in the process of therapy there would be 'violent fluctuation in the concept of self' (1959: 201) and that a major reversal in attitude or in self-perception could attend even the most minor incident. They concluded that the self is 'clearly a gestalt, a configuration in which the alteration of one minor aspect could completely alter the whole pattern' (1959: 201). Rogers ends his digression by affirming his and his colleagues' current definition of the self as 'a gestalt which is available to awareness', but acknowledges that the self might be differently defined by giving more emphasis to its 'process nature' or to a 'plural definition, indicating many specific selves' (1959: 203). We would like to reinforce the validity of a 'plural definition'. We may move suddenly from one sub-self to another, potentially bringing us closer or moving us further away from the actualizing tendency. Our conception of ourselves, and therefore the way that we relate to others, is neither static, nor even consistent.[2] By linking together the importance of discourse and fluctuating self-concepts, it becomes clear that it is not sufficient to become aware only of particular strands of socially and culturally dominant values and ideas; one must also be aware of the changes effected by relating with others. For instance, as individual counsellors we stand in a different relationship with male and female clients, heterosexual, gay and lesbian clients. Our own self-concept and the discourses that are currently operating in our lives will result in changing perceptions of our clients and ourselves, as well as the nature and potential of the relationship between us.

Beyond the self

Up to this point we have been concerned with the relationship between the organism, the self-concept(s) and our social context. In his later writings Rogers moved beyond the notion of our embodied and socially or culturally constructed selves to consider the possibility of another realm of existence which transcends the temporal and spatial limitations that normally constrict our understanding. In his 1965 dialogue with Paul Tillich he accepts Tillich's definition of a transformative level of awareness, a 'vertical line' that connects us to 'something which is infinite, unconditional, ultimate', an experience of 'the temporal invaded by the eternal in some moments of our life' (Kirschenbaum and Henderson, 1989: 73). In response to Tillich's definition, Rogers cites his own experience:

> I feel at times when I'm really being helpful to a client of mine, in those sort of rare moments when there is something approximating to an I–Thou relationship between us, and when I feel that something significant is happening, then I feel as though I am somehow in tune with the forces in the universe or that forces are operating through me in regard to this helping relationship [and that I have put myself] in line with the significant forces of the universe and thereby [am] able to trigger off a significant event. (Kirschenbaum and Henderson, 1989: 74)

Deep change takes place at a physiological level, when a felt sense is touched and the actualizing tendency activated. Trusting this level of wisdom is inimical to our culture and it is from Japan that we have gained some insight into how we may reach more precise understanding of the processes involved in recognizing and accessing the 'infinite' or 'unconditional' aspects of ourselves. F. Tomoda, who first brought client-centred work to Japan in the 1950s, has, in more recent years, been developing his own approach to the self through pursuing the study of classical Eastern philosophers. He states that it is misleading to define the self as a conceptual entity, and in 1992 presented a paper entitled '"Go", "ga" and "yo": a study on the self through the analects of Confucius, Tao Te Ching, and Chuang Tzu'. 'Go', 'ga' and 'yo' are three Chinese pronouns all representing the pronoun 'I', but Tomoda sees them as having different meanings: 'go' is the 'true' or 'essential' self; 'ga' the 'narcissistic' or 'conceptual' self; 'yo' the 'relational' self. We would see 'go' as being the self that is the actualizing tendency, whereas 'ga' and 'yo' are more akin to the conceptualized selves that we seek to fulfil in our socially constructed realities. Deep change can only take place once the introjected conditions of worth attached to 'ga' and 'yo' have been addressed.

In *A Way of Being* Rogers explains that the more fully in touch with our experience we are, the nearer we come to making a transformational shift in consciousness leading to 'a transcendent awareness of the harmony and unity of the cosmic system, including humankind' (Rogers, 1980: 133). However, if this is so, then it may be argued that concerns with the specifics of our social reality are misplaced, or at least enable us to gain only a partial improvement in our understanding of ourselves and the world. It could even be said that overly focusing on social construction and the specifics of oppression prevents access to that transformational, and potentially enormously healing, shift in awareness.

However, as Tomoda's thinking suggests, the danger is in trying to side-step the specific problems of oppression by striving for organismic change without conscious awareness. In *Beyond God the Father* feminist theologian Mary Daly aims 'to show that the women's revolution . . . is an ontological, spiritual revolution, pointing beyond the idolatries of sexist society and sparking creative action in and toward transcendence' (Daly, 1986: 6). She is deeply concerned, however, that actual social structures and discourses should not be ignored in favour of theorizing about the potential of our transcendent existence and believes that to ignore the specifics of oppression actually inhibits the growth of our awareness. She acknowledges the work of theologians such as Tillich, who show the ontological courage needed to grow away from structures which deny the true self (Rogers's actualizing tendency), but which nevertheless offer security. However, she also states that 'while Tillich analyses courage in universalist, humanist categories, he does not betray any awareness of the relevance of this to women's confrontation with the structured evil of patriarchy' (Daly, 1986: 23). There is a general point to be made here:

That is, the lack of explicit relevance of intellection to the fact of oppression in its precise forms, such as sexual hierarchy, is itself oppressive. (Daly, 1986: 20)

This is vitally important, for the failure to challenge the conceptual frameworks which constrain our thinking, and therefore our capacity for self-reflection, necessarily prevents our integration of experience not recognized within such frameworks. The trends in client-centred thinking have often centred either on our individual, phenomenological worlds or on the universal aspects of our experience, whether this be transcendent or the assertion that our deepest individual experiences are common, even if socially and culturally we are poles apart. Without examining those social and cultural differences to make explicit the power structures involved and how they fit into a client-centred framework, we may be contributing to the ability to side-step issues which foster oppression, rather than adding greater force to the move for liberation.

The recovery of lost aspects of the self

Alongside the work of feminist theorists like Irigaray and Hollway in surfacing masculine assumptions, there has been a reclamation of women's voices and the use by women writers of particular literary forms to heighten and distinguish the female voice, thereby raising awareness of the distinct experience of women. This highlights an important general consideration in counselling. What has been said by women (or any group whose experience is marginalized or hidden by dominant discourses) is significant not simply as knowledge which can be assimilated in order to give a fuller picture of the subjective world of female clients; it is also an articulation of the struggle to give voice to experience which is not recognized and which stands 'outside' language. It concerns the attempt to speak where there is an absence of adequate words.

An interesting exploration of women's attempts at articulation is contained in *The Politics of the Essay*, edited by Joeres and Mittman (1993) which gives feminist perspectives on the essay form. The editors chose to consider this form because of their awareness of the essay as being traditionally a vehicle for the views of the male European elite and yet a form which is particularly suited to giving strength and force to women's voices. They see it as 'a written form which resembles speech – that invites dialogue and connection, that is straightforward, comprehensible, yet impassioned; that allows and indeed assumes a personal presence' (Joeres and Mittman, 1993: 19).

The assumptions about the traditional background and identity of authors meant there was no necessity on the part of those writing to define their social or cultural identity: 'I' was virtually synonymous with a male, white, educated, upper-class voice (Joeres, 1993: 151). However, several feminists have consciously chosen this form precisely because of the opportunity it offers of throwing aspects of the writers' identity into relief through explicit definition. This is shown clearly by authors such as Audre Lorde, who states: 'As a forty-nine-year-old Black lesbian-feminist socialist mother of two, including one boy, and a member of an inter-racial couple' (Lorde, 1984: 114), with the result that the act of writing becomes 'certainly strategic as well as informative' (Joeres, 1993: 15). Further to this, Pamela Mittlefehldt states:

> To write an essay is to assume the validity and authority of one's voice, the significance of one's experience, and the implicit value of one's insight and perspective. To write an essay is to break silence and claim authority. It is to assume the right of speech and Being. For a Black woman in America to write an essay is an act of bodacious rebellion. (Mittlefehldt, 1993: 197)

This is crucial. The ability to speak or write directly from experience is not simply the act of delivering something to the world – it is not only 'telling about' – potentially it is a direct manifestation of a person's inner world. This again provides us with an illuminating parallel with the endeavour of clients. In the struggle to find words which feel apt in relation to their inner experience, clients are doing more than attempting to report correctly on an inner process. It is a major part of the struggle for the realization of aspects of the self, with articulation/self-expression striving towards being an undistorted manifestation of the individual.

The implications for practice and theory

The work of such theorists shows how the particular forms or structures available to us when we speak or write can either limit or assist in the exploration of other-defined, hidden or oppressed 'selves'. This has further relevance to the client-centred approach. In describing the therapeutic relationship, Rogers delineated a framework in which a client can come to redefine their experience, but this framework is described only in terms of the core conditions. The absence of a detailed theory which attempts to interpret the story of our individual psychological and emotional development means clients can be offered an empowering opportunity to attempt their own process of reconstruction. However, as is illustrated by Rogers's encounter with Gloria, client-centred therapy only presents us with a *potentially* neutral space, one in which our own cultural beliefs rather than theoretical dogma may lead us into misleading assumptions.

The challenge to the client-centred approach is to release this potential, to allow clients to recover experience and reclaim projected parts of the self, to become a being in process, free from conditions of worth and the constraints of an external locus of evaluation. In practice it will be the ability of both counsellor and client to become aware of a multiplicity of influences, and the fact that not all influences can initially be spoken of with the same eloquence or force, which will be vital in the therapeutic process. It is relatively easy to challenge client assumptions that we do not share, but it is far more difficult to see our way through assumptions, such as those embedded in discourses that define and prescribe our sexual attitudes, that are woven into the fabric of Western culture. As counsellors, we are beholden to develop our recognition of the impact of society in the construction of our selves. Lack of recognition leaves us open to perpetuating the silences that our clients bring, to limiting the potential both for individual growth and social transformation.

The core conditions offer us, as therapists, a framework for accommodating a view of the person that allows for the transcendence of limited self-concepts. To come to know a client without the bias or denial which can come through the conscious or unconscious imposition of our own perspective or values is an element both of acceptance and of empathy. It requires the acknowledgement of differences, but also a willingness to give conscious recognition to aspects of experiencing which risk being taken for granted by both client and counsellor: unaware acceptance may lead to a dropping away of elements of experience within the client that have begun to rise, for neither the counsellor nor the client may register their full significance. An example of this might be the female student client whose adherence to the 'permissive' discourse makes her feel bad for being unable to handle the emotional pressure of casual and apparently meaningless sexual encounters: a counsellor accepting permissive sexual behaviour as a 'norm' of student life might enable the client to explore her feelings of 'badness' but not to explore the deeper need for intimacy that may be finding distorted expression within a particular cultural context. Another retrospective example is the change in attitudes towards and understanding of child sexual abuse. Such abusive behaviour was previously often deemed fantasy or of small importance; recognition of its enormous impact has resulted in an increase in clients able to talk about their experiences, reminding us of just how deadly silence can be.

In the therapeutic relationship congruence should be present not just at the level of counsellor utterances, but also in terms of the counsellor's being 'freely and deeply himself, with his actual experience accurately represented by his awareness of himself' (Rogers, 1957: 224). Obviously we want to suggest that this should include awareness of the social and cultural implications of our being: that we should strive to become conscious of the contextual limitations to which we are subject.

Counsellor training is a key arena in which heightened awareness can be generated. In a recent article, Michele Crouan examines the experience of lesbian women trainees on courses which do not actively integrate a lesbian perspective into training. She believes the likelihood is that lesbian issues will be 'dealt with in the "alternative forms of sexuality" slot' and that a lesbian training on such a course will have to 'state her sexual orientation to be fully recognised. Repeatedly having to come out means repeatedly risking rejection' (Crouan, 1996: 37). This clearly illustrates how passive acceptance allows for the reproduction of social norms within training groups and therefore the risk of perpetuating oppression is high. On a more subtle level, trainer use of sexist or racist language, the incorporation of patriarchal attitudes, the failure to challenge potentially oppressive or unaware behaviour can encourage the development of oppression within an environment that is consciously seeking to activate healthy growth. Trainees quickly learn how hurtful and damaging it is not to be heard by other members of the group; it is far more difficult for the individual trainee to disentangle the unease and loneliness that may accompany recognition of her sexual invisibility or perceived deviance in a group. The dividing line between growth-promoting acceptance and potentially destructive collusion is a fine one that needs careful consideration in relation to both the experiential aspects of training and the presentation of client-centred theory.

In terms of our understanding of the theory, a greater awareness of the many ways in which cultural values are transmitted moves us beyond the need for early positive regard as the sole distorting factor in psychological development into a consideration of the ongoing social realities that we each inhabit. It would be useful to consider how active acknowledgement of discourses and oppression can be incorporated into our understanding of personality development and into our recognition of the ongoing organismic distortion that occurs through cultural endorsement of destructive patterns of living. The current promotion of 'family values' in our own culture is a simple example of a potentially oppressive structure being given higher value than more flexible and possibly more intelligent ways of living.

Finally, the later developments in Rogers's thinking suggest we have to acknowledge a transcendental dimension to our existence. Tillich, in his dialogue with Rogers, speaks of the 'two natures of man', his 'essential nature' and his 'temporal, historical nature' which 'is a distortion of his essential nature, and in attempting to reach it, he may be contradicting his true nature'. Because we are all caught up in our temporal realities we are all faced with 'a universal, tragic estrangement from [our] true being' (Kirschenbaum and Henderson, 1989: 68). Discovery of one's 'true being' may be the work of a lifetime, possibly glimpsed only momentarily in precious moments of insight. Yet, just as our socially constructed selves can operate and define themselves only in terms of their social context, so the actualizing tendency (which we would equate with our 'true being') cannot be separated from what Rogers terms 'the formative tendency'. He presents this hypothetical tendency in the following terms:

> This is an evolutionary tendency toward greater order, greater complexity, greater interrelatedness. In humankind, this tendency exhibits itself as the individual moves from a single-cell origin to complex organic functioning, to knowing and sensing below the level of consciousness, to a conscious awareness of the organism and the external world, to a transcendent awareness of the harmony and unity of the cosmic system, including humankind. (Rogers, 1980: 133)

In order to become more fully in tune with this evolutionary flow it is necessary – as Rogers points out very clearly, both here and in the earlier stages of his argument in 'The foundations of a person-centred approach' – to become more *consciously* aware of ourselves and of 'the external world' so that we can make more informed choices and move towards freeing ourselves from invalid and distorting societal constraints. This, Rogers concludes, in presenting his hypothesis for the future of the theory, 'definitely forms a base for the person-centred approach' (1980: 133).

Conclusion

Our concern in this chapter is that the client-centred approach runs the risk of colluding with prevailing oppression and hierarchies if it fails explicitly to challenge implicit power structures within our society. Feminist thinking, in the discrete areas of language and discourse that we have examined briefly in this chapter, points to some ways in which we can expand our conscious awareness of social oppression. We believe that it is only through such scrutiny that we can surface and therefore begin to address all the areas of our lives that run counter to both the actualizing and the formative tendencies.

Notes

1 It is perhaps worth noting the effects of projection onto others that can result from such misunderstanding, for our inability to tolerate conscious tension not only results in the loss of aspects of the self, but also creates a solid grounding for prejudice. A great deal of work has been done on this issue in the field of psychodynamics and for client-centred theory the mechanisms of distortion and denial can work in a similar way. Susan Griffin graphically describes the effect:

> [T]he moment I have defined another as my enemy, I lose part of myself, the complexity and subtlety of my vision. I begin to exist in a closed system. When anything goes wrong, I blame my enemy. . . . Slowly all the power in my life begins to be located outside, and my whole being is defined in relation to this outside force, which becomes daily . . . more laden with all the qualities in myself I no longer wish to own. The quality of my thought then is diminished. My imagination grows small. My self seems meagre. For my enemy has stolen all these. (Griffin, 1982: 177)

2 Within other therapeutic traditions the notion of multiple selves is more readily accepted than hitherto in the person-centred tradition. Work in this area has been documented in relation to the phenomenological approach, for example, by Sorokin (1947), Harré and Secord (1972), Gergen (1971), Middlebrook (1980) and Spinelli (1989). Spinelli acknowledges the role of language in determining our resistance to the idea of multiple selves: 'So sedimented is our stance and conviction as to the existence of a unitary core self that any alternative to this view is difficult to express in words – to speak of "self-creating selves" *sounds* like patent nonsense' (Spinelli, 1989: 95; original emphasis).

Within the person-centred approach Len Holdstock opens up the question of the self in two papers, 'Can we afford not to revision the person-centred concept of self?' (Brazier, 1993) and 'Discrepancy between the person-centred theories of self and of therapy' (Hutterer et al., 1996). The notion of multiple selves is also addressed by S. Keil from a person-centred standpoint in 'The self as a systemic process of interactions of "inner persons"' (Hutterer et al., 1996).

References

Brazier, D. (ed.) (1993) *Beyond Carl Rogers*. London: Constable.

Crouan, M. (1996) 'Pushing against the wind: the recognition of lesbians in counsellor training', *Counselling*, 7 (1): 36–9.

Daly, M. (1986) *Beyond God the Father: Towards a Philosophy of Women's Liberation*. London: The Women's Press.

Foucault, M. (1972) *The Archaeology of Knowledge*, trans. A.M. Sheridan Smith. London: Tavistock.

Gergen, K. (1971) *The Concept of Self*. New York: Holt, Reinhart & Winston.

Griffin, S. (1982) *Made from this Earth: Selections from her Writing*. London: The Women's Press.

Harré, R. and Secord, P. (1972) *The Explanation of Social Behaviour*. Oxford: Blackwell.

Holdstock, L. (1993) 'Can we afford not to revision the person-centred concept of self?', in D. Brazier (ed.), *Beyond Carl Rogers*. London: Constable.

Holdstock, L. (1996) 'Discrepancy between the person-centred theories of self and of therapy', in R. Hutterer, G. Pawlowsky, P.F. Schmid and R. Stipsits (eds), *Client-Centered and Experiential Therapy: A Paradigm in Motion*. Frankfurt-on-Main: Peter Lang.

Hollway, W. (1989) *Subjectivity and Method in Psychology: Gender, Meaning and Science*. London: Sage.

Hollway, W. (1992) 'Gender difference and the production of subjectivity', in H. Crowley and S. Himmelweit (eds), *Knowing Women: Feminism and Knowledge*. Cambridge: Polity Press.

Hutterer, R., Pawlowsky, G., Schmid, P.F. and Stipsits, R. (eds) (1996) *Client-Centered and Experiential Psychotherapy: A Paradigm in Motion*. Frankfurt-on-Main: Peter Lang.

Irigaray, L. (1985) *This Sex Which Is Not One*, trans. Catherine Porter. New York: Cornell University Press.

Joeres, R.-E.B. (1993) 'The passionate essay; radical feminist essayists', in R.-E. Boetcher Joeres and E. Mittman (eds), *The Politics of the Essay: Feminist Perspectives*. Indianapolis, IN: Indiana University Press.

Joeres, R.-E.B. and Mittman, E. (eds) (1993) *The Politics of the Essay: Feminist Perspectives*. Indianapolis: Indiana University Press.

Keil, S. (1996) 'The self as a systemic process of interactions of "inner persons"', in R. Hutterer, G. Pawlowsky, P.F. Schmid and R. Stipsits (eds), *Client-Centered and Experiential Therapy: A Paradigm in Motion*. Frankfurt-on-Main: Peter Lang.

Kirschenbaum, H. and Henderson, V. (eds) (1989) *Carl Rogers: Dialogues*. London: Constable.

Lorde, A. (1984) *Sister Outsider*. Trumansburg, NY: Crossing Press.

Middlebrook, P.N. (1980) *Social Psychology and Modern Life*, 2nd edn. New York: Knopf.

Mittlefehldt, P.K. (1993) 'A weaponry of choice: black American women writers and the essay', in R.-E. Boetcher Joeres and E. Mittman (eds), *The Politics of the Essay: Feminist Perspectives*. Indianapolis, IN: Indiana University Press.

Rogers, C. (1957) 'The necessary and sufficient conditions of therapeutic personality change', *Journal of Counseling Psychology*, 21 (2): 95–103.

Rogers, C.R. (1959) 'A theory of therapy, personality and interpersonal relationships, as developed in the client-centered framework', in S. Koch (ed.), *Psychology: A Study of a Science*, Vol. 3: *Formulations of the Person and the Social Context*. New York: McGraw-Hill. pp. 184–256.

Rogers, C.R. (1980) *A Way of Being*. Boston: Houghton Mifflin.

Rogers, C.R. and Wood, J.K. (1974) 'Client-centred theory: Carl R. Rogers', in A. Burton (ed.), *Operational Theories of Personality*. New York: Brunner/Mazel.

Sellers, S. (1991) *Language and Sexual Difference: Feminist Writing in France*. London: Macmillan.

Sorokin, P. (1947) *Society, Culture and Personality: Their Structure and Dynamics*. New York: Harper.

Spinelli, E. (1989) *The Interpreted World: An Introduction to Phenomenological Psychology*. London: Sage.

Tomoda, F. (1992) '"Go", "ga" and "yo": a study on the self through the analects of Confucius, Tao Te Ching, and Chuang Tzu', *Journal of Counselling* (Japan Counselling Centre), 11: 63–79. (Quoted in Hagashi, S., Kuno, T., Morotomi, Y., Osawa, M., Shimizu, M. and Suetake, Y. (1994) 'A re-evaluation of client-centered therapy through the work of F. Tomoda and its cultural implications in Japan'. Unpublished paper presented at the Third International Conference of Client-Centered and Experiential Therapy at Gmunden, Austria.)

9 On the Development of the Person in Relationships

Eva-Maria Biermann-Ratjen

The actualizing tendency and self-actualizing

I should like to start with a longish quotation from Robert Kegan:

> At the heart of the lens we associate with Rogers is an existential approach to the metaphors of twentieth-century evolutionary biology. In contradistinction to earlier mechanistic and homeostatic conceptions, Rogers attends to what he regards as intrinsic processes of adaptation and growth. His first principle is the 'actualizing tendency':
>
>> the inherent tendency of the organism to develop all its capacities in ways which serve to maintain or enhance the organism. . . . Angyal's statement could be used as a synonym for this term: 'Life is an autonomous event which takes place between the organism and the environment. Life processes do not merely tend to preserve life, but transcend the momentary status quo of the organism, expanding itself continually and imposing its autonomous determination upon an ever-increasing realm of events.' (Rogers, 1959: 196)
>
> This actualizing tendency Rogers regards as the sole motive of personality; there are no separate systems with motives of their own. The tensions between defence and enhancement, for example, are integrated in a single system. There is presumed to be a basic unity to personality, a unity best understood as a process rather than an entity. This process, according to Rogers's conception, gives rise to the 'self', the meaning-making system with which the process gets identified. Anxiety, defence, psychological maladjustment and the processes of psychotherapy are all understood in the context of the efforts to maintain, and the experience of transforming, the self system. (Kegan, 1982: 4–5)

Whilst in Rogers's wording the actualizing tendency 'expresses itself *also* in the actualization of that portion of the experience . . . which is symbolized in the self' (Rogers, 1959: 196), the client-centred psychotherapists who have pursued his ideas further – Kegan for instance – emphasize that human life processes in fact *are* self-actualization. Self-actualizing processes transcend, go beyond the momentary status quo of the organism, enlarging and extending it and imposing their own rules and self-regulating potential on an increasingly wider range of events. Thinking about 'the development of the person in relationships' within the client-centred framework therefore means above all thinking about the continuous process of self-actualization, whereby a growing number and range of events are given personal meaning.

Experience and symbolization

Rogers gave us the following definitions: 'The term experience is used to include all that is going on within the envelope of the organism at any given moment which is potentially available to awareness' (Rogers, 1959: 197). And 'awareness, symbolization, consciousness . . . are defined as synonymous. To use Angyal's expression, consciousness (or awareness) is the symbolization of some of our experience. Awareness is thus seen as the symbolic representation . . . of some portion of our experience' (Rogers, 1959: 198).

The process of symbolizing experience (see Gendlin, 1970) in the adult person links up physical sensations, visual imaginings, feelings, thoughts and words correlated to an experience and gives meaning to it. The successful conclusion of a symbolizing process, when the 'felt sense' is developed and a 'felt shift' occurs, is accompanied by a marked drop in tension, a sense of relief along the lines, 'That's right, that's how I feel at the moment.' The relaxation includes physical sensations. If the felt sense cannot be fully developed, there is no such sense of physical and psychic relief.

As well as bringing experience into awareness the symbolizing process enables the person to realize that he/she is experiencing or actualizing him/herself. The symbolizing process involves both mental and physical experiencing; it acts on both the mind and the body.

What are emotions?

In his recent article 'Was sind Affekte?' (What are emotions?) Mark Solms reminds us that when Freud was working out his theory on drives he took as his starting point exactly these dual aspects of conscious experience: a conscious experience is a subjective and an objective event on the one hand, and a psychic and a physical one on the other (see Freud, 1940). Just as Kant differentiated between simple awareness and self-awareness, and Bion between sensory and psychic realities, Freud, too, distinguished between experience and self-experience, between an inner and an outer 'surface of consciousness'. On the outer surface our (always only phenomenologically knowable) reality is transformed into experience via the 'conscious envelope' of our senses, by what we see, hear, taste, smell and in our physical sensations. On the inner 'surface of consciousness' we become aware of our self-experiencing through our immediate feelings. Just as we can never experience 'a thing in itself' but can only become aware of how it looks, smells and so on, equally we can never 'experience ourselves' as such but can only become aware of the emotions we are currently feeling (Solms, 1996).

Self-experience: subjective and objective

One striking feature of emotions is that they too have a dual aspect; as well as feeling them subjectively we can perceive them objectively in our own bodies. I may for instance feel frightened but I can also notice that my knees are trembling without feeling frightened; I can notice and see that I am getting goose-pimples even if I do not realize I am alarmed. This special quality of self-experience – it is bound up with the 'envelope' of emotions, which have a psychic and a physical side and can therefore be experienced both subjectively as an event in the mind and objectively as an event in the body – led Freud, according to Solms, to declare that emotional experience is the prototype of drive-determined self-experiencing. Drive-determined experience is understood to be psychic self-experience which has a physical basis. And since we cannot experience 'ourselves' psychically outside the 'envelope' of feelings, just as we cannot experience reality 'as such' but only as a phenomenon perceived via our senses, Freud postulated that drives are ultimately beyond the reach of consciousness.

The client-centred concepts of the symbolizing process and the phenomenal self and self-concept, used as synonyms, apparently draw on similar ideas; my self-experience is never 'just experiencing myself' but is always only available on a phenomenological level. Rogers took up the definition offered by Snygg and Combs, describing psychotherapy as the conveying of experience by means of which the individual is enabled to develop adequate differentiations of the phenomenal self and its relations to others. When such differentiations are made, the need of the individual to maintain and enhance the phenomenal self will lead to further development (Snygg and Combs, 1949 quoted in Rogers 1972: 143). This definition and the fundamental importance in recent work on client-centred therapy attached to the felt sense, to feelings altogether and to the body show that it is basically emotional experience we mean when we talk about self-experience. Feeling means to transcend our organismic sensations and to become aware that we are experiencing, and that we are experiencing ourselves. When undergoing an emotional experience we are both the subject and the object of our experiencing (see Kegan, 1982); as we become aware of our self-experience our self appears as a gestalt in our perceptual field.

Rogers's definition of psychotherapy

Rogers not only defined psychotherapy as providing a special kind of experience which enables the client to differentiate his/her phenomenal self.

He also defined the tendency to maintain and enhance the phenomenal self as a *need*. Furthermore he described the way the need to develop the phenomenal self is satisfied: the necessary and sufficient conditions under which the process of experiencing and thereby developing and enhancing the self can take place. In his view these conditions represent the core of his theory (Rogers, 1959: 192): 'This theory is of the if–then variety. If certain conditions exist . . . then a process . . . will occur which includes certain characteristic elements. If this process . . . occurs, then certain personality and behavioral changes . . . will occur' (Rogers, 1959: 212).

The conditions are that the therapist as part of the real outside world and the client who is in the process of differentiating his/her self-experiencing can establish a certain kind of relationship. The therapist can understand the client empathically and encounter him/her with unconditional positive regard, while the client is in psychological contact with the therapist and realizes that he/she understands him empathically and with unconditional positive regard. Understanding someone empathically means experiencing what the other is experiencing exactly as if one were the other without ever forgetting the 'as if', the realization that one is not the other. Unconditional positive regard means appreciating and accepting the other whatever he or she is experiencing without imposing judgements such as 'I like you because you are as you are, or I like you more if you are like this than if you are like that'. If the encounter between therapist and client is a genuine one founded on empathic unconditional positive regard then there is no need for the therapist to withhold any of his own perceptions or emotional reactions from consciousness, or hide behind a façade of pseudo-approval.

Rogers always described the personality and behavioural changes which take place in psychotherapy as developments in the self-concept, as changes in the meaning-making system, in the process of evaluating experience emotionally in relationships. Our wording is as follows: 'A successful psychotherapeutic process enables the client to take up the relation to himself which the therapist offers him. He can understand himself and regard his experiencing of himself in an unconditionally positive way' (Biermann-Ratjen et al., 1995: 32).

Self-development in childhood

It seems reasonable to assume that what applies to the process of self-development in psychotherapy also applies to the process of self-development in childhood. Corresponding with the definition of the necessary and sufficient conditions for the process of self-development in psychotherapy to occur, we can define the following conditions as needing to prevail if the process of developing a sense of self in early childhood is to get under way:

1   The child is in contact with a significant other person.
2   The child is preoccupied with emotional experience.
3   The significant other person is congruent in the relationship with the child, does not experience anything inconsistent with her/his self-concept while interacting with the affectively aroused child.
4   The significant other experiences unconditional positive regard for the child's emotional experience.
5   The significant other experiences an empathic understanding of the child's emotional experiencing. This 'means to sense the hurt or the pleasure of (the child) as (the child) senses it, and to perceive the causes thereof as (the child) perceives them, but without ever losing the recognition that it is *as if* I were hurt or pleased, etc. If this "as if" quality is lost, then the state is one of identification' (Rogers, 1959: 210–11) and not one of empathic understanding.
6   The child gradually perceives both the significant other's unconditional positive regard for him and his/her empathic understanding. As a result in the child's awareness a belief or prognosis gradually develops that the unconditionally positively regarding and empathically understanding object would react in a similarly accepting way to other experiences the child might have (see Rogers, 1959: 199; compare Biermann-Ratjen, 1996).

Self-development begins, it follows, with the experience of being empathically understood and unconditionally positively regarded, and this leads to a prognosis on how another person will react emotionally to one's own processing of experience.

The necessary conditions for empathic regard

Most researchers into emotions agree that an adult's consciously experienced emotions consist of at least six different components:

1   changes in the internal physiological and probably the hormone status;
2   correlated with changes in expression: facial mimicry, gestures, vocalization;
3   readiness to react on the motor level, for instance by running away;
4   the individual becoming aware of these three changes;
5   the individual's interpretation of this awareness;
6   the interpretation of the whole behaviour sequence by outside observers (see Krause, 1983).

There are inborn programmes for having and expressing the basic emotions: pleasure, interest, amazement, hurt, revulsion, rage, fear and shame (Deneke, 1992: 154). The so-called signal components of the emotions (vocalizing, mimicry, gestures) exist at birth or develop very soon after –

the human face has 46 different pairs of muscles for expressing emotions – and are recognizable to others.

This means that others can empathize with the baby's emotional experience, which is its potential self-experience. Others can feel unconditional positive regard towards the baby's organismic processes of evaluating its experience and in this way can satisfy the baby's need for unconditional positive regard from the very beginning of life. According to client-centred thinking the process of congruent (non anxious) empathic understanding is also conceived as a symbolizing process. While sensing what another person is experiencing one identifies – without ever forgetting that one is doing so – what the other is going through by referring to one's own physical sensations, images, thoughts, feelings and words. This empathic symbolizing process can be more or less complete and 'correct'. A mother may for instance grasp what her child is experiencing physically but may anxiously develop quite different images or feelings in this process than the child would if it already could do the same. This is increasingly likely the more incongruent or anxious the mother is when faced with the child's emotional messages, making her unable to accept them unconditionally. In this case the child is not given unconditional positive regard for everything it is experiencing. The effect of such incomplete empathic processing by the significant other is that the child cannot completely 'see' its experience in the responding other and is therefore unable to completely identify with it or integrate it as a self-experience into its concept of self.

The experiences which form the core of the self-concept are emotional ones. They have a physical component and can potentially reach awareness both as a subjective and as an objective experience. They contain what they mean for the enhancement of the organism. And further, the experiences which turn into the core of the self-concept are linked with experiencing that one's need for unconditional positive regard is satisfied. They contain their own personal meaning.

Sullivan and the need for tenderness

These links between the need for empathic unconditional positive regard and emotional experience in the development of the person in relationships were pointed out by Sullivan:

> The living cannot live when separated from what may be described as their necessary environment, which for the human life includes pertaining to people. Human development requires interpersonal relationships, or interchange with others. A general '*need for tenderness*' is ingrained from the very beginning of things as an interpersonal need. The necessary interchanges with others start '. . . at an indeterminately early age' with 'tensions which appear in the infant . . . marked with the prototype of what later we call emotional experience' (Sullivan, 1953: 42; original emphasis)

The 'mothering one' in reaction to the observation of the emotional experience of the child experiences 'tenderness and an impulsion to activities toward the relief of the infant's needs' (ibid.: 39). And the child in turn experiences 'the manifest activity by the mothering one toward the relief of the infant's needs . . . as the undergoing of tender behaviour; and these needs, the relaxation of which require cooperation of another, thereon take on the character of a general need for tenderness' (ibid.: 40).

Anxiety and incongruence

In Sullivan's interpersonal theory of psychiatry we do not come across the client-centred definition of the significant other in a state of incongruence and therefore unable to empathize with or give unconditional positive regard to the infant's experiencing. Nevertheless one of the central concepts of Sullivan's theory is that of the mothering one in a state of anxiety. According to this theory, anxiety is a tension in opposition to the tensions of needs and to actions appropriate to their relief. So it is also in opposition to the tension of tenderness in the mothering one. 'The tension of anxiety when present in the mothering one induces anxiety in the infant' (ibid.: 41); 'the interpersonal situation is destroyed, it breaks up' (ibid.: 95). Correspondingly, 'the relaxation of the tension of anxiety . . . is the experience not of satisfaction, but of interpersonal security', and vice versa: 'the need for interpersonal security might be said to be the need to be rid of anxiety' (ibid.: 42–3).

   This comes close to the client-centred concept of the incongruent significant other. In client-centred theory, felt incongruence is felt anxiety. The need for interpersonal security might be said to be the need for unconditional positive regard by an empathic and congruent 'mother'. The absence of these necessary interpersonal conditions for the integration of emotional experience into the self induces anxiety, which is felt incongruence.

Attachment research

Those researching into attachment along the lines initiated by Bowlby (see Main et al., 1985) stress the relevance of Sullivan's ideas for their own thinking. And they tend to use client-centred terms in describing those interpersonal experiences which are relevant to the development of representational structures. Having systematically observed the attachment behaviour of small children in great detail they have arrived at the hypothesis that depending on how sensitively the significant others respond to the child's emotional signals the child develops an 'inner working model', a representation of his/her interactions with the significant other person in situations when the child ensures that the significant other is close and available, for instance after a separation. In line with these behaviour patterns, children develop different ideas on how they themselves should behave in situations when they need support and consolation. These patterns of more or less secure attachment behaviour are not only extremely stable but also guide future behaviour and so condition certain kinds of experience and determine certain kinds of development. They enable one to predict whether the person will develop more or less social competence, and will have more or less coherent memories of interacting with significant others as a child, and more or less realistic expectations about relationships with other people and the feelings these involve.

Client-centred psychotherapists can certainly regard these results as evidence that their assumptions on how a self-concept comes about, with its intrinsic links to relating to others, are shared by researchers in other fields and have scientific backing.

Conditions of worth

The client-centred frame does not include the concept of an 'inner working model' but the corresponding idea that as soon as the self-concept – which includes a belief or prognosis concerning the reactions of objects to the experiencing child – has begun to take shape, the need for positive regard is joined by a need for positive self-regard. 'Conditions of worth' (Rogers) have begun to develop. From now on new experiences are monitored as congruent or incongruent with the self-experiences which have been integrated into the self-concept, as either confirming or questioning it. This, too, is an emotionally charged experience. Individuals feel a need to understand and accept themselves in their experiencing. They feel the need to make sense of their experiences.

Since the self-experiences which have been integrated into the self-concept are linked with being unconditionally positively regarded, every experience of not being unconditionally positively regarded means a threat to the self-concept. And since self-experience is always tinged with emotions, it is especially the emotional experience which is monitored as congruent or incongruent with the self-concept. The actualizing tendency is not only revealed in the attempt to maintain and enhance the organism as a whole but also in the attempt to maintain that part of the experience which is symbolized and represented in the self. This means 'a new experience is (not only) valued or not depending on its effectiveness in maintaining or enhancing the organism' (Rogers, 1959: 211). It is especially checked as to whether it confirms the self-concept.

The self-defending tendency

The result of this monitoring can be a split in the actualizing tendency. Efforts to develop the self-concept can collide with efforts to maintain the self-concept: an experience might possibly be enhancing to the organism as a whole. We should not forget that the self-actualizing tendency is an essential part of the actualizing tendency and the self-concept can only develop by integrating self-experience. But equally the experience may call the self-concept into question. Any experiences which are incongruent with the self-experiences integrated in the self-concept, and would contradict it if they were to reach awareness, alert that part of the actualizing tendency I call the self-defending tendency. Defence mechanisms come into play, operations which prevent experience which might question the self-concept from reaching awareness as self-experience. Experiences which do not support the self-concept may be completely banished from consciousness – that is one form of defence. Another is that experiences are symbolized only in part or in such a way that they are not identified, completely understood or accepted as self-experience. In this case as well as feeling uneasy and anxious, physically and/or psychically, the individual does not understand or accept his or her self-experience and suffers from a lack of 'positive self-regard'.

Incongruence and the fully functioning person

When the organismic process of evaluating experiences as maintaining and enhancing the organism or not runs counter to the process of evaluating experiences as confirming the self-concept, there is a state of incongruence. Being incongruent means there is a split in the evaluating processes of the actualizing tendency: the self-defending tendency runs counter to the self-actualizing tendency.

It is in this context that client-centred therapists make use of the term 'fully functioning person'. This is a person who when interacting emotionally with significant others and developing a sense of self or identity has never been frustrated in her/his need for empathic unconditionally positive regard. So there has never been an emotional and/or self-experience which could not be integrated into the self-concept. The self-concept of the fully functioning person is never really endangered by new experience, so there is no need to defend against any form of self-experience. The fully functioning person can always be congruent, can completely symbolize all self-experiences and achieve the state of relaxation which accompanies this. Of course, this person does not exist and never will. But the concept of an ideal development is important for our thinking. The client-centred concept differentiates between more or less fully functioning persons. Individuals organize their experiencing according to how poorly or well their self-concept is developed.

Different phases in the development of the self-concept

Client-centred thinking also distinguishes between early and later phases of self-development, and the corresponding forms of defence.

Building up an identity, which in client-centred terms means developing the self, is a process which inevitably involves others, whereby specific relationships with significant others become more and more distinctly integrated into a sense of self.

At the outset, when the self-concept is starting to form, self-experience means experiencing the interpersonal need for unconditional positive regard and its satisfaction. Depending on how the emotional interaction between baby and carer proceeds, a bodily felt sense of self starts to grow. It is linked to the sense of relaxation which the child feels when its expressed emotions are adequately responded to by its carers. Integrated into the core self-concept are the emotional experiences of needing positive regard and of having this need satisfied, which is an inter-personal experience. If, however, experiencing the need and the satisfaction cannot be integrated into a self-concept at this stage, later on it will not be consciously experienced as such but disguised as fears of being obliterated or destroyed – as a threat to the person's very existence. Equally, being left alone or other forms of emotional neglect will not induce sadness but instead bring on existential depression. The person will feel unable to live and will experience no right to exist. Emotional arousal and especially experiencing (possibly disappointing) close relationships will not reach awareness in the form of feelings but seem an existential threat.

Where a rudimentary self-concept has been enabled to form and gain a first 'gestalt' into which the person can integrate felt experiences of being respected and appreciated, a second phase begins. The person starts gauging experience as either confirming or threatening the self – which means above all as either satisfying or frustrating the need for positive self-regard. This, too, is an emotional experience. There may be anxiety as a warning sign that the self-concept is threatened, that there is incongruence between the experience and the self-concept, and depression as a sign of a lack of positive self-regard. In addition there are now other feelings about oneself to be discovered: pleasure in oneself, surprise about oneself, but also revulsion, fear, rage and shame.

These self-experiences may be correctly understood and symbolized or wrongly interpreted by a significant other, unconditionally or conditionally accepted, and consequently either integrated into the concept of self or not. It is during this developmental phase that the categories of good and bad emerge. If for instance significant others react to self-experiences of the child with their own corresponding interpersonal feelings rather than with unconditional positive regard – angry and aggressive towards the upset child or friendly and loving to the pleased child – which makes these experiences 'good' or 'bad' under certain circumstances, then these self-experiences will not be integrated into the self-concept. When later on the person experiences them again he/she will be alarmed. These experiences will seem threatening, as impulses to be controlled or demands to be met. In any case they will seem incompatible with the person's need for positive self-regard and capable of destroying any sense of self-respect. Whether this rating of experience as 'good' or 'bad' can be overcome in favour of a clear distinction between: 'This is how I value my self-experience' and 'This is how someone else judges it', again depends above all on the emotional reactions of the significant others. This applies in particular to the child's experiencing of impotence and defencelessness and its protest against these feelings: the desperate, frightened and mortifying rage which wells up when the child cannot make itself understood or behave 'acceptably' and cannot understand or accept itself.

The third phase is reached when the self allows the child to feel shame and doubt about itself, and its self-respect is not shattered by merely imagining it might be misunderstood or unable to behave correctly. Only then can the child focus its attention on its own potential for self-experience, for instance as a boy or girl. Integrating such experience of self into the self-concept, which is the next step to an identity, depends just like the previous steps on the child being empathically and unconditionally accepted and understood.

Daniel Stern has systematically observed the emotional interactions between babies and their significant others. He proposes differentiating between the following experiences in the development of the self:

1 the experience of the emerging self linked with impulses to express affects and to actions to reduce the physical tensions asssociated with them;
2 core self-experiences of (a) being the author (b) as a coherent being of (c) one's own emotional experiencing of (d) one's own and the same personal identity;
3 experiencing different states of emotions and the wish to communicate them and to be understood and accepted;
4 experiencing the verbal self in combination with the development of speech (Stern, 1992).

In the client-centred frame we propose distinguishing between:

1 experiencing the need for positive regard and experiencing being accepted as a living being with emotions, which means experiencing that the need for positive regard is satisfied;
2 experiencing the need for positive self-regard, experiencing being frustrated or satisfied in this respect, and
3 experiencing being able to symbolize one's individual self-experiences – also verbally.

All these aspects of self-experience can be integrated into the self-concept, provided they meet with empathic and unconditionally positive regard from significant others.

We assume it is essential that 'positive regard' in a general sense is available from the beginning of life if the child is to develop a sense of self, since its first outlines depend on the emotional reactions of significant others to the child's experience. Further, in our view, it is particularly important that significant others understand correctly what the child is feeling, and do not react with their own unreflected emotions, if the child is to be able to integrate self-reflective and self-assertive sides into its self-concept and regard itself as a coherent emotional being. Lastly, while the child is discovering its individual identity and seeking to communicate this, craving to be empathically understood and unconditionally accepted while undergoing a whole range of different emotions, the largely subconsciously conditional regard directed at its self-experience by its carers, those it loves, has a marked influence on the kind of self the person becomes identified with by her/himself and by others.

References

Biermann-Ratjen, E.-M. (1996) 'On the way to a client-centred psychopathology', in R. Hutterer, G. Pawlowsky, P.F. Schmid and R. Stipsits (eds), *Client-centered and Experiential Psychotherapy*. Frankfurt-on-Main: Peter Lang. pp. 11–24.

Biermann-Ratjen, E.-M., Eckert, J. and Schwartz, H.-J. (1995) *Verändern durch Verstehen: Gesprächspychotherapie*, 7th revised and enlarged edn. H. Bommert and S. Schmidtchen (eds), Stuttgart, Berlin and Cologne: W. Kohlhammer. First published 1979.

Deneke, F.-W. (1992) 'Die Strukturierung der subjektiven Wirklichkeit', in B. Andresen, F.-M. Stark and J. Gross (eds), *Mensch, Psychiatrie, Umwelt*. Bonn: Psychiatrie-Verlag. pp. 143–60.

Freud, S. (1940) *Abriß der Psychoanalyse*. Gesammelte Werke 14, in A. Freud, E. Bibrzing, W. Hoffer, E. Kris and O. Isakower (eds), *Werke aus den Jahren 1925–1931*. Frankfurt-on-Main: Fischer. pp. 63–138.

Gendlin, E.T. (1970) 'A theory of personality change', in J.T. Hart and T.M. Tomlinson (eds), *New Directions in Client-Centered Psychotherapy*. Boston: Houghton Mifflin. pp. 129–73.

Kegan, R. (1982) *The Evolving Self: Problem and Process in Human Development*. Cambridge, MA: Harvard University Press.

Krause, R. (1983) 'Zur Onto- und Phylogenese des Affektsystems und ihrer Beziehungen zu psychischen Störungen', *Psyche*, 37: 1016–43.

Main, M., Kaplan, N. and Cassidy, J. (1985) 'Security in infancy, childhood, and adulthood: a move to the level of representation', in I. Bretherton and E. Waters (eds), *Growing Points in Attachment Theory and Research*. (Monographs of the Society for Research in Child Development, 50): 66–106.

Rogers, C.R. (1959) 'A theory of therapy, personality and interpersonal relationships, as developed in the client-centered framework', in S. Koch (ed.), *Psychology: A Study of a Science*, Vol. 3: *Formulations of the Person and the Social Context*. New York and Boston: McGraw-Hill. pp. 184–256.

Rogers, C.R. (1972) *Client-Centred Therapy (Die klient-bezogene Gesprächstherapie)*. Munich: Kindler. First published 1951.

Snygg, D. and Combs, A.W. (1949) *Individual Behavior: A New Frame of Reference for Psychology*. New York: Harper.

Solms, M. (1996) 'Was sind Affekte?', *Psyche*, 6 (50): 486–522.

Stern, D.N. (1992) *Die Lebenserfahrung des Säuglings*. Stuttgart: Klett-Cotta. First published 1986.

Sullivan, H.S. (1953) *The Interpersonal Theory of Psychiatry*. New York: W.W. Norton.

10 Incongruence and Psychopathology

Eva-Maria Biermann-Ratjen

The naively optimistic client-centred therapist

Client-centred therapists are very often alleged to have a rather naive idea about human nature which in their opinion is motivated by nothing more than the 'actualizing tendency', 'the inherent tendency of the organism to develop all its capacities in ways which serve to maintain or enhance the organism' (Rogers, 1959: 196). Similarly client-centred psychotherapists constantly find themselves accused of having no theory on psychopathology and being in no position to invent one as long as they proclaim, for instance, that 'Anxiety, defence, psychological maladjustment, and the processes of psychotherapy are all understood in the context of the efforts to maintain, and the experience of transforming, the self system' (Kegan, 1982: 5).

It is true that client-centred psychotherapists tend to see human development in a positive light in terms of growth and growth potential rather than in negative terms of illness and development deficits. This can mean that they forget that the idea of the fully functioning person is an ideal – something which will never really exist – serving as a definition of the completely healthy person. It will never apply to a concrete individual's thinking and feeling and personally motivated behaviour. Thinking about human development in terms of growth may also seduce us into forgetting that the fully functioning person in the client-centred frame is not the description of any form of human growth. Rather the term describes the process of establishing congruence between the experience of the organism as a whole and the experience represented in the concept of self, or in other words of achieving complete awareness of one's self-experiencing and of integrating it into the self-concept.

Unconditional positive regard and the integration of self-experience

Exactly what the person may become aware of, which may then be represented in the self-concept, is rarely closely defined in client-centred literature. It is termed experience. This in turn is defined as everything going on within the organism as a whole which is potentially available to awareness. It becomes more precise when we remember that according to client-centred theory human experiencing is understood to be a process which organizes itself under the conditions offered by certain social relationships. The person develops by becoming increasingly aware of him/herself in the regard others give to his/her experiencing processes and by identifying with this unconditionally positively regarded self-experience, by integrating it into a self-concept, which then represents his/her experience of him/herself.

Identifying with self-experience or integrating it into the self-concept depends on 'unconditional positive regard'. According to client-centred thinking the person's one overriding need – other needs are not specified – is for empathic unconditionally positive regard. Encountering another person in this way means understanding empathically how he/she experiences him/herself and reacting towards this both consciously and unconsciously – congruently – with no other feelings than unconditional positive regard.

The organism as a whole distinguishes between experiences of being maintained and enhanced and those of being not supported and not respected. This process of evaluating experience from the very beginning of life involves emotions, as we have seen in the previous chapter. There are inborn programmes for having and expressing the basic emotions: pleasure, interest, amazement, hurt, revulsion, rage, fear and shame (Deneke, 1992: 154). The so-called signal components of the emotions (vocalizing, mimicry, gestures) exist at birth and are recognizable to others (see Krause, 1983). This means that others can empathize with the baby's emotional experience, which is its potential self-experience, and can feel unconditional positive regard for the baby's organismic processes of evaluating its experience. They can satisfy the baby's need for positive regard from the first days of life onwards.

Since self-experience can only be integrated into a concept of self if the individual realizes in some way or other that the experience is being given unconditional positive regard, the experiences which become part of the self-concept always include interactions with others and involve evaluating emotionally whether the experience is supporting and enhancing or limiting and threatening. Furthermore they are self-experiences which meet with unconditional positive regard.

As soon as the self-concept has started to take shape, the organism does not just evaluate experience as to whether it is *felt* to be supporting or hindering. In addition each experience is checked emotionally as to whether it confirms the self-concept. To repeat, in the client-centred frame we assume that only those experiences can be integrated into the self-concept which have met with unconditional positive regard. From this it follows that when a core self-concept has been established any experience which does not meet with unconditional positive regard presents a threat to the self-concept, and every time an experience is repeated which did not meet with unconditional positive regard when it first occurred, this is felt to be a threat to the self.

Incongruence

The process of monitoring self-experience for its component unconditional positive regard past and present can result in a split in the actualizing tendency. Efforts to develop the self can collide with efforts to maintain the self-concept. Self-actualizing processes enhance the organism as a whole; the self-concept develops by integrating self-experience. On the other hand an experience may fail to meet the person's conditions of worth, her/his need for positive self-regard. Becoming aware of that experience threatens the person's self-concept.

Being incongruent means there is a split in the evaluating processes of the organism as a whole: the tendency to defend the self-concept runs counter to the tendency to actualize the self. The fully functioning person in client-centred thinking is invariably congruent. There is no incongruence between the total experience past and present and the self-experience represented in the self-concept. The fully functioning person can 'objectively' be aware of her/his bodily felt state and can 'subjectively' feel how she/he is, identify her/his feelings as her/his own and accept or integrate them into the self-concept, that is identify with them. The fully functioning person is completely open to experience, can understand and accept her/himself with all feelings and be aware of her/himself as coherent. She/he can equally be open to the feelings of others, can sense empathically how others are feeling, can value their experiences and by definition never becomes incongruent or identifies with what the other person is experiencing.

A state of incongruence comes about when someone is forced to discover that his/her need for unconditional positive regard is not satisfied, that he/she is not understood or not unconditionally accepted, when significant others show feelings towards his/her experience which cannot be reconciled with unconditional positive regard. A state of incongruence also comes about, however, when the person discovers that she/he does not understand her/himself and/or cannot accept his/her self-experience. The person will then feel that she/he is going through something which is incongruent with the experience integrated in her/his self-concept.

Trauma, incongruence and self-defence

In what follows I should like to show that the human reaction to a threat to one's self-concept and self-esteem brought about by an experience incongruent with the experiences integrated into the self-concept is modelled on the reaction shown when the organism as a whole is endangered. We react to experiences which imperil our self as if they were enemies from the outside world. As an answer to unusually upsetting events which seriously threaten our own safety or well-being or that of someone close to us (catastrophes, accidents, war, crime, rape, but also unusual sudden changes in our social position or network, for instance a series of deaths in the family), the individual develops what is termed an acute stress reaction (see WHO, 1991). Within a few moments the individual typically develops a kind of anaesthesia, limiting his/her awareness and narrowing her/his range of perception; the person is usually unable to cope with stimuli and becomes disorientated. This condition can be succeeded by a further withdrawal from potential experience of any kind into a stupor, or by the opposite: restlessness and hyperactivity, attempts to escape and actual flight. Usually there are vegetative signs of panic such as tachycardia, sweating and flushing. Following this initial anaesthetized state, depression, anxiety, anger, despair, hyperactivity and withdrawal appear. None of these self-experiences lasts long. The acute reaction usually starts to abate after a few hours and the symptoms usually subside gradually 12–24 hours after the disaster and are almost imperceptible after three days. There may be partial or complete amnesia about the episode.

It is important to realize that 'traumatic' situations are those in which the organism as a whole is faced with an existential threat and/or there is a dramatic absence or loss of 'positive regard', which is the condition for integrating self-experience into the self-concept. The acute stress reaction represents a form of defence against having to realize what is happening and results in an acute state of incongruence between experience and awareness. Faced with a 'traumatic' event the person develops anxiety in conjunction with the prototype of defence against experience, namely reduced awareness; the experience is not permitted to reach consciousness and is blotted out. The emotional reaction, anxiety, is often manifested only as a physical phenomenon, physiological reactions or reactions in the motor programmes well known to ethologists as forms of self-defence: running away, attacking, feigning and playing dead. Such reactions are at the same time social appeals to fellow beings, are understood as such and awaken certain responses toward the individual's plight.

We assume that while the self is developing during early childhood, acute stress reactions – which engender the experience that one is defending oneself – are not just brought about by situations which are life-threatening. Stress reactions also come about when there is a lack of empathic understanding and positive regard for the child and in all other situations in which the capacity of the self-concept to integrate experience is subjected to too much strain. This can be the case when a self-experience repeats itself which was not accompanied by positive regard when it first occurred and which therefore could not be integrated into the self-concept. A lack of unconditional positive regard plus self-experience which cannot be reconciled with the self-concept constitute a severe threat to the self, and the child reacts by showing signs of self-defence: anaesthesia, which may include concentration deficit, emotional withdrawal, depressive moods, doubting its own value, and/or with readiness to defend itself by attacking or fleeing.

We assume that for the child's further growth as a person it is especially important that these reactions to a threat to the self – in German, as in English, one can express this neatly by saying someone is beside or outside himself – are understood for what they are and not interpreted and evaluated as something else by the significant others. It is, however, very likely that the significant others will react to the child's emotional experiences according to their own emotions and therefore be blind and deaf, failing to give the child's feelings – actually they are symptoms, indicating incongruence – the positive regard they require, or that they will respond in a very conditional way. Later on the child will regard these stress reactions as conditions of worth which belong to him, or as conditions of no worth, alien and not part of him, depending on the degree of empathic understanding and unconditional positive regard these affective experiences received from others. When adult the person will be more or less vulnerable to stress or, more precisely, his/her self-concept will be more or less threatened by experiencing the need to defend him/herself against mortal dangers to body and mind.

It is characteristic of neurotic experience that some or all of the symptoms of acute incongruence cannot be fully symbolized or understood and accepted as self-experiences. When maladjusted persons suffer from limited consciousness, fear, depression or hostility they are usually unable to develop any sense of these experiences. They may become aware of them only in the form of physical sensations, alien fantasies, recurring thoughts or strange motor reactions. They do not realize or accept that they are experiencing their own defence against experiences which threaten their self-concept. They cannot perceive that their acute stress reactions are an expression of the value they put on their experience emotionally, namely as endangering their self-respect or idea of themselves.

We as therapists should help them to discover that the acute stress reaction is a completely intelligible and logical message conveying how the whole organism reacts to finding itself physically or psychically in danger: it makes sense. The reaction awakens an impulse to flee; it protects consciousness against the traumatic experience; it mobilizes aggressive impulses in order for us to defend ourselves, and in depression it adopts submissive behaviour which is also intended as self-defence. The empathic client-centred therapist conveys exactly this understanding of the symptoms to his/her client.

Post-traumatic stress disorder and developmental stagnation

Post-traumatic stress disorder, also known as the traumatic neurosis, may occur after a latency period of weeks or months after a 'traumatic' experience and can result in a lasting change of personality.

In a post-traumatic neurosis the 'traumatic' experience repeatedly crops up in awareness, flashes across the inner eye in daydreams or in dreams. At the same time the patient feels numb and emotionally paralysed, has no interest in other people, is passive, bleak and avoids situations and activities which might remind her/him of the trauma. Often the vegetative system is on constant alert, making the person hypervigilant, and his or her mood can be anything from gloomy to suicidal. Now and then he/she experiences sudden dramatic outbursts of fear, panic or aggression, brought about by sudden reminders or a repeat of the trauma or the original reaction to it.

In post-traumatic stress disorder we can see what happens when someone remains unable to integrate a self-experience. This disorder can be regarded as the prototype of experiencing that self-actualizing tendencies run counter to self-defending tendencies. Again and again efforts are made to become aware of what happened but the symbolization remains restricted to the physical and imagery level. The feelings cannot be tolerated or accepted or integrated as self-experience. Efforts are made to overcome the state of incongruence, to become aware of experience and to integrate it as self-experience on the one hand, while on the other there is a persistent effort to defend the self, as shown by signs of stagnation in its development. The danger of a 'traumatic' experience is that it may lead to a permanent stagnation in self-development, that defending oneself against experience becomes habitual and general. What began as a limited form of anaesthesia can turn into emotional withdrawal and numbness where experiences of every kind are ignored. What began as an impulse to escape from danger can turn into excessive vigilance, with the person avoiding or being on the alert to flee from any kind of new experience. If an individual has sensed that his/her own life and feelings are deemed utterly worthless by the powers threatening him, then a tendency to play dead may turn into depression combined with or culminating in a desire to be really dead. Additionally and alternatively, reacting aggressively as a form of self-defence or feigning socially desirable feelings may turn into strategies applied under all circumstances.

Hans Swildens (1991) has shown in incomparable manner how we can see the symptoms of chronic incongruence from a phenomenological and ethological point of view as acute stress reactions or symptoms of acute incongruence frozen into neurotic ways of life:

- The 'anxious' patient chronically runs away from experiencing anxiety and so avoids developing further.
- The hysterical patient insists on being approved of for what he/she regards as socially desirable feelings while ignoring his/her real feelings, the equivalent of refusing to live a real life.
- The obsessive patient is concerned with keeping every possible inimical experience under control and in this way hampers his/her own growth.

● The depressive patient attempts to relinquish all responsibility for whatever she or he is experiencing to avoid any guilt, and this prevents her or him from being properly alive.

Traditionally, neurotic disorders have been classified as anxiety neurosis, dissociative disorders, obsessional neurosis or depressions, in line with the stress reactions frozen into neurotic behaviour patterns.

As well as knowing that self-experience can only be integrated by accepting it, we also know nowadays that the best way of treating post-traumatic disorders is to help the traumatized person to remember the traumatic experience in the safety of a therapeutic relationship marked by empathic unconditionally positive regard. In this frame the experience which has been repeatedly driven out of consciousness can be retrieved piece by piece and reach awareness, and the person can come to accept and understand his/her own behaviour and feelings in reaction to the traumatic experience as a form of self-defence.

Psychogenic illnesses and incongruence

What applies to the treatment of post-traumatic stress disorders according to client-centred theory also applies to the treatment of every other form of psychological maladjustment. In line with their core assumption that anxiety, defence and psychological maladjustment are all to be understood in the context of the efforts to maintain the self system (see Kegan, 1982: 5), client-centred therapists regard different psychogenic illnesses as different ways of experiencing different kinds of incongruence, or as different signs of different efforts to defend oneself against self-experience which is incompatible with the self-concept and therefore seems inimical. Client-centred therapists consequently assume that the therapists' interventions are only effective when they act 'as channels for fulfilling one of the conditions' (Rogers, 1957) for the psychotherapeutic process on the therapist's side of the relationship. These conditions are that the therapist does not regard the client's self-experience as dangerous in the way the client does but understands his or her plight empathically, realizing for instance that clients feel threatened by their own experiencing of themselves and fight in some way or other while trying to defend their self-concepts.

In Chapter 9 I have shown that developing a self is a process of increasingly differentiating ourselves and our relations to significant others in the safety of certain relationships. At the outset when the self starts to form, self-experiences are largely physical ones of being acknowledged and accepted, including the emotional experience of the satisfaction of the need for unconditional positive regard. Depending on how reliably this need in particular is accepted and satisfied during the earliest phase, a self-concept emerges in which more or less emotional experience is integrated; to put it another way, the child develops a self-concept, an idea of itself, into which both feeling the need for unreserved approval and feeling this need satisfied can be integrated. If no self-experience of this sort can be integrated into the self-concept the person defends herself/himself in a schizoid, depressive or narcissistic way against experiencing feelings, in particular the need for unconditional positive regard. She/he cannot integrate the experience of being frustrated into her/his self-experience. If the person cannot ignore feeling interpersonal dependency, when for instance she/he loses a significant other, she/he experiences her/himself as overwhelmed or even destroyed by feelings alien to her/him and dangerous to her/himself and others.

In a second developmental stage the child starts monitoring experience: does it confirm the sense of self or not, and does it satisfy the vital need to accept oneself or not? Perhaps the experience also induces the urge to assert or defend the self. Experiencing that one is not being understood and accepted as one is and the frightening feelings this brings about may either be integrated or not into the self-concept, depending on whether these 'stress reactions' or experiences of acute incongruence are understood and accepted by significant others for what they are. If these emotional experiences cannot be integrated into the self-concept, then later on when the person encounters these feelings again they will seem to be threatening impulses or demands to cope in a specific way, for instance to be con-trolled, fearless, happy, sensitive, and so on under all circumstances. If, however, the developing person has been able to integrate feelings of doubt and shame into the self-concept, so that his or her self-respect does not crumble away at the very idea of being unable to make him/herself understood and accepted, and he or she can experience feeling angry, anxious, depressed or irritated by this, then the child will be free to turn its interest to its own individual self-experiencing. Whether such individual self-experiences can be integrated into the self-concept depends, too, on whether they meet with unconditional positive regard. This for instance applies to suffering from concentration problems, emotional withdrawal, depression, aggressiveness, shyness and other forms of reaction to the stress of being only conditionally accepted for what we are.

Stern (1992) emphasized that these developmental steps of the self succeed one another but do not vanish in the sense of the next wiping out the previous one. Every self-experience entails physical tension and relaxa-tion when it is fully symbolized and integrated. The questions: 'Am I the author of my self-experiences, do they belong to me, do they fit in with me and my self-image?' always play a role as well as the question: 'Am I understood and accepted as I experience myself in my own way?', and, starting with the development of speech, the question: 'Can I understand and accept my self-experiences and communicate them in full, and in words to myself and to others?'

Any symptom of psychogenic illness is the expression of experiencing incongruence:

1   The person may be unable to symbolize completely and communicate verbally certain experiences.
2   The person may be unable to understand and/or accept certain experiences as self-experiences.
3   The person may experience certain ways of defending against experience (stress reactions, acute incongruence) or different forms of stagnation in self-development (chronic incongruence).
4   In any case experiencing incongruence will include experiencing physical tension.

Depending on the phase in which self-development was interrupted, different forms of anxiety will dominate a person's life. They range from sensing that one's very existence is under threat when the defence is overwhelmed by emotional experience or by experiencing a frustration of the need for positive regard, to feelings of worthlessness and absolute wickedness when feeling the urge to assert oneself, and to being afraid of losing one's self-esteem when undergoing certain alarm reactions.

Neurosis and the client-centred process-oriented therapist

In the language of the client-centred approach, neurotics, for instance, suffer from a vulnerable self-concept brought about by experiences in early childhood when they had to contend with conditional positive regard or when they had to experience incongruence from a significant other. If such not unconditionally positively regarded experiences repeated themselves the child's inability to integrate them as self-experience into the self-concept induced a state of alarm and uneasiness. This state of mind, too, may be more or less adequately grasped and accepted by significant others and thus more or less adequately integrated into the self-concept: 'That is how I feel and think and fantasize if I am not understood or not unconditionally accepted, if I upset someone with my feelings and induce him to react emotionally.'

When in later life an experience endangers the self, the person will find himself or herself suffering from this state of alarm and uneasiness again. Because the symptoms or some aspects of the initial state of alarm have not been completely understood and/or unconditionally positively regarded, the neurotic person equally cannot symbolize or understand and accept them or can do so only partially. The neurotic disposition usually does not develop as a result of a single traumatic event but as the outcome of years of living with significant others who are unable to accept the child for its own sake but only if it meets with certain expectations, or can only conditionally accept it, for instance when it is the intelligent and brave child they expect. The significant others for persons who later become neurotic, as well as only accepting their child in a conditional way were unable wholly to understand or accept its emotional alarm reactions.

Instead they themselves responded emotionally, because they sensed that their own self-concept and self-respect were under attack when their child was upset.

A neurotic disorder develops when the experiences which could not be integrated are repeated, reactivating the defence and/or the stress reactions. These, or at least some of them, cannot fade away because the neurotic person is unable to accept or symbolize them accurately and completely and so become aware of them as his/her own experiences. And so the neurotic remains burdened with one or other of the neurotic 'symptoms' which are unaccepted and/or only partially symbolized emotional stress reactions.

As therapists working with neurotics we should therefore first of all focus on the client's symptoms, which are a sign of a state of alarm, of defence, and grasp their significance so that we can help the client to symbolize them and to accept and understand them. Only then can we proceed to join the client in exploring which experiences are repeats of earlier ones that he or she has so far been unable to integrate into the self-concept. Client-centred therapy with a neurotic client must always be process oriented, as Hans Swildens (1991) has recommended: first comes the symptom phase, where the symptoms have to be understood as a sign that the client has got stuck in the process of becoming him/herself and only after that can one start off on the real journey of client-centred therapy.

Client-centred and psychoanalytic concepts of psychopathology

In this concluding section I would like to summarize and clarify some client-centred ideas on self-development and psychopathology by comparing them to those of the psychoanalytic ego psychology, self-psychology and object relations models.

In the psychoanalytic ego-psychological model 'behavior, mediated by the ego, is viewed as a defensive compromise among: 1) wishes and impulses; 2) inner conscience, self-observation, and criticism; and 3) the potentialities and demands of reality. Effective ego functions allow an appropriate delay between peremptory wishes and actions and protect the individual from excessive anxiety or depression while providing for security, pleasure, and effectiveness' (Perry et al., 1987: 547).

In client-centred theory normal development as well as psychological maladjustment, anxiety and defence against experience are all understood in the context of efforts to develop and maintain a sense of self. Experience and behaviour are mediated by self-actualizing and self-defending tendencies and may be symptoms of incongruence, where the tendency to actualize the self runs counter to the tendency to defend the self. Effective self-actualization protects the individual from anxiety or depression, which are the extremes of felt incongruence between what an experience means to the organism as a whole and what it means to the self-concept.

'The ego-psychological model gives special focus to derivatives of forbidden sexual and aggressive strivings, their resolution during the oedipal phase, and the ongoing residual intrapsychic conflicts and defensive compromises that determine character and symptoms' (Perry et al., 1987: 547). The client-centred model gives special focus to the interpersonal relationship which is the essential condition of self-development. This relationship is characterized by unconditional positive regard by a significant other for the experiencing developing person. Experience which does not meet with positive regard when it first occurs cannot be integrated into the self-concept and means a threat to the self-concept so it is fended off when it occurs again.

The experience of defending oneself against experience is modelled on the acute stress reaction which includes self-defence in the guise of attack – not the aggressive strivings of the psychoanalytical model. 'The psychoanalytic self-psychological model postulates a psychological structure, the self, that develops toward the realization of goals that are both innate and learned. Two broad classes of these goals can be identified: one consists of the individual's ambitions, the other of his or her ideals' (Perry et al., 1987: 547). By contrast the client-centred model postulates one and only one motive: the actualization of the total organism. 'Normal' development does not involve 'the child's grandiose idealization of self and others, the exhibitionistic expression of strivings and ambitions, and the empathic responsiveness of parents and others to these needs' (ibid.). Normal development in the client-centred frame involves the emotional expression of the child's experiencing its need for unconditional positive regard and the empathic understanding of these expressions by significant others. The self-concept develops by integrating the experiences which have met with unconditional positive regard.

'The object relations model conceives of psychic structures as developing through the child's construction of internal representations of self and others. These representations range from the primitive and fantastic to the relatively realistic; they are associated with widely varying affects (e.g., anger, sadness, feelings of safety, fear, pleasure) as well as with various wishes and fantasies (e.g., of sex, of control, or of devouring and being devoured)' (ibid.). The client-centred model understands psychic structures as self-organized internal representations of self-experiencing in relation to others including affective experience. But in client-centred theory these representations do not 'range from the primitive and fantastic to the relatively realistic'. They range from a state of congruence between the experience of the total organism and its representation in awareness in the fully functioning person to a state of extreme incongruence between what experience means to the self-actualizing organism and to the self-concept in the vulnerable person.

Psychopathological phenomena in client-centred theory are symptoms of various forms of stagnation in the development of the self. These correspond to different levels of incongruence in a range of affects, which may be more or less completely represented in awareness. Both intellectually and in clinical practice the client-centred theory of psychopathological phenomena possesses an elegance and a clarity which are currently unrivalled. The theory deserves to be more generally acknowledged and applied – especially by client-centred therapists and researchers themselves.

References

Deneke, F.-W. (1992) 'Die Strukturierung der subjektiven Wirklichkeit', in B. Andresen, F.-M. Stark and J. Gross (eds), *Mensch, Psychiatrie, Umwelt*. Bonn: Psychiatrie-Verlag. pp. 143–60.

Kegan, R. (1982) *The Evolving Self: Problem and Process in Human Development*. Cambridge, MA: Harvard University Press.

Krause, R. (1983) 'Zur Onto- und Phylogenese des Affektsystems und ihrer Beziehungen zu psychischen Störungen', *Psyche*, 37: 1016–43.

Perry, S., Cooper, A.M. and Michels, R. (1987) 'The psychodynamic formulation: its purpose, structure, and clinical application', *American Journal of Psychiatry*, 144: 543–50.

Rogers, C.R. (1957) 'The necessary and sufficient conditions of therapeutic personality change', *Journal of Consulting Psychology*, 21: 95–103.

Rogers, C.R. (1959) 'A theory of therapy, personality and interpersonal relationships, as developed in the client-centered framework', in S. Koch (ed.), *Psychology: A Study of a Science*, Vol. 3: *Formulations of the Person and the Social Context*. New York and Boston: McGraw-Hill. pp. 184–256.

Stern, D.N. (1992) *Die Lebenserfahrung des Säuglings*. Stuttgart: Klett-Cotta. First published 1986.

Swildens, H. (1991) *Prozeßorientierte Gesprächspsychotherapie*. Cologne: GwG. First published 1988.

WHO: World Health Organization (1991) *Internationale Klassifikation psychischer Störungen. ICD-10 Kapitel V (F). Klinisch-diagnostische Leitlinien*, ed. H. Dilling, W. Mombour and M.H. Schmidt. Bern, Göttingen and Toronto: Hans Huber.

PART II

PRACTICE

---

11 Focusing: Interpersonal and Intrapersonal Conditions of Growth

Mia Leijssen

Interpersonal – intrapersonal – interactional

Following in Carl Rogers's footsteps (1961), client-centred therapists have put a great deal of effort into offering an interpersonal relationship in which the client can recover and grow. However, the therapist–client relationship is not the therapeutic goal; the intention is rather to have the client develop a relationship with him or herself capable of processing life events, of discovering meaning and of generating symbols and actions beneficial to both the client and the environment. This process implies that clients should not only be 'outward' directed when looking for solutions to problems but that they should be capable of searching 'within' themselves for a source of knowledge that is richer than logical rational thought. The experience of relating to this inner experience is unknown to many clients. Yet some research (Gendlin et al., 1968) shows that successful clients – defined in terms of change on independent pre- and post-therapy psychometric measures – are different from unsuccessful ones precisely in their use of a specific form of self-exploration in which they turn to a vague bodily felt sensation from which further meaning emerges.

Focusing

Gendlin (1978, 1981, 1984, 1996) has studied this self-exploratory behaviour and has called it *focusing*. 'It is a process in which you make contact with a special kind of internal bodily awareness' (Gendlin, 1978: 11). That body sense or felt sense is like an implicit source, which at first is unclear but is nevertheless sensed distinctly as soon as one turns one's attention inward and waits for a special kind of bodily sensation. 'The body referred to here is not the physiological machine of the usual reductive thinking. Here it is the body as sensed from inside' (Gendlin, 1996: 2). It is a bodily sense of some situation, problem or aspect of one's life, felt as a whole complexity, a multiplicity implicit in a single sense. Through interactions with symbols, the felt experience can become more precise, it can move and change, it can achieve a felt shift: the experience of a real change or bodily resolution of the issue. Gendlin (1984: 83–4) has described the required attitude to interact with the felt sense very evocatively by calling the felt sense 'the client's client'. The client's 'inner therapist' gives friendly attention and silent waiting time, refrains from interpretations, receives and resonates whatever comes from a felt sense and lets it be, at least for a while. Successful clients seem to have the crucial skills to make contact with their felt sense. As Ann Weiser Cornell formulates it:

Focusing is a natural skill that was discovered, not invented. It was discovered by looking at what people are doing when they are changing successfully. Focusing ability is the birthright of every person: we were all born with the ability to know how we feel from moment to moment. But for most of us, the experience of hurt and alienation in our childhood and from our culture have caused us to lose trust in our bodies and our feelings. We need to re-learn Focusing. (Weiser Cornell, 1996: 5)

In order to teach focusing Gendlin described a model which involves six process steps: (1) clearing a space; (2) getting a felt sense; (3) finding a handle; (4) resonating handle and felt sense; (5) asking; (6) receiving. Many therapists use this model in order to guide people through a focusing process.

However, it is not helpful to teach focusing during therapy. It is preferable that the therapist model the more general focusing attitude of waiting in the presence of the not yet speakable, being receptive to the not yet formed, listening in a gentle, accepting way, honouring and trusting the wisdom that speaks through the body, helping the client hear the messages that the inner self is sending, finding the right symbolizations in which the bodily experience can move further into meaning. The focusing steps can be referred to as 'sub-tasks' or 'microprocesses' offered at certain moments in psychotherapy, to help establish the conditions that are optimal for facilitating particular kinds of self-exploration. This requires a process diagnosis, in which the therapist recognizes the signals heralding the emergence of a microprocess in need of facilitation. The combination of focusing attitude and focusing steps leads to several types of focusing situation which have a broad applicability.

Focusing processes/life stages

Of course, in the complexity of the living process – which psychotherapy always is – the phenomena I'll distinguish are not so neatly separated. Nevertheless, for 'didactic purposes' it might be helpful to highlight dominant aspects of different sub-processes.

A research project (Leijssen, 1996a), including an analysis of transcripts of therapy sessions of 40 cases, brought three comprehensive *focusing processes* – which require various attitudes and skills on the part of the client – to the fore: (1) finding the right distance to bodily sensations; (2) symbolizing a felt sense; (3) dealing with interfering characters.

The case studies led to the hypothesis that these skills are connected to three main *stages in life*, in each of which 'significant others' make up the relational context: (1) contact with mothering – which can also be given by male persons; (2) contact with fathering – which can also be done by female persons; (3) the broader social context. From the various interpersonal interactions in each stage of life, specific ways of relating to oneself seem to develop which will determine, later on, whether or not a person is able to use the focusing skills and thus aid the emergence of a healthy inner relationship. It became obvious that successful clients had sufficient high-quality interpersonal relationships in their past to serve as models for the relationship which they developed with themselves.

I relate the essential focusing skills to processes that take place in a healthy developmental process and I will explain how the 'missed opportunities' can be lived over again within the therapeutic relationship, which gives an opportunity to internalize 'good parenthood' or a nurturing, growth-stimulating interpersonal environment. In the psychoanalytical literature there are theories that seem to be based on similar observations (Stern, 1985). There is no need, however, to borrow the sophisticated concepts of our psychoanalytical colleagues. My reason for utilizing the metaphors 'mothering' and 'fathering' is that it is a language which everyone can recognize as a description of their experience. It can help therapists and clients to capture the attitudinal qualities of focusing rather than the technical steps. By introducing certain aspects of the focusing process during therapy, taking clues from markers in the client's experiencing healing may be facilitated.

Person-centred attitudes

I also see a link between the stages in the focusing process and the well-known person-centred attitudes of empathy, authenticity and unconditional positive regard. I will show how facilitating focusing can stay very close to the kind of interactions 'good' person-centred practitioners have always offered. Facilitating various focusing processes can be seen as a further differentiation of the basic person-centred attitudes, making more concrete how we can implement the general principles of Rogers's metatheory in our practice with clients whose therapy process is not successful. In fact, focusing therapy is person-centred therapy, further elaborated and described in distinctive therapeutic actions. I will try to demonstrate the truth of Gendlin's (1996: 301) statement: 'Focusing-oriented therapy is Client-Centered therapy', and: 'Focusing-oriented therapy is not therapy that includes brief bits of focusing instruction. Rather it means letting that which arises from the focusing depths within a person define the therapist's activity, the relationship, and the process in the client' (ibid.: 304). A passage from Iberg's inspiring article can illuminate the spirit of working in focusing-oriented therapy:

> We do not abandon the client-centered axiom that the client is the final authority about what is 'really' going on. . . . I hope to guide the client to more effective introspection. Ideally the interaction should be non-directive: the client makes improvements, rather than being directed to do so by the therapist. The specific method I use to minimize directiveness is a two step approach. The first step is a simple empathic reflection of the event. . . . The second step may not be needed, since when a process event is well reflected, the problem may resolve itself. . . . If the client does not find an improvement in the process, I then make guiding suggestions. . . . The kind of process improvement in question here is evaluated by the client. . . . I recommend reaching a confirmed understanding of a process event to give the improvement every chance to come spontaneously from within the client, but if it does not, I make a suggestion, rather than letting the client proceed oblivious to a small change which might bring improvement. (Iberg, 1996: 22–3)

Adding focusing suggestions may be totally consistent with the way many therapists are already working, or it may represent somewhat of a shift in attitude and language. Wiltschko warns, and I agree with him:

> The combination of any therapeutic method with Focusing is not as easy as it seems at first glance, because the point with Focusing is not the technique but rather specific Focusing attitudes, and they cannnot be achieved so easily. . . .
>
> A Focusing therapist is in contact with his/her body, with his/her bodily resonance, the felt sense, about the whole person of the client, the client's ongoing experiencing and self-expressing. This is because all therapeutic 'techniques' emerge from this implicit resonance. The therapist's felt sense is the source of Focusing Therapy techniques (provided that the therapist is exactly perceiving the client's verbal and non-verbal expression). These 'techniques' are not only listening and guiding methods but also *authentic responses* towards the client's person. (Wiltschko, 1995: 2–6; original emphasis)

Interactive

Before differentiating types of focusing process and going into details of interpersonal and intrapersonal ingredients of 'successful self-exploration', I would like to emphasize that focusing can only happen if the inter-personal conditions are right. 'The relational space between client and therapist is the living space in which the client's developmental process can occur. In fact, internal and interpersonal processes are not separate, rather they are two aspects of one process. . . . If the relational conditions are not good, focusing is almost useless because the inner process is very much a function of the ongoing interactional process' (Wiltschko, 1996: 5, 1). The essentially interactive nature of the formation of a bodily felt sense in the client is what Rogers stressed when he said that the client must to some degree perceive the empathy, genuineness and positive regard from the therapist. The inner process is always a function of the interpersonal process.

Finding the right distance to bodily sensations – good mothering – empathy

In the first stage of life, bodily sensations are paramount to the child. The small child is unable to put into words what these sensations mean and is dependent on an environment that 'receives with understanding' his or her non-verbal expressions. Mother's reactions can either turn the child's bodily sensations into a meaningful worthwhile experiencing process or impede such a process. Children who have not known an environment in which the sometimes overwhelming bodily sensations are accepted and responded to may have a deeply disturbed reaction to them. They do not have a friendly, receptive curiosity towards feelings and an 'appropriate way of dealing' with bodily sensations: either they are overwhelmed by unmanageable experiences or else have learned to ignore them.

In therapy we see these clients either fusing with overwhelming experiences or else 'feeling nothing'. These *client dimensions* – cutting across diagnostic categories of disorder – are called in focusing terminology: 'too close/too distant processes' (Weiser Cornell, 1991). Gendlin (1996: 7–15) describes these states as two kinds of dead end that can happen in psychotherapy: the first occurs when there are quite concrete emotions, but they are repeated over and over; the second dead end happens when the therapy consists only of interpretation and inference without an experiential process. Margaret Warner speaks of a 'fragile style of processing': clients who have this style of processing 'tend to experience core issues at very high or low levels of intensity. They have difficulty starting or stopping experiences that are personally significant or emotionally connected' (Warner, 1996: 140).

Good mothering/empathic responding

At the level of 'good mothering' the therapist has to offer a first elementary remedial response. This means: being present in a warm-hearted, friendly and affectionate way and receiving empathically what the client tries to express:

Empathic understanding plays a particularly crucial role in therapy with clients who have suffered empathic failure in childhood to the point that their ability to hold and process experience has been severely compromised. . . . Empathic understanding responses are often the only sorts of responses people with a fragile style of processing can receive without feeling traumatized or disconnected from their experience. The ongoing presence of a soothing, empathic person is often essential to the person's ability to stay connected without feeling overwhelmed. . . . The communication of empathy tends to facilitate change because it generates a particular sense of experiential recognition within the other person. . . . This is a value in itself as a form of human connection and it also tends to shift one's relation to implicit, bodily felt, non-conscious aspects of experience, opening these to awareness and change. (Warner, 1996: 140, 130)

Good mothering in therapy also means realizing that the client's verbal expressions convey only part of the truth and that there are deeper layers of experiencing to which the client no longer has access. The body of the client is speaking, but the client doesn't hear its message. The therapist tries to bring the client's bodily knowledge back into the spotlight and into the client's awareness by valuing non-verbal expressions, by directing responses at the client's 'inner side', by allowing time for the vague to become more precise:

Much of therapy involves starting with what is explicitly in the client's conscious awareness and going on a search together to find that part of the client's experiencing which is pregnant with meaning that is not consciously understood, but which relates to the problems with which the client wants help. These pregnant spots in the client's experiencing are phenomenologically like 'hot spots', or 'buttons that can be pushed', or 'sore spots', or 'ripe places', which, when the search comes to one, usually reveal themselves with a bodily development: feeling 'wells up,' and the person's face changes, or their voice or rhythm of speaking changes. There is often a sense of vulnerability. The conscious client may not make much of such spots, or may even seem to prefer to veer away from them. Almost every instance of non-conscious experiencing occurring as part of the discussion of the client's feelings, if brought empathically into the client's awareness will be a step in the direction of the important pregnant spots. (Iberg, 1996: 14)

The *essentials* about this first stage in developing a focusing attitude – which the therapist tries to model and facilitate in the client – can be summarized as: a friendly, empathic, welcoming attitude; an awareness of the ongoing bodily experiencing; a certain distance between the mindful 'I' and the inner datum; taking time and making space to allow a felt sense to form (see also Wiltschko, 1995: 3–7).

Too much distance

Peter, a 30-year-old man, comes for therapy with complaints of compulsiveness: he has to control everything in his environment and is continuously worried that he may let someone down. Feelings are foreign to him; he does not know what people mean when they say they are sad or happy. He never pays attention to his body: eating is a quick snack between other occupations. In winter or summer he wears the same sober clothes; any kind of comfort is forbidden. He does not acknowledge his body as a place where he can experience how things affect him, he only knows it as something you have to keep clean; his only bodily experience is that of suffering intestinal pain, something for which he consults a physician regularly. The image of his mother is that of an anxious woman who was always cleaning. He remembers how, at bedtime, her main concern was about the sheets being pulled neatly and tidily, and that there was never time for a hug or a kiss.

Peter's face blushes at the therapist's warm greeting and he moves uneasily when she tells him to take his time and make himself comfortable when he arrives. When he talks about an aunt who played the piano, his gestures become a bit more lively. The therapist mirrors his lively gestures with her own body and lets him know that she understands that he experienced something which felt good; she invites him to give this bodily liveliness a bit more room and see how that feels. It is very unusual for Peter to see the therapist refraining from passing judgement when he speaks about his compulsive rituals, but instead showing that she has heard exactly what he may experience in himself about them.

The therapist's way of wording looks recognizable and yet different to Peter. For example: 'Something in you becomes worried that you may have overlooked something and the only way you know to placate that awful inner feeling is to wash your hands once more.' With these words, Peter's attention – at first totally absorbed in his actions – has been shifted to 'that awful feeling inside'.

As a next step the therapist asks compassionately and curiously if Peter can give some more attention to his bodily experience and describe what the sensation inside feels like. Peter looks surprised: he had never been encouraged to bring his awareness into his body, to notice how it feels there and to name it. He answers: 'Painful, of course. . . . But the doctor told me there is nothing wrong.' Therapist: 'It wants to let us know that there is something painful. . . . Can you acknowledge that. . . . Even if the doctor says there is no reason . . . there might be some good reason for the painful feeling. . . . Let's listen to it and invite the feeling to tell us a little bit more.' Peter hits on a memory of his mother punishing him for making clothes dirty. There is a painful expression on his face and his body is in a cramped position. Therapist: 'That must be painful, being punished when you were just enjoying yourself and then feeling it is not OK to be dirty.' Peter relaxes, as if something inside him is saying: 'I'm glad you heard me.'

Clients like Peter have learned to *feel nothing*. From the process-diagnostic point of view it could be said that the inner relationship remains absent because the client remains 'too far from his experience'; the client is not aware of the possiblility of an inner referent. In the focusing process, special attention is paid to this 'wrong inner distance' by guiding the client more explicitly when making contact with the body as it can be felt from inside. It may be useful to start a therapy session with such clients by asking them to follow their breathing or to check systematically how the various parts of the body are feeling. Non-verbal approaches (music, movement, drawing) can also be very facilitative (see Leijssen, 1992).

With predominantly rationalizing people or those who have established no contact with what is felt inside, talk during the session may become more meaningful when attention is first turned to being physically present. The point is not to have the client reach a state of 'bodily relaxation' but to switch attention from thinking to experiencing, from talking to silence, from outside to inside. 'The client must become able to inwardly sense his/her body as a space in which he/she can walk around, look around, sense around, in which he/she is able to direct his/her attention to different places' (Wiltschko, 1995: 3). This can be helped along by repeatedly communicating and modelling the focusing attitude which consists of listening to the body with compassion and receiving in a friendly manner what emerges from the bodily knowledge. Thus the client learns to adopt the position of a non-judging, observing self which can relate to certain inner experiences.

Too little distance

Good mothering also means that one can experience that there is a safe place in which to receive the vehemence or threat of some feelings. When a child fails to learn that *intense experiences* can receive a place and will subsequently be acknowledged in their meaning, they will, as an adult, be easily overwhelmed and get lost in unmanageable feelings.

> *Ilse, a woman of 27, was sent for therapy by her employer who was worried about her panic attacks. She lives with a man who beats her but has to stay with him lest her life should become total chaos. When he is away for a few days, she sinks into 'daydreams' in which the distinction between reality and fantasy becomes totally blurred. The only way of coping with these frightening experiences is to plunge into hard labour, which she continues until she collapses. She can/may not focus on her body lest she should be flooded by anxiety or rage. The memory of her childhood is dominated by a depressed mother, who was often in hospital.*
>
> *Ilse says in therapy that she does not want to visit her mother because she 'could kill' her when she starts nagging about her problems. While telling this, she rants and raves continuously against the 'stupidity' of her mother. The therapist withstands the verbal storm and keeps letting Ilse know that she understands her anger. By being able to contain the rage and linking fragments of it again and again to specific situations which have touched her deeply, the client becomes calmer, her rage ceases to be a chaotic stream of emotions and becomes a meaningful response to parts of her reality. For example, the therapist's reflection: 'You cannot tolerate any longer your mother ignoring your needs; you deserve a mother who is willing to listen to you at least once' gives Ilse substantial relief. She feels her need accepted. In another session, Ilse is flooded with painful memories of the time when her mother was admitted to a psychiatric hospital shortly after the death of Ilse's older sister. Ilse relives the event as if the whole world were about to crumble any minute. Her anxiety and deep sadness become more tolerable when she expresses them for the first time in all their intensity in the supportive presence of the therapist.*

When the therapist receives and understands what the client goes through and responds in such a way as to enable the client to give it a place and a meaning, then the feelings lose their overwhelming character and the client becomes capable of relating to what has happened to her rather than being carried away by it.

In the focusing process, special attention is given to this way of relating characterized by 'too little distance' by actively encouraging the client to find an appropriate distance to the overwhelming experiences. Indeed, here too an inner relationship is impossible because the client 'disappears' under the stormy feelings; there is no more 'self' which could relate to the experiences: the client 'fuses' with what is felt. 'In fact, real progress seems to involve maintaining a part of oneself that is apart from the intensity, and supporting that part as one explores the intense emotion' (Iberg, 1996: 24). The therapist helps the client to be *with* the feelings, not *in* them. Focusing works best when the client can 'sit next to' his or her feelings instead of plunging into them. Ann Weiser Cornell gives various tips to facilitate this *being with* instead of letting the client feel engulfed. When for example the client says: 'I am sad', the therapist can slightly change the verbal expression to: 'You're aware of something in you that feels sad' (Weiser Cornel, 1996: 17). This special way of formulating invites the client to turn to the content, to get in touch with this content, to establish a relationship between 'I' and the content. The content has an explicit part, the part that is already known, already communicable ('sad'), and an implicit part, an aspect that is indefinite yet, not yet unfolded, which is mentioned by the word 'something'. By saying 'in you', the therapist indicates that besides the content, there is an 'I' that has a content: it is not the content, this 'I' is bigger than the content (see also Wiltschko, 1996: 61–2). This *dis-identification* is a step towards gentleness, it helps the client to develop a relationship to an inner part. 'Those familiar with inner child work will see the similarity. The difference is that there is no need to personify the felt sense as a child. If it feels like a child to the client, that is welcome, but if not, it can still be given gentleness, acceptance and listening' (Weiser Cornell, 1996: 100).

Procedures to find the right distance

The facilitating of the inner relationship can also be introduced in a more directive way. In the focusing literature there are descriptions of several ways to help the client find the 'right inner distance' when there is 'too little distance'.

The first way is by asking the client to *give a place* in the room to the overwhelming content. Here, the client is given the opportunity to contact briefly the experience and then asked to find a place for 'it'. This can be done in fantasy or, more concretely, by writing or drawing the problem on a piece of paper and putting it in the room at some distance from the client. It is amazing how liberating such a 'simple' move can be. Therapists often forget the therapeutic value of this kind of distancing work and focus unilaterally on the content of the problem. Yet working with content may only be meaningful after a new way of relating to the problem has been found.

This way of working is poignantly illustrated in the following example (a transcript of the session can be found in Leijssen, 1993).

Angela hyperventilates at the beginning of the session and is overwhelmed by anxiety. The therapist asks her 'to put whatever makes her so anxious some distance away'. Angela goes along with the proposal and says she wants to push 'it' away. When she has given 'it' a place in a corner of the therapy room, she quietens down, the hyperventilation stops and she feels stronger. From this new position she can then look at it and attribute symbols to what she 'sees': she experiences it as a threatening fog capable of creeping inside her and occupying her totally, causing her to lose herself. She can subsequently link this up with past experiences with people which she now relives in all their hurtfulness. Reliving the pain is no longer overwhelming; now it is the recognition of something which has deeply affected her and to which she had no access before. Only after we had put 'it' some distance away and after the client had made contact again with a 'self' capable of relating to 'it' was she capable of discovering the meaning of her experience.

Another way of creating distance from an overwhelming problem is to let the client modify his or her position by, say, *stepping back* or moving to another chair from which a 'broader view' of the problem can be had.

Rudy experiences a stabbing pain in the region of the heart during a session and cannot breathe any more; he feels an 'enormous block of concrete' crushing him. The therapist says: 'Try to imagine going backwards; imagine making the step which gets you from under the block of concrete'. The client sighs deeply, which is a sign that the distance-creating process had indeed created a felt shift in the client. Then the client says: 'All of a sudden, I see that this block of concrete is my mother, who always stops me from living my own life!'

In those cases where it is difficult to put the thing in question at a distance, one can encourage the inner relationship by creating *breathing space in one's body* by means of one's breath. The therapist asks the client to breathe in a friendly way towards the spot in the body where the specific feeling or the pain is located. One may even emphasize this by using metaphors such as: 'Could you put a bandage around the spot with your breath . . .' or 'Could you make a cradle in your body in which to put "it" down?' Experiences dealing with something fragile, something precious or something which is literally present in the body, such as an illness, are especially suited to such an approach. Besides, something like a 'healing energy' is conveyed to the spot in question by means of one's breath. One client, who felt an enormous void in her belly after the death of her baby, was unable to tolerate her sadness and pain about that. The suggestion to 'breathe lovingly towards that part of her body which had to carry such a big void' was experienced as particularly helpful to her. In this way, she was helped to enter into a relationship with the pain instead of fusing with it.

A fourth way of creating distance is sometimes mentioned in which a 'good spot' is created by *recalling something positive* in the client's life. On the basis of the accompanying feeling of strength, the overwhelming or painful experience is then explored. For this form of creating a healing inner relationship, I refer to the inspired illustrations of McGuire (1982–3, 1984), McDonald (1987), Grindler (1985) and Kanter (1982–3).

Facilitating the appropriate distance between 'I' and 'the inner experience' can never be a stereotyped procedure. It will always come down to the therapist exploring and testing out what could be the right way of relating for the client. The therapist's directivity in the process consists of showing possible alternatives for the process-blocking patterns which cause the client either to remain too far removed from experiences or to fuse with them, and by which one stops oneself from reaching a healing inner relationship. Once the right distance is discovered, the problem at hand can be explored further. There are times, however, when one chooses to go deeper into the experience of inner peace and strength, which can come from finding the right distance. This can lead to intense experiences of a spiritual-transcendental nature.

Symbolizing the felt sense – good fathering – authenticity

The bodily felt experiencing process subsequently acquires its shape through interaction with *structures outside* the person. External structures are often first represented in our culture by the father. Good fathering means that structure emerges from chaos, that the shapeless will acquire shape, that experiences get named, something which makes communication with the outside world clear. Interaction with the 'outside' completes the experience:

> Early on most parents begin to engage in a particular sort of empathic inter-
> action in which they begin to name the infant's experiences and to offer
> hypothesized reasons for these experiences. . . . Essentially parents are offering
> verbal symbols that could carry the infant's implicitly felt experience forward
> into explicit meaning if the infant had words. At some point children come to
> recognize a matching between words and their own felt experience. I remember
> seeing such a moment of dawning recognition in my three-year-old nephew. His
> mother had left the room to pay attention to his younger brother and he had
> begun throwing his toys. I said 'you feel angry'. He looked at me with a sense of
> surprise and discovery and tried on the words 'I feel angry'. He threw his toys a
> few more times, saying the words with greater conviction each time. Then he
> went into the kitchen to tell his mother triumphantly about his new discovery,

that he felt 'angry'. . . . Some parents are relatively inattentive or have difficulty leaving their own perspectives. Hence, experiences may go unnamed or be systematically misnamed. (Warner, 1996: 134)

Inadequate fathering

Inadequate fathering causes the child to acquire too little structure and to remain stuck at the diffuse level of bodily sensation. Bodily discomfort will then be stilled by activities connected with Mother (e.g. oral gratification or a search for increased comfort); things will not be named by their name; experiences may be labelled in ways that are most calming or least threatening; reality will not be faced and there will be no authentic communication with the external world.

Here is an example of a client whose problems appear to go back to inadequate fathering.

> *Louis is 46 and seeks therapy for problems of alcoholism. During Louis's childhood his father totally vanished into building a career, bringing home substantial sums of money. His mother had learned to run the household without a man and found his 'intrusions' undesirable. Louis himself has built a successful career which he is now in danger of ruining through excessive alcohol consumption. His social contacts consist of, on the one hand, a number of dominant women who like to use him and to whom he cannot say 'no', and, on the other hand, a few 'friends' from work who only know his façade as a 'friendly, helpful colleague' who is generally willing to tackle any job. In his communication with the therapist, Louis has enormous difficulty being honest and open about his problems and cannot, or does not dare to, name things by their name. When he cannot boast about his achievements ('look, Mam how well I do that') or about the latest fads acquired the previous week, he falls silent; there is only the bodily felt uneasiness which is relieved by the next cigarette. Louis also tries to become 'friends' with the therapist: he invites the therapist to his birthday party and when the therapist refuses to come, he brings a bottle of wine to the session, with the invitation that it might stimulate their social intercourse.*

Inadequate fathering – which is always the case with clients who are victims of incest with the father or when the fatherly role was not embodied by someone in the client's life – leaves the client somehow incapable of using clear verbal expressions to conceptualize what is going on inside and outside and of setting limits. If the therapist waits in a non-directive attitude, these clients often lose themselves in rather vague, endless talking, without really coming to the point.

Therapy can suffer through inadequate fathering as well when the therapist does not set limits and endlessly gives in to the client's feelings and needs, without stimulating the client to conceptualize the experiencing process. When the therapist does not promote the verbal elaboration of the client's experiences, then no links can be made between these experiences and the situation in the outside world. A therapist who shrinks away from 'getting down to business' and structuring the therapeutic happening can cause therapy to become an unproductive and formless process with much unnecessary waste of time.

Authentic communication/congruent symbols

In therapy the therapist will endeavour to restore meaning by offering a form-providing, limit-setting interaction and by furthering authentic communication.

> Realness does not equate therapy with friendship, or deprive it of its distinctive structure and limits. The structure and limits protect the client. The therapist carries certain responsibilities. . . . All feelings are welcomed, but possible actions are highly restricted. That keeps therapy from becoming like other relationships. The limits on actions make depth possible. Limiting the relationship in breadth, fencing it off on the left and right, defines a central channel between client and therapist in which they can relate more deeply and in a more real way than we usually do in our needful and twisted personal relationships where we hear each other so poorly, and so much of what we say and feel is projection. (Gendlin, 1996: 303)

Authentic communication only becomes possible when one's organismic experiencing is well represented by the symbols therapist and client use. 'Focusing is the process of developing more congruent symbols for organismic experiencing. The point is not to publicly reveal one's inner-most reality indiscriminately; rather the point is that one can make more intelligent choices about what to reveal publicly when one is not deceiving oneself' (Iberg, 1996: 32). The therapist will facilitate linking up the client's internal world with the external world by helping to find words, images, body movements or postures, actions fitting the implicitly felt. In therapy things are named and expressed to capture exactly the experience of the client. The process of symbolizing isn't something magical or strange. It's something we are all familiar with and what many clients spontaneously do. But clients who are unfamiliar with the vocabulary of feeling or who are inhibited about moving may need this process modelled. The therapist may need to guess at the feelings of the client, and make sure there is room for the client to amend the therapist's guess. Descriptions and expressions help the client find the way to the centre of the maze. Continuing to search for good descriptions or expressions keeps the client pointed toward the centre.

So, when Louis gives evidence of being ill at ease, the therapist invites him to put into words what he feels rather than promptly pushing the feelings away. Louis doesn't have words to name it. It is only something 'annoying' which he wants to get rid of as soon as possible. However, the therapist will not allow him to be led astray: 'As if you were coming across something difficult to feel and have learned only to treat it as if it did not exist.' *Client*: 'Oh, my life is fine.' The client's angry, nervous gaze and the stamping of his foot don't escape the therapist: 'You're telling me your life is fine, but when I see your body expression I imagine there might be some anger? . . . It is OK to feel anger, you may well have good reasons.' Whereupon the client continues vehemently about colleagues who impose upon his kindness. But the word 'anger' does not figure in his repertoire. Neither did it at home where any dissatisfaction was quickly suppressed by eating something sweet or buying something nice. The therapist also names some more of Louis's unmentionable feelings, such as his sadness, his loneliness and his shame. Gradually, Louis learns that he can differentiate between various 'annoying' feelings and that he does not have to take everything that comes his way. The therapist provides a model of limit-setting and honest communication, whereby Louis realizes that those sessions in which he is challenged to show himself as he is, satisfy him more than the endless tirades where he upholds the appearance of the 'lucky boy'.

The therapist helps the client to enter a new and more congruent relationship with himself and the outside world by being authentically present as well as by providing names for feelings the client has learned to avoid or deny, because they were undesirable. Finally Louis can acknowledge serious dissatisfactions and feels tremendous relief when, after many years, he has the courage to move towards more authentic choices in his life.

A *full felt sense*

A felt sense only comes to *completion* when bodily sensations and emotions are symbolized and linked to external situations. The full felt sense has four aspects: body sensations, emotional quality, imagery or symbolism, and life connection or story (Weiser Cornell, 1996). Studying fragments of therapy sessions, I discovered that clients can start with one of these four components. Regardless of the entry chosen, the felt sense fully emerges when contact is made with all four components. It is the therapist's task to evoke the missing component. (For clinical illustration of the four components and how a therapist can invite the missing aspects, see Leijssen, 1996b, 1997). In the case of insufficient fathering, the client often spontaneously omits the exact symbols and situations to which bodily sensations and emotions pertain. Here the therapist needs to insist on calling feelings and events by their name. Only when these 'truths' can see the light of day will the client be capable of further development.

Vera, a woman of 35, notices an uncomfortable feeling in the middle of her body and she feels sadness, which develops into a feeling of hate and horror. The therapist asks: 'If you direct your hate to someone or something, to whom or what would that be directed?' After much hesitancy, the client answers: 'I don't know how to name it; shall I say "him" or "that man" or should I say "father" or *"that specimen"* . . . *I never know what word to use.'* Therapist: *'The normal words don't seem to fit with your experience. . . . Let's look for words that really express your experience. . . . Is it something like "swine" or . . .'* Client: *'Yes! "Swine" and even worse, "beastly", "brutal", "vulgar"!'* Therapist: *'What your father did with you was beastly, brutal, vulgar, not how a father should behave with a child.'* Client: *'Ah . . . this is a relief . . . I feel less guilty and cramped!'*

Felt shift

When the right symbols that fit the experience are found, the client feels a satisfying sense of rightness; this is a 'felt shift'. There are many kinds of shift. On the continuum of *intensities* at the 'low end' there are 'small shifts' which may be very minimal, very subtle: one could easily skip over them if one didn't know about them. At the 'high end' the shift is intense, dramatic, obvious: it's a 'big shift', no one would miss it. There are also different *kinds* of shift: sometimes the client feels a release or a relief in the body (a sigh, tears); sometimes it is a sharpening of some vague experience or the sense becomes stronger (a general feeling of confusion becomes a clear feeling of anger); sometimes the client feels something moving from one location in the body to another (a choking sensation in the throat becomes a warm feeling around the heart); sometimes it is an experience of more energy, excitement, enthusiasm, personal power or new life awakening and stirring in some parts of the body or the whole body; at other times it's feeling more peace, clarity, groundedness, a warm, spacious well-being. The client might also have a new insight about an issue, but we consider this only as a felt shift or a new step if the insight happens not only in the mind, but is also in some way a bodily felt resolution (see Friedman, 1995: 24–5; Weiser Cornell, 1996: 30–2, 90). When what is felt in the body becomes more and more accurately symbolized, one is achieving congruence, which seems to bring back the 'spirit' in life.

Overvaluation of the fatherly

When the fatherly is overrated – an easy thing to happen in a patriarchal society – the danger of symbols and explanations of situations taking the upper hand, without them being in touch with bodily sensations or being accompanied by emotions, is a real one. For people who experience this, a body is something which they 'own' and which they bring to the 'experts' for repairs 'as a machine'. Their verbal expressions and actions are not authentic, because they emerge no longer from something 'underneath' thinking, namely the bodily felt experience.

Hilde is 42 and was sent for therapy by her doctor after repeated attacks of hyperventilation. She admires her father a lot and speaks with disdain about her mother who was 'stupid and weak' in contrast with her father who managed to fascinate her from childhood on with his books. Father was proud of his daughter, who was very verbal. Hilde was intelligent but failed in the studies which she would have liked to complete according to Father's wishes. In therapy she talks very quickly and has always a pat answer ready; she has a bookish explanation for every problem. Her life proceeds in a very orderly way: everything follows a logically built sequence, until it becomes 'path-o-logical'.

Hilde, who shows overvaluation of the fatherly, needs help to connect her multitude of symbols and concepts with the bodily felt experiential flow. Here the therapist tries to reconnect external authority – such as books, rationalizations, logical structures – with the inner authority. In such a situation the therapist occasionally has to interrupt the client's word flow and invite her to remain quiet for a while and feel how the words touch her inside. Thus Hilde tells of having heard in a lecture how numerous problems find their roots in a fear of dying and of finding this a suitable explanation for her own hyperventilation.

Therapist: *'You talk about fear of dying. Could you try to spot where in your body you most experience that?'* Client: *'In the region of my heart.'* Therapist: *'Is there a word or an image that fits exactly the quality of what you are feeling there?'* Client: *'That's fear of dying.'* (There is no visible bodily relief.) Therapist: *'Take your time, does "fear of dying" really fit? Or is there something else that you can sense? Maybe the sense in the region of your heart can bring a word that feels right?'* [Silence] Client [with more energetic voice]: *'As if the vehemence of my heart beating is saying: "Hey when are we going to live really!"'* Therapist: *'Ah there seems to be an urge in you to live really! That's how it feels?'* Client: *'Yes, it feels like urgent, like I have lost so many years to please the men in my life, I have never thought about what I wanted to do with my life!'* Therapist: *'Does it feel now like: "I want to stop pleasing the men and I'm up to looking for what I want with my life?"'* Client [laughs]: *'I don't know if I can stop pleasing the men, but I surely want to look more for things I like to do.'* Therapist: *'You might take some time to notice how that feels in your body, if you commit yourself to look more for what you want to do with your life . . . .'*. Client [sighs]: *'There is a warm and bright feeling in my heart and even in my whole body.'*

After some more interactions, the therapist asks: *'If you let your imagination go forward to the week to come, are there some specific steps you feel you would like to take?'* [Silence] Client: *'For such a long time I have thought of buying a telescope, because I like to observe birds. I never did because I was always with partners who are not interested in nature. . . . It feels like a big gift to myself to take that step!'* *In another session, Hilde says that her doctor advised her to do more physical exercise since she is suffering a lot from back pain. The therapist asks:* *'How do you experience your back?'* Hilde: *'Everything is rigid, especially the right side.'* Therapist: *'Could you check what you associate with your right side?'* *After a period of silence, Hilde laughs, surprised:* *'That is masculine, strong, controlled, related to working . . . .'*. *After reflecting this back, the therapist wonders:* *'Could it be that your body tries to tell you that you suffer from a rigid right side, or that the masculine, the strong part is not flexible enough?'* Hilde: *'I do feel that I am not balanced . . . but if I were to lean towards the other side . . . there is the more feminine and I don't dare going there. . . . I never want to be like my mother!'* Therapist: *'The feminine and your experience of your mother brings something you feel as threatening? Or how is it for you?'* Hilde: *'I have always found it terrible to be a woman and thus to be weak; I don't want anything to do with that . . . I was glad that I had good control over that . . . but now, something does not seem to fit. . .'.* Therapist: *'Nature doesn't allow full control. . . . Maybe your body cannot accept any longer that the feminine is out of balance with the masculine . . . I don't know if that fits with how it feels for you?'*

Because her back pain eases after this session, Hilde gradually starts to believe in consulting a source of knowledge other than 'Father's logic'. Her very sophisticated vocabulary now became an aid in expressing her experiences in a differentiated way instead of using words not fed from within. Here, too, honest communication on the part of the therapist is important. Thus, when Hilde asks the therapist's opinion about a certain book, the therapist admits not knowing it. Hilde looks a little condescending and says: 'I thought you would have to read this for your job!' Therapist: 'You seem disappointed about the fact that I cannot talk about it . . . I don't have a great need for that sort of literature but I'm interested in what you would like me to understand about you through this book.' The therapist invites the client repeatedly, in a friendly way, to enliven her 'bookish wisdom' by sensations in her body and to establish a relationship with the internally felt authority.

The therapist, too, has to be careful not to take over the client's authority by offering many concepts and logical explanations which do not help the client in his or her search for the internally felt authority. When fathering dominates the therapy too much, therapy may be too cold, too rational, overstructured, too verbal, insufficiently fed by bodily sensation.

Many people are not so clear about the authority their feelings should have over the words that are spoken about them. Some people have an attitude that 'if you say so, it must be right.' This is especially true for some people who as children were consistently told how they felt. . . . You may detect this problem by watching carefully to see the client's reactions to your 'less than your best' responses. . . . take the initiative to say something to the effect of 'I don't think I got that quite right. It doesn't seem to fit. Did my wording seem incorrect somehow?' In this way you can invite the client to seek more precision of expression, and you model an attitude of respect for the authority of their own experiencing. (Iberg, 1996: 25)

In the focusing process *checking with the body*, over and over, all through the session, is an important way to look for confirmation of the words from the felt sense of the client. In this 'resonating step' we ask the body: 'Does this word fit? Is it like this?' or we simply reflect the expression of the client with the implicit invitation to offer it back to the felt experience, from where the client may correct the former expression or move forward in a deeper and centred way.

A healthy inner relationship is a *balanced* one: 'within' interacts with 'without'; nature and culture cross-fertilize; mothering and fathering are equally valuable; bodily sensations, emotions, symbols and external situations all belong to the complete experiencing cycle.

Dealing with interfering characters – following one's own sense of direction – unconditional positive regard

Once children have sufficiently internalized both mothering and fathering, they are ready for *puberty* in which their own sense of direction is developed in interaction with the broader social context. In this period one is usually given room to experiment, take risks, make mistakes, discover what one really wants – even if it goes against social conventions – take responsibilities and bear the consequences of one's decisions. It is a time of many choices: lifestyle, profession, partner. . . . From the hormonal point of view this period is situated between the ages of 12 and 18, but in our increasingly complex culture, the psychosocial process of letting go and acquiring personal independence can take until well past the age of 20.

Hindrances in puberty

Problems at this stage often result from a lack of adequate mothering and/ or fathering, thus leaving the adolescent without trust in an inner source and/or without the ability to structure and limit him or herself. The young person is then unable to detach him or herself from mother and/or father and does not feel the inner strength to develop his or her own structure. Sometimes a lack of balance or a deficit in the parenting is accompanied by a bad or absent relationship between the parents whereby the adolescent feels called upon to supply Father or Mother with the missing partnership. The adolescent can also be confronted with the parents' (unspoken) needs to such an extent that he or she does not arrive at making personal choices. Thus in the case of unfulfilled parental dreams, educational and professional choices may be made in such a way as to fill as yet unmet parental needs. Parents who want to keep a strong grip on their children fail to give them room to experiment, to fall and get up, to design their own life. Conforming to family norms then takes precedence over searching for an authentic, creative lifestyle. When no inner source (adequate mothering) and/or suitable symbolization process (adequate fathering) has developed, one may become exceptionally vulnerable to outside influences during this period of life. To protect the vulnerable self, the person develops behavioural patterns designed to please important others or else imprisons the real self by playing roles copied from idolized models, while increasingly fusing with these inauthentic choices without being aware of it.

> *Ann is 30 and comes for therapy after a suicidal attempt. Mother became ill when Ann was nine and died when Ann was 16. Together with Father, Ann took care of Mother and took on the household tasks (there were two younger children). Later she got a job as an employee in the business where her father works. In the meantime, the two younger children married. Ann was occasionally*

approached by prospective partners but they were quickly ruled out by Father's criticism. In recent years, she has often been ill, believes sometimes that, just like her mother, she will die of cancer, and she complains of depression.

Acknowledging different parts

In therapy, autonomy is encouraged by leaving the client room to find her own direction, which is done by not interfering on the basis of the therapist's needs. The therapist does not 'stand in the way' with advice and personal opinions. The therapist helps – without any judging – the client to acknowledge the roles she has learned to play or the sorts of reactions she has learned to use in order to protect herself.

Ann discovers that she is 'married' to her father and that she wants to develop a different life to the one she is living now. She enters then into a crazy stage in which she tries out all sorts of relationships. After several confrontations with her father, she chooses to go and live alone. She starts evening classes, seeking extra skills in order to get another job. She asks the therapist's advice about every decision but the therapist's answer is consistently one of reflecting the material which the client brings herself and encouraging her to feel inside how it resonates there. For example, Ann would ask: 'I have met a man who is in the process of separating and who can see something come off with me. Do you think I should take the risk?' Therapist: *'Can you bring your awareness down into your body . . . and try asking in there, "How do I feel in here about the relationship with this man?"' Especially when Ann is down after the break-up of yet another relationship, the therapist reminds her that the growth process is a matter of falling and getting up, and helps her to discover what she can learn from her experiences.*

Client: *'I am so disappointed – yet another man with whom it does not work out. I want to meet a man, but when it gets close, I seem to run away. I'll always fail. I feel stuck.'* Therapist: *'Take your time . . . sensing how different feelings are there. . . . Maybe we can allow the different parts to be heard and listen to the complexity, the variety and subtlety. . . . The first thing you mentioned was the feeling of disappointment. . . . Is that the best description of how it feels right now? Or whatever gets closest to how that sense feels right now?'* Client: *'Well, it is not exactly disappointment . . . [silence] it's I'm scared I'll have to stay in my loneliness for ever.'* [Some tears are coming.] Therapist: *'Being in contact with the feeling of loneliness brings this scary feeling and also some sadness. . . .'* [more crying and silence] *Is there something more in it, that it wants you to know or that it might need?'* [silence] Client: *'I can't stand any longer the feeling of having a close contact with someone and then facing the danger of losing someone who has become dear to me . . .'* Therapist: *'As if it lets you know that that place in you is already too much hurt to take more of that.'* Client: *'Yes . . . it has been too much . . . after my mother's death I can't face another loss . . .* [sigh]. *But I don't want to stay without a partner!'* Therapist: *'You can acknowledge the part that is so deeply hurt that it can take no more risks, and at the same time, there is the longing for a partner.'* Client: *'It's relieving to separate these two . . . maybe I can give them both their own space.'*

The therapist uses focusing interventions to release the client from different forms of inner sabotage. 'Evaluative reactions to feelings are the most common alternative to friendly receptivity to feelings. . . . Sometimes clients have quite obviously critical reactions toward what they feel' (Iberg, 1996: 24). Focusing helps the client to step back and to be more accepting of all feelings as various parts of a complicated reaction. This *self-acceptance* allows deeper and faster change in the areas of life that need to change. 'Focusing is being a good listener to your inner self. There are parts of you that want to be heard, without judgment, without criticism, without advice. In focusing, you can give yourself that non-judgmental listening that feels good and brings greater clarity. . . . Focusing is about having a positive and supportive relationship with yourself' (Weiser Cornell, 1996: 17).

Friendly interest/welcoming new steps

Sometimes the therapist might choose to ask some *open-ended questions* to the felt sense of the client, for example: 'What does it need?' or 'What's the worst of it?' or 'What is most important about this?' Asking can be a natural next step if the client seems not to know what to do. The purpose of the questions is to hold an attitude of friendly interest and respectful curiosity, and to direct the attention to what more is there. Asking implies that the client is the one to feel best what the next step can be. The 'response' from the felt sense takes some time; it can take a minute before it opens and gives a new step. 'Old information' will be there immediately, but what the felt sense can create is infinitely better, more creative and richer than anything the conscious mind of the client (or the therapist) can think up. The questions create a welcome for new ways of being, a new meaning, new action steps. The experience that the felt sense 'knows the answer', and that the body is able to unfold the next step if we approach it in a loving attitude, can be seen as a confirmation of the person-centred belief in the actualizing tendency in the human organism. The actualizing tendency is experienced immediately and bodily. As an illustration of this, Ann Weiser Cornell (1996: 8) points out that focusing is a great tool for decision-making because it helps to sense the rightness of choice-making, at a level beyond logical analysis. It helps the client to make a choice that is right holistically, that is, taking in and integrating all factors at once.

Luc is 28 and comes for therapy, pushed by his parents. In high school he was known as a good boy and model student. His parents, simple labourers, dreamt of having their only son become a doctor. Luc enrolled to study medicine but did not qualify in spite of hard work. Pushed by his parents, he started studying nursing but regularly passed out at the sight of blood and switched to social work. Then he met 'bad' friends, experimented with drugs, occasionally committed minor thefts, neglected his studies and was eventually dismissed from college. He now wanders about in town, intermittently has a job as a waiter or a dishwasher and only goes home when in financial difficulties. His parents have now made their financial aid contingent on his seeing a psychologist. In therapy, Luc initially plays the role of the nice boy who obeys his parents. Either he awaits the therapist's move by silently looking at her or tells superficial anecdotes from the previous week.

Therapist: *'I understand that you want to make a handsome gesture towards your parents. If it were me, I would perhaps be prepared to spend an hour at the psychologist's myself if I were to get extra pocket money for it. . . . You don't have to fill the hour with talk. Just be quiet, if you wish . . . perhaps you can notice how you feel inside . . . you can spend time with just feeling that and if you wish, we can try finding out more about the things you notice inside.'* The therapist does not moralize, nor does she take the responsibility for the client's life. Because there is no interference from the therapist's needs, the client gradually feels an open space in which he is free to discover what he wants for himself and what suits his inner deeper needs and wishes. Client: *'What will I do with my life? . . . Shall I continue by having all these little jobs . . . it gives me some freedom . . . or shall I go back to studying. . . . If yes . . . what kind of study?'* Therapist: *'How does having these jobs feel in your body?'* Client: *'Worthless . . . a heavy feeling, especially in my arms and legs . . . being a nobody.'* Therapist: *'When you check that back with your body, worthless, being a nobody . . . how does it feel from its point of view?'* Client: *'It says: shut up, you're able to do more with your life!'* Therapist: *'You have a feeling of being able to do more with your life. . . . How does that "more" feel like?'* Client: *'Some excitement in my arms and legs when I imagine starting some studies that could really be something for me.'* Therapist: *'Some kind of studies might be exciting for you.'* [Silence] Client: *'Maybe studying something like economics . . . that's something I was good at in secondary school.'* As the client stayed with this idea, more energy came into his body. He focused several more times on this issue and it resulted in a clear sense that studying economics might be the right decision.

Therapists, too, may behave as needy, overprotective parents who need their clients for themselves or who want to keep the client's life in their own hands. They may be angry or disappointed when clients have not followed their advice or they provide them with all sorts of addresses and information and thus steer, in a subtle way, the client's life in the direction considered by the therapist to be the right one. The therapist's value judgements then become the norm for the client's choices.

Interfering character/inner critic/superego

When the client has identified with some inner critic and grants it a higher authority than other parts of his or her experience, more process-directive interventions may be needed in order to help the client develop his or her own sense of direction. The attitude of unconditional positive regard doesn't mean that we agree or are glad about whatever is coming, it means that we acknowledge what's there and try to understand what might be its reason for being there. For the therapist to direct the client towards focusing is not the same thing as steering the client's life in a certain direction or telling the client what to do. It aims at bringing to the fore the client's deeper knowledge which has been suppressed by unfavourable growing-up conditions. Gendlin (1996: 247–58) uses the term 'superego' to describe the part that attacks from within and interrupts a person's every hopeful move. 'Everyone who has studied people has found this part of a person. We recognize it under various names: "the superego", "the inner critic", "the bad parent"' (Gendlin, 1996: 249). When the therapist does not recognize the interfering behaviour patterns, the chances are that the client will get stuck in his or her process, always in the same way, and will boycott every emergence of something new in him or herself. 'The pattern is characterized by guilt, shame, humiliation, blame, fear, the inability to act freely, the avoidance of competition, the wish to give up one's power, the conviction that one can never get what one needs, the habit of stopping oneself from acting to get what one wants, and many other variants. These avoidances of life and living are related to superego attacks' (Gendlin, 1996: 256). 'The superego . . . has attitudes. It is usually negative, angry, hostile, attacking, mean, petty; it enjoys oppressing a person' (ibid.: 255). 'When thought of as a manner of experiencing, the superego is inherently "not me". What we call "me" pulls back, defends itself, hides, and becomes constricted under the attack' (ibid.: 250).

Brigit, 28, was sexually abused by her father between the ages of 6 and 16. In one therapy session, she gets in touch with a 'deeply hurt feeling inside'. While talking about that, a shrill, scornful voice suddenly comes up in her, saying: 'Don't exaggerate! Are you really sure it's true what you are saying?' She knows this voice very well because it is the one with which she always sweeps her feelings under the carpet. The therapist invites her to place this voice in front of her and see whether she can put a face to it. The client almost immediately 'sees' the face of her mother who always reacted in this way when the client, as a young girl, tried to inform Mother of what Father did. The therapist invites her to put the image of Mother saying such things even further away and gives a message, inviting the inner knowledge to come to the fore: 'You feel deeply hurt inside; give this more space; let us listen to that some more . . .'. The client is then capable of expressing her anger and pain about what Father did to her as well as about Mother's reaction to it. The client terminates the session discarding the 'voice' which denies her feelings and replacing it by an encouraging message in which she 'hears' that it is all right to express her pain and anger.

Ian, 32, lives isolated and cut off from people. While exploring his feelings towards a friend in a therapy session, a voice saying: 'Watch it, don't trust anybody' comes up in him. The therapist enquires whether there is an image matching this voice. The client 'sees a watchman always guarding the entrance'. The therapist invites him to start a conversation with this watchman and find out about his intentions. The client discovers that he protects him from intruders. Further exploration of the watchman's function makes the client understand that he himself took the watchman on in order to avoid being hurt as he had been as a child. The therapist agrees that the watchman has indeed been very helpful in protecting the child in the client and has thus rendered a very good service, for which thanks should be expressed. Next, the therapist invites the client to 'create a new job for this dutiful, faithful servant'. The client laughs and answers that this would be possible: 'Perhaps I could consult with my watchman about whether or not he is needed at a given time and send him on leave when I am with my best friends.' Therapist: 'How does that feel when you imagine that?' Client: 'It has something liberating, less lonely and boring, because I was in fact always isolated with this watchman at my door.'

Recognizing and processing the inner critic

At first the therapist needs to help the client recognize interfering patterns of behaviour – or interfering characters, or inner critics, or superego attacks – which put the client off track. Interfering characters can take on a multitude of shapes and can be distinguished from inner knowledge by their predictability and stereotyped expressions. 'It is felt as a thud, a constriction, a collapse of energy in the body' (Gendlin, 1996: 252). Besides, they are characterized by their typically unfriendly, degrading, sharp, demanding, humiliating, ridiculing, negative tone of voice. They make sure that the person will feel worse, will fail to fulfil his or her potential and be prevented from living fully. They act in 'all or nothing' terms, know no nuances or differentiations and keep governing a person's life even when circumstances no longer call for them. The therapist has to intervene here in a friendly but resolute manner in order to help the client find a 'new balance of power' inside. Therapists can use different strategies for counteracting the inner critic. 'The main procedure is to move the superego out of the way of the process. The simplest way is to restore and respond to what the client was feeling just before the superego attack' (Gendlin, 1996: 258). Although Gendlin believes that rapid progress can be made with simple procedures, chronic severe inner attacks are not so easily bypassed. More often the therapist has to intervene by giving the client the possibility of identifying the emergence of the interfering character in him or herself and of exploring from the right distance – thus without fusing with it – its function in the past and the present.

Inner critics have become powerful components of the personality because they are often introjections of important authority figures or have been called into being in order to manage certain feelings that are to be avoided at all costs:

Although the superego has a lot to do with one's parents, it is more unreasonable and destructive than one's parents ever were. It contains a residue of parental preaching and criticism, but it is much more than that. . . . The superego absorbs the aggression and violence that the conscious person rejects. . . . Many lovely, sensitive people are inwardly brutalised and oppressed by their superegos. They would never treat others as their superego treats them. (Gendlin, 1996: 249)

Often there is an important dynamic behind an inner critic; it may have been a protection in very difficult circumstances, it may have been a way to survive otherwise unbearable traumas. Many times the interfering characters are unhealed parts of the client that have been cut off from love and acceptance. By gently and compassionately asking it what it is doing in the client's life, it might reveal old wounds of hurt and anger. When the client can receive what the *function* of the critic was in his or her life, and has been able to sense what the critic wanted or wants, his or her body can find better ways to take care, more in tune with the circumstances in the actual life of the client. The exploration of the critic subsequently can lead to the discovery of the part of oneself that has been *kept suppressed* by the interfering character. Finally, a new way of relating emerges in which the suppressed part is acknowledged and the interfering character is given a more appropriate place in the client's life. This 'better place' may mean: thanking it for services rendered and sending it on leave; it may also mean keeping it in active service but then under the client's more differentiated control (see also Leijssen, 1997; Müller, 1995).

How a better integration can take place is something that can only come from the felt sense of the client. When we prevent quick and hard conclusions and respect and revere what the felt sense has to tell, new life, that was *under* the critic, can be restored and the client can grow in love and acceptance towards the different parts of him or herself.

Maturity – the inner relationship – spirituality

The psychological stage of life in which a person makes his or her own unique contribution to society is called adulthood. This stage is not experienced by everybody – age notwithstanding – because certain aptitudes (e.g. the internalization of good mothering and fathering and the development of one's own sense of direction) may not have been mastered, or not sufficiently mastered, in previous stages. For such people, therapy may create new opportunities in which the most important life ingredients may yet be offered.

However, it is only when the therapist is capable of establishing an authentic and loving relationship with him or herself – perhaps not all the time, but at least most of the time – that he or she will be sufficiently mature to accompany others in their process of growth. A healthy maturity enables a person to be in touch with him or herself in such a way as to be capable of receiving and acknowledging what is present in the deeper experiential flow. Felt meanings can be accepted without distortion and symbolized properly. Life's medley of experiences can be lived in freedom and with integrity.

An increase in internalization should not be seen as selfishly contemplating one's navel. On the contrary, it is a powerful source from which a person, purified and healed, may emerge feeling genuine concern about what others really need and it may provide the vital force needed to devote oneself with increased dedication to one's fellow human beings. An inner sense of purpose and importance is a greater motivating force than imposed duties or the imitation of a role model. Deep down, human beings know their destinies and know what they have to do when relating to the world around them. When a person starts from an inner centre, reaching out to others becomes more meaningful. Thanks to this inner anchorage others are no longer needed for security and thus room becomes available for more fruitful relationships.

Bio-spiritual horizons

Once some clients have explored and alleviated the worst of their sufferings through therapeutic contact, and once they start to see a way out of their problems, a period is likely to ensue in which they discover that the search within themselves can be a most fascinating adventure. Such clients learn to experience this inner adventure in therapy with the therapist as a guide. But sooner or later, this guide has to disappear from the client's life and then the client has to be capable of taking over. The task is to replace the therapist by an observing, reflecting, experiencing self which makes contact with what is felt inside but does not fuse with it, a self which gives careful attention to the inner experience in order for the inner knowledge to go on revealing its meanings, a self that is able to occupy the position of *detached witnessing*. With this attitude the person enters an inner relationship which can open an extraordinary doorway into the realm of spiritual awareness. 'The opening of broader bio-spiritual horizons can spontaneously occur as a gratifying component within human development itself' (Campbell and McMahon, 1985: 12). Gendlin points to this when he writes: 'Your physically felt body is in fact part of a gigantic system of here and other spaces, now and other times, you and other people – in fact the whole universe. This sense of being bodily alive in a vast system is the body as it is felt from inside' (Gendlin, 1981: 77). 'The felt sense comes between the conscious person and the deep universal reaches of human nature where we are no longer ourselves. It is open to what comes from those universals, but it feels like "really me"' (Gendlin, 1984: 81). What is felt in the human organism leads to a broadening of the experiential field and a finding of meaning.

The felt sense seems to know more than can be expressed or explained. The inner relationship opens up a process which implies more than we can describe in words and which incites us to reach for metaphors to express that 'more'. The chosen metaphors are never independent of what 'appeals' to us in our environment. Every culture provides cognitive structures by which experiences may be put into words. Similar deep experiences will receive different 'names' according to the words available in a person's environment which are capable of stirring emotions to such an extent that they are recognized as the 'right expression' for the experience at hand.

Many 'focusing therapists' speak of the focusing process resulting in a *spiritual, transcendental* experience, when the inner sense is treated with attention and respect. The spiritual experience originates in the body but reaches beyond the body's limits: the person feels him or herself to be part of a greater whole. 'The process of focusing touches into a level of humanity united in a single evolving world, a "gifted" or "graced" unity that is not caused by ego efforts but rather by surrender to this common underlying process. . . . As one moves more deeply into it, every event, every "felt meaning" can become a religious event' (Campbell and McMahon, 1985: vi–vii). During their focusing process, people can experience a surge of spiritual energy, the presence of a force greater than their own self, something that stands above time and space, a mystery which some call 'God' or contact with their 'Soul' or a 'Higher Reality' (Hinterkopf, 1990, 1996; Jaison, 1991; Leijssen, 1995; Lukens, 1991). As focusing experiences accumulate, one tends to move in the direction of having a characteristic attitude.

> In an advanced condition of maturity, one has the ability to accept surrender at a moment's notice, trusting something larger than oneself to assert true and accurate representation of reality. . . . this attitude of sacredness seems very much a part of healing and growing experiences. . . . By an attitude of sacredness, I mean a respect for the unknown and a respect for the meaning in pain and unpleasant experiences, as well as in pleasant experiences. This attitude involves something like faith that what one feels and experiences can become part of a constructive life process if one approaches it properly and is willing to learn. It involves something like awe for the creative power of things beyond one's small personal sense of 'me'. (Iberg, 1996: 37)

However, the inner relationship points in the direction of a deeper cosmic process and the experiencing process found in focusing may have a transcendent dimension.

> The transcendent dimension may, but does not necessarily, involve a deity or higher power. . . . 'Transcendent' means moving beyond one's former frame of reference in a direction of higher or broader scope. The transcendent dimension, found in all human beings, involves moving beyond one's own unhealthy egocentricity, duality, and exclusively towards more healthy egocentricity, inclusivity, unity and capacity to love. (Hinterkopf, 1996: 10)

Thus, in the middle of ordinary external life, a person may feel carried along in an exciting inner adventure, unique to each individual, which may contain an inexhaustible source of caring for oneself and the world. It may lead to increased self-confidence and confidence in the 'mystery of life' which refers to 'more' than our human thoughts can encompass.

References

Campbell, P.A. and McMahon, E.M. (1985) *Bio-spirituality: Focusing as a Way to Grow*. Chicago: Loyola University Press.

Friedman, N. (1995) 'On focusing: how to access your own and other people's direct experience'. Unpublished manuscript, can be ordered from Massachusetts Avenue, Arlington, MA 02174, USA.

Gendlin, E.T. (1978) *Focusing*. New York: Everest House.

Gendlin, E.T. (1981) *Focusing*, revised edn. New York: Bantam Books.

Gendlin, E.T. (1984) 'The client's client: the edge of awareness', in F.R. Levant and J.M. Shlien (eds), *Client-centered Therapy and the Person-centered Approach: New Directions in Theory, Research and Practice*. New York: Praeger. pp. 76–107.

Gendlin, E.T. (1996) *Focusing-oriented Psychotherapy: A Manual of the Experiential Method*. New York: Guilford Press.

Gendlin, E.T., Beebe, J., Cassens, J., Klein, M. and Oberlander, R. (1968) 'Focusing ability in psychotherapy, personality and creativity', in J.M. Shlien (ed.), *Research in Psychotherapy*, Vol. 3. Washington, DC: APA. pp. 217–41.

Grindler, D. (1985) 'Research perspectives on "clearing a space" with someone who had cancer', *The Focusing Folio*, 4 (3): 98–124.

Hinterkopf, E. (1990) 'Focusing and spirituality in counseling', *The Focusing Folio*, 9 (3): 81–96.

Hinterkopf, E. (1996) 'A process definition of spirituality: implications for focusing therapy', *The Folio: A Journal for Focusing and Experiential Therapy*, 15 (1): 9–12.

Iberg, J.R. (1996) 'Finding the body's next step: ingredients and hindrances', *The Folio: A Journal for Focusing and Experiential Therapy*, 15 (1): 13–42.

Jaison, B. (1991) 'Focusing and spirituality', *The Focusing Folio*, 10 (4): 54–8.

Kanter, M. (1982–3) 'Clearing a space with four cancer patients', *The Focusing Folio*, 2 (4): 23–7.

Leijssen, M. (1992) 'Experiential focusing through drawing', *The Focusing Folio*, 11 (2): 35–40.

Leijssen, M. (1993) 'Creating a workable distance to overwhelming images', in D. Brazier (ed.), *Beyond Carl Rogers: Towards a Psychotherapy for the Twenty-first Century*. London: Constable. pp. 129–48.

Leijssen, M. (1995) 'Focusing: psychotherapeutisch proces en religieuze ervaring', *Tijdschrift voor Psychotherapie*, 21: 24–36.

Leijssen, M. (1996a) 'Focusingprocessen in cliëntgericht-experiëntiële psychotherapie'. Proefschrift aangeboden tot het verkrijgen van de graad van Doctor in de Psychologische Wetenschappen. Catholic University, Leuven.

Leijssen, M. (1996b) 'Characteristics of a healing inner relationship', in R. Hutterer, G. Pawlowsky, P. F. Schmid and R. Stipsits (eds), *Client-centered and Experiential Psychotherapy: A Paradigm in Motion*. Vienna: Peter Lang. pp. 427–38.

Leijssen, M. (1997) 'Focusing processes', in L.S. Greenberg, G. Lietaer and J. Watson (eds), *Experiential Psychotherapy: Differential Intervention*. New York: Guilford.

Lukens, L. (1991) 'Focusing: another way to spirituality', *The Focusing Folio*, 10 (4): 65–72.

McDonald, M. (1987) 'Teaching focusing to disturbed, inner city adolescents', *The Focusing Folio*, 6 (1): 29–37.

McGuire, M. (1982–3) '"Clearing a space" with two suicidal clients', *The Focusing Folio*, 2 (1): 1–4.

McGuire, M. (1984) 'Part II of an excerpt from: "Experiential focusing with severely depressed suicidal clients"', *The Focusing Folio*, 3 (3): 104–19.

Müller, D. (1995) 'Dealing with self-criticism: the critic within us and the criticized one', *The Folio: Journal for Focusing and Experiential Psychotherapy*, 14 (1): 1–9.

Rogers, C.R. (1961) *On Becoming a Person*. Boston: Houghton Mifflin.

Stern, D.N. (1985) *The Interpersonal World of the Infant: A View from Psychoanalysis and Developmental Psychology*. New York: Basic Books.

Warner, M.S. (1996) 'How does empathy cure? A theoretical consideration of empathy, processing and personal narrative', in R. Hutterer, G. Pawlowsky, P.F. Schmid and R. Stipsits (eds), *Client-Centered and Experiential Psychotherapy: A Paradigm in Motion*. Vienna: Peter Lang. pp. 127–44.

Weiser Cornell, A. (1991) 'Too close/too distant: toward a typology of focusing process'. Paper presented at the Second International Conference on Client-centered and Experiential Psychotherapy, University of Stirling, Scotland.

Weiser Cornell, A. (1996) *The Power of Focusing*. Oakland, CA: New Harbinger.

Wiltschko, J. (1995) 'Focusing therapy: some basic statements', *The Folio: A Journal for Focusing and Experiential Therapy*, 14 (3): 1–12.

Wiltschko, J. (1996) 'Focusing therapy II: some fragments in which the whole can become visible', *The Folio: A Journal for Focusing and Experiential Therapy*, 15 (1): 55–78.

12 Client-Centred Therapy for Adolescents: An Interactional Point of View

Lidwien Geertjens and Olga Waaldijk

Adolescence is a developmental phase in which far-reaching physical, emotional, cognitive and social changes take place. For a thorough assessment of adolescence a substantial knowledge of normal, as well as of pathological development, is a prerequisite. The same applies to therapeutic treatment.

In a now classical article Rutter et al. (1976) contends that adolescence is indeed a tempestuous period, but that most youngsters go through it without much damage. Weiner (1988) states that 'normal' maladjustment in adolescence is a myth, that emotional confusion and commotion reflect a disturbed adaptation and that psychological symptoms in adolescents are an indication of pathology. But it's also true that already existing problems manifest themselves, especially in this phase, because of the demands the young person is confronted with. In addition to this their personal resilience may prove to be too weak to stand the vicissitudes of adolescence, or this phase may see a resurgence of pathology from earlier stages. Nagera (1966) distinguishes:

- developmental conflicts (phase-related problems);
- developmental disorders (problems resulting from disturbances in earlier phases);
- developmental interferences (problems as a result of extreme factors or outside influences).

It has been claimed that there are specific requirements for the attitude of the psychotherapist treating adolescents (Driessen, 1984). This attitude can be described as being more active and more direct than is usual in therapy with adults. The reason is that the self-concept of youngsters in this phase is just beginning to take shape and does not yet have a stable structure. The therapist is guiding them in the exploration of possibilities and impossibilities. The therapist can be a model, a parental figure as well as a 'congruent and transparent other'.

Aspects of developmental theory

Adolescence can be roughly divided into three phases with each having a different colour and character and implying different developmental tasks: early, mid- and late adolescence (Blos, 1962; De Wit et al., 1995). Around the age of 12 clear changes are appearing in the child. The beginning of adolescence coincides with the transition to secondary education: the world becomes wider and the cognitive capacities expand. At the same time physical changes are taking place: in hormonal equilibrium and physical appearance, menarche and so on. From that moment on the youngster is confronted with the task of discovering: who am I? what am I capable of? who do I like to be? Through the enlarging of their thinking adolescents are gradually becoming aware of the norms and values which have been transferred to them. Some of these the adolescent wishes to maintain and to internalize, but they also will adopt new concepts, new ideas from outside. Contacts with peers, the confrontation with more or less familiar sub-cultures and the experiencing of influences different from the parental environment play an important role in this process. The youngster discovers what he or she is able to do and by implication what he or she is not able to do; what are the limits and the impossibilities. In this sense adolescence can be seen as a 'point of no return' for further development: the choice of an educational course or school and the joining of a specific social group have important implications for the rest of life.

Early adolescence

The popular name for this phase is puberty. We prefer to speak of 'early adolescence' because 'puberty' generally refers to the physical aspects only and we want to examine this phase from a broader point of view. Early adolescence is above all a period of transition and of strong changes, both in physical and in psychosexual, cognitive and social respect. The body grows rapidly and becomes an area to discover once more. The power of drives and impulses becomes stronger and restraints are becoming weaker. Fluctuations of basic mood are a daily affair. The way of thinking changes. The range of problem-solving strategies becomes wider and hypothetical-deductive reasoning becomes possible. According to Piaget (1970) the stage of formal-operational thinking is reached.

The family as a safe haven becomes less important and association with the peer group has to be achieved. To put it briefly: the young adolescents' world is being overturned! With this loss of everything that used to be self-evident they are feeling quite insecure. They are inclined to hide this insecurity from others. But not only are the early adolescents themselves insecure: the people around often don't know how to deal with them. At which level should they approach them? What will be understood, and what not? How to deal with the changing moods? Which responsibilities are they able to manage?

Mid-adolescence

After early adolescence, approximately at the age of 14 or 15, the so-called mid-adolescence (Blos, 1962 speaks of adolescence proper) arrives. Gradually, impulsive outbursts diminish. The adolescent acquires more and more a feeling of self-control. The changes in cognitive functioning, in abstract thinking for example, help in this respect. In the preceding phase much was invested emotionally in the parents. Now the adolescent tries to become more independent of parents both in thought and in wishes and deeds. With regard to relationships, attention is shifting more and more to peers. They become the new frame of reference. Through contact with other people adolescents become acquainted with new ways of life, other customs and with up till now unknown ideas. They are beginning to look at their own families in a different light. This is stimulating for the process of self-reflection. The intensive contact with themselves makes adolescents withdraw from time to time, perhaps with favourite music or into writing poems or a diary. There is a growing awareness of their own body and of its similarity or difference in comparison with others. The nostalgic longing for and the loss of childhood become more bearable.

Late adolescence

After passing through the phase of 'identity versus role-diffusion' (Erikson, 1950), which started around the age of 13, the adolescent arrives round 17 or 18 years at the phase of 'intimacy versus isolation'. On the progressive scale of attachment the most characteristic concept is that of reciprocity. In this phase of late adolescence the sexual identity takes its definitive shape. The same is true of the ultimate direction of study and profession. The relationship with the parents has lost its flavour of revolt as well as of adoration and a new and more mature balance develops. The preoccupation with their own world and the exaggerated belief in themselves, for a long time a driving force in their development, disappears and reality becomes dominant. The world of the adolescent has become larger: friends, fellow students and colleagues are at least as important as parents and siblings.

Entering psychotherapy

The manifestations of the problems of adolescents looking for help are varied and complex. Adolescents can be depressive, suicidal, psychotic. They can exhibit behaviour problems ranging from being withdrawn and inaccessible to passionate acting out. They struggle with their identity, have conflicts with their parents, are unsure in their relationships with peers or exhibit psychosomatic symptoms. In a diagnostic assessment of how the adolescent is presenting him- or herself the psychotherapist will differentiate between what is normal and in accordance with the age and what is deviant. 'That's enough for me! I can't stand it any longer!!' can be a relatively normal reaction to a confrontation with a teacher, expressed perhaps a little vehemently. But it can also be a signal of an overwhelming feeling of depression and meaninglessness.

> *Albert is 14 years old. Since the death of his grandfather he has withdrawn more and more to his room. There he sits playing the guitar for hours and hours. His school achievements are deteriorating and his friends are staying away. He agrees with his parents and his class tutor that something should be done to help him out of his depressive moods. After a diagnostic assessment he enters psychotherapy.*

> *Mary, a 16-year-old, drives those around her to despair. She ran away from her mother to go and live at her father's place. She doesn't stick to any agreement and plays truant frequently. When, after a couple of months, she returns home again very late at night an argument escalates to a physical fight. After this Mary takes one of her father's sleeping pills. The family doctor succeeds in motivating her to see a specialist.*

Albert and Mary are two of the many 12- to 20-year-olds asking for psychotherapeutic help. They are doing this not so much because they are suffering from being an adolescent as because there is a burden of suffering in their environment. More often than not youngsters are coming because their parents or other important adults in their lives are seriously concerned.

Consequences for psychotherapy

Adolescence is a time of substantial physical, cognitive, emotional and social development. The psychotherapist will have to take this into account and her response has to be informed by her understanding of the distinction between normal development and signs of pathology. In the following section we shall describe which elements play a role in the development and in the maintenance of a working alliance with the adolescent (Anbeek, 1983; Geertjens, 1990; Graafsma, 1988; Meeks, 1986; Waaldijk, 1983).

Characteristics of psychotherapy with young adolescents

- Young adolescents rarely come asking for help of their own accord. Although they are able to recognize and to admit that they have problems, they often hardly dare to let this become manifest to people around them. They are afraid of losing their grip on the situation. Their self-esteem is by definition weak during this period.
- The parents almost always play a role in the therapy and a good working alliance with them is therefore a precondition for the success of the therapy. Without their co-operation there is not sufficient room to make real therapeutic work possible. This has implications for the

confidentiality of the therapy. Often the balance between openness and confidentiality is a delicate one.

- Young adolescents regard adults quite often as an extension of their parents, especially when an adult is invited by the parents to help them. The therapist cannot consider herself from the beginning as an independent person in the eyes of the client. She will have to take this into account from the very start of the contact, otherwise she will be ignoring the young client's experience and perception of the situation. Within the therapy the adolescent is in a position of dual dependency: as a client and as a child.

- The newly developed capacity for formal thinking implies opportunities and restrictions for the therapy: young adolescents are not yet very capable of self-reflection. Their thinking is often still quite egocentric (Piaget, 1970). Distancing oneself from oneself is quite a task for them.

- Another characteristic of young adolescents is that they are very action oriented and not very inclined to dwell on, or reflect on the things they are doing. They live mainly in the present. Describing or articulating their inner experiences and feelings is not easy for them. This requires from the therapist the ability to introduce into the therapy play, or playful moments. Just as in child psychotherapy, important things can be dealt with through this approach. But it should be done in a way which fits with the client's age, because nothing is as frightening for a young adolescent as being belittled (Waaldijk, 1983).

The above-mentioned age-related restriction has often led in the past to the conclusion that psychotherapy for this age group is not appropriate. Over the last 20 years a lot has changed in this respect, at least in the Netherlands. There have been many experiments and discussions but unfortunately too little has been published about both the opportunities for and the impossibility of offering therapeutic help to this age group.

Characteristics and adaptations of psychotherapy for mid- and late adolescents

It is good to be aware of how the mid- or late adolescent perceives the therapist. However young she looks or feels herself, the therapist is an adult and is experienced as such by adolescents, though some of them adopt the attitude 'we are adults together' and seem to have more life experience than the therapist believes herself to have had at that age. In this context the mid-adolescent will be looking for a substitute parent and the late adolescent more for an 'older friend'. In both situations this implies for the therapist a more active role in the shaping of the relationship than is usual in psychotherapy with an adult.

- For adolescents it is difficult to be in therapy: since their (conscious) aspirations tend primarily towards autonomy and independence, it is almost against nature to place themselves 'under treatment'. This is reinforced by the ambivalence of this phase: 'either–or' is still prevailing over 'as well as' (Anbeek, 1983). According to Swildens (1988) the asking for help has at first an element of ambivalence, of manoeuvring and sometimes of claiming or demanding. Being active, flexible, creative, not afraid of discussion, knowing how to use humour, but also being able to maintain limits and structure are abilities which the therapist cannot do without.

- In addition to this, adolescents are still developing. Their self-image, their self-concept is still in the making and therefore exposed to influences from outside. Adolescents are still learning and they are still able to develop their cognitive and emotional understanding of others and of themselves. The therapist's attitude and behaviour need to be appropriate to this context. Direct concrete questions about the adolescent's behaviour are helpful and stimulate reflection on the inner experience of their actions and reactions. Self-exploration, as it happens, may not yet have begun, but it can gradually develop in the process with the therapist. In this phase action often replaces thought or emotion (Geertjens, 1990).

- Adolescents often expect an immediate reaction from the therapist. They may do something which cannot be ignored or avoided, say something, ask for a response without delay; they may challenge. This kind of behaviour may mean a variety of things: it may be about exploring and testing boundaries, or about exploring real issues and views by protesting against others. It may be an 'expression through action' of what cannot yet be put into words. There may also be genuine direct questions such as 'How would you do this?' or 'What do you think about this?' or 'What do you think I should do?' As the adolescent becomes older and more mature such questions may become less direct and more exploratory.

The three basic conditions

In the preceding sections we have described some general considerations regarding therapeutic work with young people. Now we will explore the meaning and importance of the well-known basic conditions of client-centred psychotherapy in working with this age group.

Genuineness

Genuineness has in the description of Lietaer (1991) an inner and outer aspect, related respectively with *congruence* and *transparency*. When the therapist is open to all aspects of her own stream of emotional experience, in other words, when she is congruent, she will have an eye and an ear for the adolescent experiences stored in herself and activated by the therapeutic interaction with the adolescent. The therapist needs to be aware of 'parental feelings': not only the archaic paternal and maternal feelings which the therapist carries in herself, but also the real feelings evoked in the present therapeutic situation. The therapist expresses in a transparent way, in words understandable to the adolescent, her personal understanding. She will do this as specifically and concretely as possible, translating if necessary the personal into more universal categories and constantly being aware of the impact which a 'transparent' adult can have on a dependent, not yet fully individualized youngster.

> *Joseph, 16 years old, is referred for behavioural problems and social isolation. Hardly seated, he fires away: it was again a terrible week at home. His mother was unbearable and his father commented on everything he did. Then he talks extensively about ongoing conflicts, especially over the rules at home. He considers these rules too strict and therefore he violates them. The therapist expresses his understanding that Joseph becomes furious when he is obliged to do something and that this is very difficult in a phase in your life in which adults confront you with so many obligations. Joseph agrees, he feels understood. After this the therapist can put into words that in his view Joseph too has a role in the expanding rules and restrictions. Without feeling attacked (once more!) by an adult, Joseph begins to explore his own role in the conflicts. He discovers that he doesn't always have himself under control and that rules and agreements are still a necessary evil.*

Unconditional positive regard

Without unconditional positive regard, a therapist of adolescents cannot get far. It will be self-evident that unconditionality will not result in an attitude in which all boundaries, norms and values have disappeared. Adolescents are in search of who they are and who they will be and of what they are expecting from life. In this searching they need the therapist as a model and as a sounding board. In many ways the adolescent is demanding: 'Let me know you, therapist, as a person, so that I can recognise myself in you and can discover who I am, where I stand and where I have to go' (Driessen, 1993). Unconditional positive regard will therefore above all aim at the recognition of the uniqueness, the particularity of the single adolescent at this moment of their life. The 'here and now' prevails in their daily life over the past and, to a lesser degree, over the future.

'Positive regard' refers to concepts such as 'good enough mother' and 'the gleam in the mother's eye' (Winnicott, 1971) or in the words of Yalom, to a phase further back in time: 'the therapist's raison d'être is to be midwife to the birth of the patient's yet unlived life' (Yalom, 1980: 408).

> *Yvonne, a 16-year-old grammar school pupil, enters the therapist's room looking pale and tired. She is doing her written exams at the moment. This makes her tense and uncertain. It is difficult for her to express something of her experiences about all that in words. In fact, she doesn't want to talk about anything at all.*

The therapist doesn't push her and respects the burden of her present situation. A week later she is cheerful and says a lot about searching for a holiday job. She is very talkative. When the therapist notes the differences from her self-presentation a week ago, she becomes silent. She is embarrassed because so much in her life is changing, which frightens her.

Empathy

Empathy is an ongoing process of checking hypotheses, in which the therapist becomes acquainted with the inner world of the client in cognitive as well as in emotional respects: 'I know how you are experiencing things' and 'I am feeling what you are feeling' (Vanaerschot and Van Balen, 1991). The therapist learns to understand the client in a more and more subtle way as a unique unity of cognitions, affectivity and behaviour, situated in culture and time (De Vries, 1993). For the therapist the step to the inner world of the adult is a smaller one than the step to the inner world of the adolescent. Being able to make the connection with her own experience makes this step easier for the therapist. Besides this, knowledge of normal and pathological aspects of this developmental phase can facilitate a more accurate empathy. Interest in the rapidly changing world of adolescence enhances the empathy but identification should be avoided. De Vries (1993) mentions the necessity for the therapist to notice the deficiencies in the development of the self and the gaps in the frame of reference of the client as an aspect of empathy. Understanding the immaturity of the client's frame of reference and guiding the client in developing this is a specific task in adolescent psychotherapy.

Sabina, 16 years old, is referred because she cannot succeed in making contact with peers. She withdraws and is still very dependent on her mother. Her parents insisted strongly on treatment. In the 15th session she enters with an angry expression on her face. She says it's annoying for her to be obliged to come every week. She proposes to come only when something has happened and she has something to tell. The therapist understands that she feels forced to come and that this must be very annoying for the almost-adult she is. She proposes to explore together how the conditions can be changed so that Sabina feels free to come of her own accord, while at the same time the agreed continuity is maintained.

The interactional view

The interactional point of view stems from the interpersonal approaches to personality. H.S. Sullivan was one of the first to formulate this interpersonal theory clearly: human personality is 'the relatively enduring pattern of recurrent interpersonal situations which characterise human life' (1953: 110–11). In the interactional approach experiencing, just like thinking and acting, is seen as a process which is structured from the beginning in interaction with other people. In accordance with that view psychopathological phenomena are described using concepts of disturbed interpersonal behaviour (Kiesler, 1982): there is a reciprocal connection between someone's psychological problems and complaints and their specific attitude towards people around them.

In the Netherlands this interactional point of view is fully accepted as part of the client-centred approach. In the Dutch/Belgian textbook on the client-centred approach (Swildens et al., 1991) the interactional perspective is included and respected as an approach in client-centred work which focuses specifically on what happens between client and therapist. For those for whom this inclusion of the interactional view in a client-centred framework is new we shall first give an explanation of the interactional approach. Next we will argue why we have the conviction that especially for the age group we are speaking of here this approach is so worth while.

Short description of the interactional theory

Kiesler wrote, together with J.C. Anchin, the *Handbook of Interpersonal Psychotherapy* in 1982. As 'An Interpersonal Manifesto, Part II' is a good summary we shall quote from it as follows:

1 Problems in living are defined as disordered transactions, resulting originally and cumulatively from a person's neither attending to nor correcting the self-defeating aspects of his communications to others. The disturbed person consistently communicates, largely by non-verbal messages, a rigid and extreme self presentation and simultaneously draws a rigid and constricted response from others.

2 Despite its unique characteristics, the client–therapist interaction has major similarities to other human transactions. The client communicates to the therapist, sends the same rigid and extreme evoking messages in the same duplicitous way that he communicates with important others in his life. As a result, the therapist experiences 'live' in the sessions the client's distinctive interpersonal problems.

3 The central assessment task of the interpersonal therapist is to attend to and to identify, the client's evoking style as it unfolds over the therapy session. Central to this assessment are the therapist's own emotional and other engagements experienced with the client.

4 The therapist's priority interventions are first to stop responding in kind, in a complementary fashion, to the client's duplicitous communications. The therapist breaks the vicious transactional cycle when not continuing to be hooked or trapped by the client's engagements or pulls. Second, the therapist meta-communicates with the client about the client's evoking style and its self-defeating consequences, both with the therapist and with others outside therapy. The goal of interpersonal therapy is for the client and therapist to

discover more adaptive options, to replace constricted and extreme transactions with more flexible and congruent communications adaptive to the changing realities of specific encounters. In other words, to make him more free.

5 Statements offered to clarify the client's disordered transactions are more or less useful hypotheses, or guesses at best. To attain more adjusted living the client needs more consensually validated hypotheses about relating to others. Validation of these hypotheses comes from changes in the client's pattern of communication with both the therapist and others.

6 General propositions of interpersonal assessment and therapy need to be translated as they apply to distinct groups of clients or to distinct problems in living. (Anchin and Kiesler, 1982: 19)

This manifesto, somewhat shortened by us, offers a good overview of the theory behind interactional therapy. There is little doubt that by shifting the emphasis to the dialogue between therapist and client, the interactional approach seems to deviate somewhat from Rogers, especially from his notion of the actualizing tendency. During his lifetime, however, there was already considerable debate about the role of 'the other' in the growth process and both Martin Buber, in the famous dialogue with Rogers in 1960, and Eugene Gendlin are leading examples of those who questioned his understanding of the therapeutic relationship. What is clear, however, is that the interactional approach shares Rogers's emphasis on the import-ance of the presence of the therapist as a real person and on the importance of the 'here and now' relationship. There is, too, the same concern for deep empathic understanding and the same belief in the trustworthiness of the therapeutic process. In practice, the differences are more to do with the therapist's preparedness to be more directly active in the relationship and to confront strongly where this is appropriate. These changes in emphasis are discernible in other followers of Rogers and spring from a realization that a more extensive repertoire of responses offers more options to the therapist and more possibilities for furthering the thera-peutic process.

Psychotherapy with adolescents from an interactional point of view:
worthwhile or not?

Adolescence is the period in which the search for identity is the most pressing developmental task. This search occurs principally in an intensive interaction with the environment. External dialogue plays a vital role in this development. This dialogue takes place both with adults who are important for the adolescent, for instance parents, teachers and with peers. In no other phase of life is the focus on peers so strong and decisive. Given this overriding emphasis on the interpersonal, it seems worthwhile to find out if the therapeutic possibilities of the interactional view are especially suitable for this phase of human development. In exploring this question we refer to van Kessel and van der Linden (1991a, 1991b), two Dutch representatives of the interactional way of thinking. They contend that the therapeutic dialogue can be seen as the medium through which the interpersonal rigidified structure can be actualized, explored and then revised. Rigid interaction can be experienced in the process and once it is loosened up the internal dialogue, too, will become more open and more free. Van Kessel and van der Linden describe four characteristics which are necessary for the therapeutic dialogue to make the therapeutic process effective. We shall summarize these characteristics briefly and then explore how they can be used and eventually adapted in psychotherapy, especially with young adolescents. It is self-evident that the older the adolescent, the more the therapeutic relationship can resemble the relationship with the adult client.

The therapist works with a different priority regarding levels of communication

Communication takes place on two levels: the level of content, which is normally explicit in the foreground, and the level of relationship, which is normally implicit, unspoken, in the background. The interactional therapist turns the usual relationship between content and relational aspects upside down, and gives priority to relationship above content in the communication. The role of the therapist is characterized by Sullivan as that of 'participant observer': participating in the conversation as well as being open to her own feelings, so that she can better perceive the appeal the client is making to her and therefore be better able to articulate and respond to the relational aspect.

> *Sandra, a 13-year-old, is for the first time in a therapy session. After diagnostic assessment and an advisory interview with Sandra and her parents the decision was taken to start individual psychotherapy. The therapist starts with her usual statement about the how and why of psychotherapy, but is quite soon interrupted by Sandra: 'First of all, I would like to know who you are!*

How to respond? To begin with, the therapist brings into her awareness how this question touches her. Does she feel attacked by the youngster? Is she embarrassed? Is she angry? Has she any idea why the client is asking this? Her answer will depend on her hypothesis in response to these questions. With adults it will probably be a question of exploring why the client is asking this question. In doing so, the relational aspect is given priority over the content. With young adolescents this will probably result in their soon leaving the therapy room. Generally, especially at the beginning of therapy, it is advisable to give a direct answer before finding out cautiously what makes the client ask the question. The young person's still very concrete way of thinking, as well as the easily triggered anxiety (resulting from uncertainty about their own situation, and from their need for control) makes such a direct response necessary. In any form of therapy with young adolescents and thus also in the interactional method, their developmental phase must always be taken into account. Heuves in his dissertation about depression in male young adolescents writes that

> much epidemiological research about the psychological well-being of (young) adolescents overlooks the clinically stated fact that these youngsters are not able, or only under specific conditions, prepared to describe their inner feelings adequately before an adult. This makes the validity of this research far from satisfactory. (Heuves, 1990)

The young adolescent often is so busy with controlling or hiding their own feelings behind the façade of indifference that explicit articulation is not advisable, and certainly not at the beginning of therapy. It is often better to start with discussing fixed patterns of behaviour or to explore difficult situations. In doing so, the therapist learns a lot about the 'external dialogue' of the youngster, their way of behaving and making contact. Besides this talking together, joining in shared practical activities with the young adolescent during therapy is sometimes desirable. Often used are the so-called 'action techniques' such as drawing, making cartoon stories, games, and so on. The motto is: we do not just talk; we also do (Waaldijk, 1983). Later on in the therapy, when the working alliance is established, the client can more easily go into interactional feelings, naming them and discussing them. Young adolescents very much need a safe situation before being able to confront their own behaviour and feelings.

In late adolescence the client is, thanks to increased control over body and emotions, better able to perceive and to describe feelings and to reflect on them. This is particularly true with regard to the perception of other people, of important peers or adults. Adolescents are engaged in a journey of exploration, looking for themselves with themselves. Therefore they 'use' the therapist who might be a guide in this process. Not a guide walking ahead and indicating the road, but a guide who helps to discover opportunities and impossibilities, chances and risks. The content of the communication (equivalent of the 'doing together' in the case of the young adolescent) will regularly be the vehicle to explore the relational aspects. This implies, of course, much discussion about situations with friends, about school experiences, and so on. When therapist and youngster become more acquainted and at ease with each other, when the therapy situation becomes safe enough, when the young client becomes accustomed to the different kind of dialogue, there will be more room for explicit attention to relational aspects of the therapy situation itself.

The therapist avoids reinforcing the habitual interactional style of the client

Instead of giving in to the interactional appeal, the therapist tries to let the client discover what the significance of that appeal is and how the client tries to involve the other (the therapist) in it, how they try to get the other to react in an acceptable way for them. The therapist's attitude is not so much to give a client answers as to confront them with themselves. This will give rise to anxiety and confusion in the client. It is the therapist's task to regulate the intensity of these emotions. Beier (1966) speaks in this context of 'beneficial uncertainty'.

> *Charles, 15 years old, enters the therapy room and sits somewhat crouched and silent in his chair. The invitation of the therapist to indicate what he would like to talk about today is followed only by a shrug. It is not the first time that this has occurred; it is a recurrent pattern in every session. To the next question, whether anything special happened this week, he answers also in the negative: 'as usual, nothing special . . .'.*

For many therapists of adolescents this is a recognizable situation. The youngster tries to force the initiative upon the therapist. Probably this is the habitual style of interaction with adults. His parents, too, get the same answer to their question about how things were at school: 'As usual, nothing special!'

This second principle of interactional therapy is particularly relevant in working with this age group, and easily creates tension in this relationship, too. As the therapist's response contributes to an increase in uncertainty and confusion the risk of the client quitting, shutting up or denying becomes greater, especially when the therapist persists in implying that it is the task of the client to propose the theme for the session and refuses to help the youngster to do this. Should she give in to the client's resistance and start to enquire into the school, the client's mood and such things, then she runs the risk of meeting the same dilemma in the next session. So it is important that she makes it clear that the initiative is up to the client and why, but that she is also prepared to help him to learn to take the initiative and that she understands that taking responsibility for the therapy is frightening. Being silent may originate from the client's feeling that he has been made to go to therapy.

Apart from this, another characteristic of the young adolescent may block the therapy: in the search for their own identity they are very much experimenting. Patterns are not yet that fixed so it is a pitfall for the therapist to get swept along by the different 'roles' played by the client. Some adolescents can surprise the therapist time and time again by entering in an outfit or mood or with an attitude totally different from the last session.

In the older adolescent identity is more or less shaped. They are more oriented towards the world outside them and are in search of contact with other people. After a period of introvertedness in early adolescence there comes a period of extrovertedness in mid- and late adolescence (Gemengde GHIGV Werkgroep, 1991). The client is experimenting with interactions. Although there is now a more stable formation of identity, the therapist must nevertheless be alert to the difference between 'the identity in evolution' and 'exercises in identity' presented by the youngster. She should be aware that her presence and her position as therapist are influencing these 'identity experiments'.

The therapist can give interpretations, but only in an interactional way

Traditionally a basic principle of the client-centred approach is that no interpretations are given but that the therapist only creates the conditions under which the client can give new meaning to their experience. The interactional view is not content to leave it at that. The hope of renewal originating from the client is too restricted, because they can stay imprisoned in the logic and self-evidence of their own restricted style of interaction. The passing of new meanings to them is therefore permitted. The interactional analysis of the problems (developed by the therapist during the process) may clarify much for the client and can become meaningful for them. Quite often the relationships with key figures in the client's past will be dealt with in this context. This third characteristic of the interactional approach will at first sight imply little difficulty for our target group. The more active, more directive role seems to be quite fitting for the therapist of adolescents. But for these youngsters, interpretations may often have the connotation of 'the adult who always knows better'. They may easily feel restricted. The therapist should also be aware that young adolescents in particular are often too automatically prepared to give in, to be influenced and to adopt such suggestions without having chosen them themselves. In this context techniques working more indirectly may be helpful. For instance: an older person appearing in an imaginative story, created by the client and the therapist together, pondering on the advantages and disadvantages of different solutions is stimulating the young adolescent more towards their own personal decision. A somewhat older adolescent, being in a process of separation and individualization, will sometimes refuse explicitly to be influenced by the therapist. In that case, interventions aimed at uncovering, exploring and expressing meaning with the client or offering a new perspective on their experience may be more helpful.

The therapeutic relationship is handled as the medium of change

Psychotherapy is here conceived as a social process of influencing in which the interaction of client and therapist is handled as an instrument for diagnostic clarification as well as for therapeutic change. The therapist's 'anti-social' responses, that is, responses which are different from what is socially expected and which are challenging of the client's normal interactional style (Beier, 1966) are not only frustrating in that they compel the client to react in a different way than usual, which is frightening, but they are also positively appealing as an invitation to a renewal and expansion of communication.

> *Barry, 14 years old, is referred for a second time to the Outpatient Clinic, because according to his parents he is not doing well. He is obstinate, does poorly at school and is difficult to approach. He agreed to have individual therapy but not with much enthusiasm. The first sessions prove difficult, with a poor contribution from Barry himself. The therapist has to drag things out of him. At a certain moment the therapist says: 'That seems to be pretty awful, your parents being really concerned about you and you not at all understanding really why. That must be a very annoying feeling indeed.' For the first time Barry looks the therapist in the eye, sits up straight and says, more or less surprised: 'Yes, that is how it is.' From that moment on the therapy takes a more constructive course.*

The giving of anti-social responses from the very beginning enlarges the opportunities for the client to learn. This is all the more desirable because young adolescents generally are not inclined to stick long to therapy. As soon as they have the slightest idea that they can manage they will want to stop. The challenge to the youngster to invent time and time again alternative responses obviously meets their need for experimentation. Here the question can be raised whether for young adolescents the group as the medium for change should not have an important place. Some people take the view that the inclination of this age group to act quickly, instead of to think and talk, often intensifies the problem of keeping order in the group, so much so that therapeutic activity is blocked. Others, however, see many opportunities for learning, by verbal and non-verbal techniques from and with peers (Dijkhuizen, 1993; Eijkman, 1993; Tijhuis, 1988). The combination of individual and group therapy with adolescents is often used in psychiatric clinics (Geertjens, 1994). In a somewhat later stage of development the relationship between client and therapist can be used in a more direct and active way as a means to therapeutic change. The mid-adolescent still harbours a strong need for identification with the therapist, whereas the late adolescent is often already able to distinguish between the concrete here-and-now interaction with the therapist and the more general aspects of relating with an adult other. The therapeutic relationship then becomes increasingly an instrument for change.

Conclusion

The basic conditions of client-centred psychotherapy are valuable in the treatment of adolescents on the condition that they are adapted to the developmental phase of the client. The interactional psychotherapeutic view within this approach appears to be quite useful for this age group: the growing involvement with peers, the strong focus on the present, on the here and now, the self-development in the interaction with the other – all this finds much resonance with the interactional outlook. But there are problems too: the therapist is often confronted with the still weak capacity for self-reflection and the strong action-directedness of the young adolescent and with the changing, developing self of the mid- and late adolescent.

Experimentation will almost certainly be a continuing part of the process for client-centred therapists who choose to work with this volatile age group for whom experimentation is a necessary path to self-discovery.

References

Anbeek, M. (1983) 'De werkrelatie in de psychotherapie met adolescenten, een trias', in *Psychotherapie met adolescenten, verslagboek Twents Symposium Adolescenten Psychotherapie*. Hengelo: Stichting STAP. pp. 76–106.

Anchin, Jack C. and Kiesler, Donald J. (1982) *Handbook of Interpersonal Psychotherapy*. New York: Pergamon.

Beier, Ernst G. (1966) *The Silent Language of Psychotherapy: Social Reinforcement of Unconscious Processes*. Chigago: Aldine.

Blos, Peter (1962) *On Adolescence*. New York: Free Press.

Buber, Martin and Rogers, Carl (1960) 'Dialogue between Martin Buber and Carl Rogers', *Psychologia*, 3: 208–21.

De Vries, J.H.P. (1993) 'Empathie in de procesgerichte gesprekstherapie', *Tijdschrift voor Psychotherapie*, 19 (6): 334–48.

De Wit, J. van der Veer, G. and Slot, N.W. (1995) *Psychologie van de adolescentie*. Baarn: Intro.

Driessen, A.C. (1984) 'Opleiding in de psychotherapie met adolescenten', *Kind en Adolescent*, 5 (3): 118–32.

Driessen, A.C. (1993) 'Separatie en individuatie bij adolescenten en de communicatie met de therapeut', *Tijdschrift voor Cliëntgerichte Gesprekstherapie*, 31 (3): 19–31.

Dijkhuizen, G. (1993) 'Creatieve therapie drama in de jeugdpsychiatrische kliniek: laveren tussen hoofdrol en rekwisietenlaatje', in F. Verhey, R. Eijsberg and A. van Strien (eds), *Klinische Kinder- en Jeugpsychiatrie, Praktijk en Visie*. Assen: Van Gorcum.

Eijkman, J.C.B. (1993) 'Groepstherapie met adolescenten', in *Praktijkboek Groepspsychotherapie*. Amersfoort: Academische Uitgeverij.

Erikson, E.H. (1950) *Childhood and Society*. New York: Norton.

Geertjens, L. (1990) 'Adolescenten', *Maandblad Geestelijke Volksgezondheid*, 45 (7/8): 744–6.

Geertjens, L. (1994) 'Individuele psychotherapie met adolescenten in een klinisch-psychiatrische setting', *Kinder- en Jeugdpsychotherapie*, 21 (4): 151–70.

Gemengde GHIGV Werkgroep (1991) *Klinische Psychotherapie voor Adolescenten*. Ministerie WVC.

Graafsma, T. (1988) 'De adolescent in de analytische situatie', in B. Driessen and H. de Hoogh (eds), *Psychotherapie met Adolescenten*. Den Haag: Van Loghum Slaterus. pp. 143–69.

Heuves, W. (1990) 'Depression in young male adolescents: theoretical and clinical aspects'. PhD dissertation, University of Leiden.

Kiesler, D.J. (1982) 'Interpersonal theory for personality and psychology', in J.C. Anchin and D.J. Kiesler (eds), *Handbook of Interpersonal Psychotherapy*. New York: Pergamon Press.

Lietaer, G. (1991) 'Authenticiteit en onvoorwaardelijke positieve gezindheid', in H. Swildens (chief ed.), *Leerboek Gesprekstherapie: De Cliëntgerichte Benadering.* Amersfoort and Leuven: Acco. pp. 27–65.

Meeks, J.E. (1986) *The Fragile Alliance.* Malabar: Krieger.

Nagera, H. (1966) *Stoornissen in de vroege jeugd, de neurose in de kindertijd en de stoornissen van volwassenen.* Rotterdam: Donker.

Piaget, J. (1970) *De Psychologie van de Intelligentie.* Amsterdam: J.H. de Bussy.

Rutter, M., Graham, P., Chadwick, O.F.D. and Yule, W. (1976) 'Adolescent turmoil: fact or fiction?', *Journal of Child Psychology and Psychiatry*, 17: 35–56.

Sullivan, H.S. (1953) *Interpersonal Theory of Psychiatry.* New York: Norton.

Swildens, H. (1988) 'Client-centered psychotherapie bij adolescenten: het begeleiden van een crisis', in B. Driessen and H. de Hoogh (eds), *Psychotherapie met Adolescenten.* Den Haag: Van Loghum Slaterus. pp. 169–83.

Swildens, H. et al. (1991) *Leerboek Gesprekstherapie: De Cliëntgerichte Benadering.* Amersfoort and Leuven: Acco.

Tijhuis, L. (1988) 'Groepspsychotherapie met adolescenten', in B. Driessen and H. de Hoogh (eds), *Psychotherapie met Adolescenten.* Den Haag: Van Loghum Slaterus. pp. 200–27.

Vanaerschot, G. and Van Balen, R. (1991) 'Empathie', in H. Swildens (chief ed.), *Leerboek Gesprekstherapie. De Cliëntgerichte Benadering.* Amersfoort and Leuven: Acco. pp. 93–139.

Van Kessel, W. and van der Linden, P. (1991a) 'De hier-en-nu relatie in cliëntgerichte therapie; het interactionele gezichtspunt', in H. Swildens (chief ed.), *Leerboek Gesprekstherapie: De Cliëntgerichte Benadering.* Amersfoort and Leuven: Acco. pp. 223–50.

Van Kessel, W. and van der Linden, P. (1991b) 'De interactioneel gerichte therapeut aan het werk', in H. Swildens (chief ed.), *Leerboek Gesprekstherapie: De Cliëntgerichte Benadering.* Amersfoort and Leuven: Acco. pp. 377–95.

Waaldijk, O.(1983) 'Niet (alleen) praten maar (ook) doen', in *Congresboek Twents Symposium Adolescenten.* uitgave Stichting STAP Hengelo. Verkort verschenen in *Kind en Adolescent*, 5 (3): 209–24.

Weiner, I. (1988) 'De mythe van de normale onaangepastheid in de adolescentie', in B. Driessen and H. de Hoogh (eds), *Psychotherapie met Adolescenten.* Den Haag: Van Loghum Slaterus. pp. 99–141.

Winnicott, D.W. (1971) *Playing and Reality.* Harmondsworth: Penguin.

Yalom, I. (1980) *Existential Psychotherapy.* New York: Basic Books.

13   A Person-Centred Perspective on Leadership and Team-Building

Leif J. Braaten

After more than 20 years of clinical work with the 'losers' of society I have switched over the last 15 years to offering group therapy to and consulting with the 'winners' in business and industry. One approach is to run year-long self development groups with top and middle-range leaders. The other approach is to initiate self- and organizational development through consulting with groups of leaders who actually work together. Participants for such groups are recruited through an advertisement lodged in the Norwegian equivalent of the London *Financial Times*. The text of the advertisement for the most recent group reads as follows:

> New Self Development Group for Leaders in Business and Industry facilitated by L.J.B. and K.I. starts Sept. 3, 1996 under our joint leadership. We meet downtown Oslo eight Tuesdays 5.–8. p. m. during the Fall, with eight follow-up meeetings from Jan. 14, 1997. The target group is women and men in leadership positions who need professional assistance in order to exploit even more effectively their leadership resources and their personal qualities, or who at times are functioning below their desired level of performance. Contact the group leaders . . .

This text has been carefully developed so as not to put off potential candidates by implying that we are seeking clients for therapy. Typically those who respond are performing at least reasonably well in their positions, but they have the mature judgement that they want to improve further, both as leaders and in their private lives.

Why work with leaders?

The history of my interest in group work is perhaps revealing. After my postgraduate training in Chicago in the late 1950s with Rogers and his staff and four years as a professor of clinical psychology at Cornell University, Ithaca, New York, I returned to my native country, Norway, in 1964. From then on I was a professor at the Institute of Psychology, training students to become professional psychologists. Simultaneously I pioneered a Student Mental Health Service from 1967, where in addition to individual therapy I started offering group therapy to students and staff with emotional problems.

Some years later I began offering group therapy to colleagues in leadership positions in the mental health field, mainly psychiatrists, psychologists and social workers. Like myself they had leadership positions which involved considerable stress, and needed a place to work on their self-improvement.

A few years later a professor colleague of mine at the Institute asked me on behalf of a friend and leader in the insurance business if I could offer a self-development programme to a team of ten leaders in that business. I accepted the challenge, and in this way I got started with leadership training and team-building in business and industry. Like many of my colleagues, I also tried to make use of my services outside the university, in order to broaden my experience and usefulness.

It seems fitting now to say a few words about leaders as a client group, and how they are similar to and different from other categories of help-seekers. Leaders, like everyone else, have their share of life's successes and miseries, even if they tend in public to minimize stresses and strains. Many of them have the humility to believe that they can become better leaders. They know, too, that they have at times worked below their desired capacities. Effective and humane leadership is more important than ever in our time, both in politics and in business and administration. Leaders are the key people who shape the organizational culture, which again determines in part the mental and physical health of all employees.

Furthermore, it is a challenge to try to cultivate positive self-development in persons, and not merely to correct emotional problems. Knowledge about positive mental health is actually of general interest and relevance for helping all kinds of clients. It has been exciting and rewarding to work with this client group, because they often improve themselves, and in addition they influence in a positive way the functioning of their leadership teams.

Brief historical note about person-centred group work

Before I proceed further, it is constructive to offer a brief review of group work within the person-centred tradition. At the Counseling Center in Chicago during the 1950s we were trained with a student-centred group approach. It was a blend of a traditional didactic education and experiential learning through the group process. But there was no formal training in group therapy.

At the Institute of Psychology in Oslo I have further developed this type of training, making considerable use of role-playing and self-development groups for students. Inspired by Rogers's classic *Freedom to Learn* (1969)

I wrote a book with the title *Psychotherapeutic Learning through the Group Process* (1974), which reported on my attempts to facilitate experiential learning for psychology students so that they could become better professionals.

The interested reader is referred to an excellent historical summary of the group as an instrument for person-centred clinical work by Lietaer and Dierick (1996). I agree with these writers that there has been little emphasis on group therapy within the person-centred tradition, with the notable exception of Rogers's influential book *On Encounter Groups* (1970). Another influential arena has been person-centred work with large groups which has taken place in many different parts of the world (Rogers, 1980). The principles of individual client-centred therapy have, however, been applied somewhat uncritically to the group approach. I shall attempt in this chapter to present a viable model of person-centred group therapy which can be a legitimate alternative to the action-oriented and psycho-analytically oriented group therapies which dominate the field today.

General process themes of leaders

I have emphasized the need to offer a coherent presentation of person-centred group therapy, precisely because I believe we actually have a viable alternative worth considering, both for professionals and for members of the public. In my new book *Leader Development and Team-Building in Norwegian Organizations* I describe more fully certain process themes of leaders (Braaten, 1997). Here I can only present such themes in brief outline.

Early themes of process

Most groups manage to develop a good team spirit during the first few sessions, and participants are thrilled by this accomplishment. Early themes of process will include universalism, that is the discovery that we are actually more similar than different in our make-up. Clients learn most through self disclosure, but they also gain by listening to others and vicariously learning through their experiencing. Norms and rules are developed to facilitate the group process. Test results are shared to provide the group with useful baselines for self-development projects and the resolution of emotional problems. Role possibilities and limitations are discovered, for example, co-leader, door opener, care person, provider of law and order, and being the clown.

Advanced themes of process

Intrapsychic tasks may include: the search for one's true identity, learning to express feelings more spontaneously, honest self-confrontation, developing a sense of humour, daring to risk oneself in business and in private life, overcoming the tyranny of perfectionism, and developing a proper self-care.

Interpersonal concerns deal with issues such as the following: fear of authorities, too much emotional control while in the company of others, fear of intimacy, loyalty versus confrontation, the significance of support and alliances, learning to really care for each other, and developing a professional attitude to conflict resolution.

Finally, there are 'whole group' matters that surface: too much dependency in relation to the formal leader, the challenge of sharing the responsibility for the group, the experience of we-ness, the necesssity of differentiating the self from others, learning to offer constructive feedback, and dealing with the dangers of scapegoating.

Long-term themes of process

A basic, long-range goal is to help participants develop increased vitality, and to foster access to life energy and resources. Personal and professional maturity is seen in terms of a balanced integration of the child self and the grown-up self. Such a person is better able to take overall responsibility for himself/herself.

The mature person learns to exploit constructively the perhaps small margin of freedom of choice. It is important to be able to be one's own person, as well as being able to build healthy and stable attachments to significant other people in one's life. It is desirable to achieve a good integration of the intellect, the heart, and intuitive gut feelings.

Such a person finds it easier to do what he/she really enjoys, without this being at the cost of other people. He/she has a positive sense of appreciating the new and unknown and understands the importance of both to be your own best friend and to be truly interested in others. Finally, many clients discover the paradox that closeness gives freedom, and freedom creates an appetite for intimacy.

Personal themes in a particular group

There now follow vignettes of members drawn from a group I facilitated some years ago, who are in many ways representative of the 500 or so leaders with whom I have worked during the past decade.

A woman, who often appeared in touch with others and with her sense of humour, wanted to become less tense and rational in her relationships. She had to learn to perceive the anxieties of others, which was often difficult for her because of her own personal power. She further hoped to become less of a workaholic and to develop her sense of intimacy. She had to work through her depression, her compulsiveness and her ritualism. At the profoundest level she struggled to overcome her great shame about her father's alcoholism in her childhood home.

A man, who was generous, attentive, and an especially good 'student', was preoccupied with becoming less overly impressed by people with an academic background, because he lacked that himself, although he had had outstanding success in business. He became less fanatical about directing everybody and everything. He became less dependent upon others for praise and recognition and more naturally accepting of his own great competence at his job and in life generally. Deep inside he attempted to overcome his bitterness about the poverty he experienced in his childhood, which persisted despite his demonstrable financial success later in life.

Another man, with considerable courage and integrity, wished to become less reserved, authoritarian and conformist. He tried to develop greater tolerance for feelings – both within himself and in others. He tried to reduce his habit of pointing out the problems of others, and to cultivate instead his role as the 'house philosopher and elder statesman'.

A woman, with natural professional authority and confidence, wanted no longer simply to be nice and well dressed. A major theme for her was to establish a better balance between being withdrawn, inferior and not self-assertive enough, and an exaggerated sense of pride and ambition. She wanted to become less overly sensitive when criticized or when she was experiencing difficult times, and to reduce the bitterness in connection with her very traumatic childhood.

A caring and self-sacrificing man was always eager to learn and struggled to really change for the better. He also wanted to become less impressed by authorities, and able to accept himself as an authority. He worked to become less weak and super-dependent, more able to be properly self-assertive, both socially and in life generally.

A woman was professionally capable, trustworthy, always someone who wanted to work hard, and was eager to learn. But she was no longer content just to be young, pretty and a conformist, and wished to stop yielding so much in a male-dominated social environment. She tried to become less formal, rational, less the great harmonizer, and to become less impressed by all kinds of authority. She wanted to exploit her own considerable authority, rather than submitting to others.

Another man had a big heart, great charm and a sense of humour, but needed to have more insight into his disabling depression and his sense of burnout. He struggled with his personal style as a pioneer in business, and his tendency to resist delegating appropriate reponsibility to his excellent staff. In a similar manner to quite a few of the others he tried hard to overcome his feeling of inferiority because he did not have much higher education. As far as self-esteem went, it did not matter that he had obtained great success in his maritime business. He became better at establishing intimacy in his daily interactions. He ceased to idealize so persistently his gifted friends all around the globe.

Another male participant, who was kind, attentive and service-minded, worked to become more trusting of other people. He was vulnerable in his sense of self-esteem, and became depressed and experienced a midlife crisis. He wanted to improve a destructive relationship with his twin brother, who operated in the same business as himself. He was also concerned about some problems connected with being a pioneer in his branch of business, especially his inability to let go of his control of everybody and everything.

The next man was personally independent and occasionally offered creative comments to the group, which impressed us all. He made great efforts to become more intimate, instead of impressing us as a philosophizing word manipulator. He also struggled to obtain better control over his rage and his rebelliousness, and to dampen down his extreme criticism and suspiciousness.

The last man in this group was very loyal, supportive, warm and, in addition, willing to risk himself. He made great efforts to become less vague, more direct, not always the one who offered compliments to everybody. Behind this pleasing façade he discovered considerable hostility, which he tried to get out of his system. In contrast to the business pioneers described above he delegated too much responsibility, and did not follow up properly. He realized that he literally had to get used to looking people in the eye in order to establish good contact and communication.

An insightful and professional woman worked to become less passive-aggressive, less systematically naughty in order to prove that she was not the excessive harmonizer. In her own words she said that she was searching to rediscover her real self. She desired to take more responsibility for herself, develop a greater tolerance for taking risks, and work through her midlife crisis.

Finally, there was a woman who was seductive, charming and creative, but struggled to train herself to adopt the framework of the other, that is to improve her empathic understanding. She also desired to develop more equality in human interaction generally, and had a need to become clear about the boundaries between the I and Thou. A related theme for her was to increase her credibility regarding all kinds of transactions in life, not least in relation to economic matters.

These participants, as is clear from the above vignettes, were concerned with a mixture of leadership themes and emotional problems from their private lives, revealing the fact that human beings are basically one and the same at work and at home. However, the emphasis in such self-development groups is always on the work arena. Problems relating to authority and delegation were central themes. Difficulties in interaction and bad communication were often focused upon. Several clients struggled to develop the significant leader qualities necessary in modern society. Finally, a common theme was the shame harboured deep down in the human mind, which typically had its origin in deficits and traumas in childhood and gave rise to bitter memories that often poisoned the lives of these now grown-up people.

Core therapy conditions and techniques

I shall now turn to describing the person-centred model for group work, and shall attempt to clarify the similarities and differences compared to individual work. Hopefully this model may serve as an inspiration for those wishing to apply the person-centred approach in other spheres.

During the late 1950s I was a doctoral student at the Counseling Center at the University of Chicago, with Rogers as the inspiring leader. It appears in retrospect a happy coincidence of history that we, the doctoral students, were actually present when he first presented his classical model of the necessary and sufficient conditions for psychotherapeutic personality change (1957). At the time we were politely impressed, but argued as critical graduate students that he was greatly oversimplifying a serious matter. Only as the decades passed did we realize his stroke of genius, as he advocated heuristically that the famous conditions actually were necessary and sufficient.

More comprehensive discussions of this model are offered by Mearns and Thorne (1988), Prouty (1994), Raskin (1985), Meador and Rogers (1979), and for the group therapy format Lietaer and Dierick (1996), and Schmid (1994). In the following paragraphs I have attempted to follow the advice of Watson (1984) who appealed to therapy researchers to attempt to describe and evaluate the model as a whole, not just parts of it.

In this spirit, about ten years ago, I constructed a *Group Climate Questionnaire – Person-Centred Form* (Braaten, 1986a) with 15 items tapping the famous Rogers (1957) model of 'the necessary and sufficient conditions for psychotherapeutic personality change': client anxiety and vulnerability, therapist genuineness, therapist unconditional positive regard, and therapist accurate empathy. This questionnaire was routinely filled out during the last five minutes of each group session. The results were fed back to the group at the beginning of the next session in terms of a mean group climate profile, and a print-out which showed individual group climate evaluations.

Client anxiety and vulnerability

It will be recalled that Rogers claimed that the only condition necessary for the client was his or her anxiety or vulnerability. The group climate items anchoring this dimension read as follows: 'The members became anxious when difficult problems were touched on.' 'The members appeared in fact vulnerable or insecure.'

I have checked empirically this hypothesis and found that *there exists a curvilinear relationship between anxiety and the positive effects of therapy* (Braaten, 1994b). In other words, there appears to exist a moderate range of anxiety which triggers serious, dedicated therapeutic work, whereas too little or too much anxiety does not produce good results. Similar current concepts are: depth of self-exploration, self-relatedness, and psychological-mindedness.

I found, somewhat surprisingly in the light of Rogers's hypothesis, that anxiety was not related to an explicit item about motivation for treatment. Instead motivation was clearly related to the client's experience of the therapist conditions of unconditional positive regard and accurate empathy.

Therapist genuineness

I found that genuineness sets an upper limit to the other therapeutic conditions (Braaten, 1994a). These group climate items operationalize this condition: 'The members were open and honest toward each other.' 'The members told each other exactly what they actually thought and felt.' 'The members challenged and confronted each other in order to expose the true self.'

Let me now turn to the relationship between the conditions. You cannot be more acceptant and empathic than you actually feel toward a particular client at any one time. I have struggled throughout my career to become increasingly more of what is harboured within me as a person. Thus I have opened myself progressively to anxiety, anger, sadness, spontaneity and humour. In addition to the satisfaction of experiencing personal development, it has become apparent to me that the personality of the therapist sets limits to his or her usefulness for clients. *The richer, broader, more mature person you are, the better you can mirror back to your client every kind of human quality.* In principle, as a therapist, you are also, in some measure, available to disclose aspects of your own person, but only in the spirit of being committed to facilitating the growth process of your client. To be genuine means that you are integrated, that you are your real self, not a pretence, that you can serve as a reasonably mature model of the good life for your client.

Therapist unconditional positive regard

Most colleagues within the person-centred tradition have emphasized accurate empathy as the most significant core condition. *I have always felt acceptance to be the more basic condition of the two.* Here some relevant group climate items should be mentioned: 'The members liked and cared for each other.' 'The members confirmed each other as unique persons.' 'The members valued each other regardless of whether the communication was positive or negative.'

The essence of the false self is that the client has been forced to introject conditions of worth in order to be shown positive regard, which psychologically is so vital for one's mental survival and growth. From the current perspective of Kohut (1977) the typical client is deprived of adequate acceptant mirroring during the crucial pre-Oedipal period of life. Interestingly, I found that clients cannot actually discriminate between positive regard and empathy (Braaten, 1994a). Therefore, in honour of Rogers, I call a new combined core condition *empathic positive regard*. This does not mean, however, that we should no longer distinguish between the two. Rather it means that usually they go together for both the sender and the receiver. Related concepts to unconditional positive regard are the following: to really care, show compassion, be non-judgemental, offer nurturance and support, and respect for positive resources.

Therapist accurate empathy

In order to accept a person you must clearly know him or her. Therefore, accurate empathy can be seen as the main vehicle for building acceptance and positive regard. The group climate empathy items are: 'The members showed understanding for the special self-experience of each other.' 'The members attempted to get at the meaning each one attributed to their experience.' 'The members understood each other spontaneously and immediately without any special efforts.'

When as a group leader I occasionally have trouble in accepting a participant, I work diligently at empathy in order to arrive at a break-through in acceptance. *'Now that I really know you, I can also accept you'*. Related concepts include: accurate understanding, appreciation of affective experiencing, focusing on felt experiencing, and emotional resonance.

The interrelationship of the conditions

Meador and Rogers argue that the three conditions are not distinct states of being; they are interdependent and logically related:

> In the first place, the therapist must achieve a strong, accurate empathy. But such deep sensitivity to the moment-to-moment 'being' of another person requires that the therapist accepts, and to some degree prizes, the other person. That is to say, a sufficiently strong empathy can scarcely exist without a considerable degree of unconditional positive regard. However, since neither of these conditions can possibly be meaningful in the relationship unless they are real, the therapist must be . . . integrated and genuine. . . . Therefore, it seems to me that *genuineness or congruence is the most basic of the three conditions*. (Meador and Rogers, 1979: 132; italics added)

To the alert reader Rogers confirms a certain bias towards empathy among the conditions, but appears not to be far from appreciating the integration of empathy and positive regard, what I am now calling empathic positive regard. We both agree that the therapist must be genuinely acceptant and empathic in order to reach a client effectively.

Implementing conditions through techniques

I have for many years taken the position that the therapeutic conditions are basic, whereas the clinician can feel free to exploit the large variety of techniques which have been offered by countless innovators from different orientations. Because of space limitations only a few examples can be mentioned. *Humour* can occasionally show the client genuineness. *Touch* is once in a while the means of expressing that you really care. *Reframing* can sometimes be quite effective in conveying accurate empathy.

Intrapsychic interventions

The old client-centred self-concept was more intrapsychic, whereas the new, evolving person-centred self-concept emphasizes more a dimension of bonding and connectedness. I have recently proposed a revised notion of the self-concept with an equal emphasis on the unique, private self and the dependent, social self (Braaten, 1996). Although Rogers always thought of the relationship between the therapist and the client as a major source of psychological growth, he placed emphasis, like Freud and Jung, on an intrapsychic self. Therefore, he was surprised when, in my new instrument to measure positive self-development, I documented that *the self appeared to have three interpersonal dimensions first, and only then two intrapsychic dispositions* (Braaten, 1989b).

A minority of contemporary group therapists are actually performing what is almost individual therapy in a group setting. In such groups therapist interventions might include: 'When under pressure, you sometimes turn pale because you are afraid.' 'You have not cried real tears ever since you were a child.' 'If you are not perfect, you become panicky.' I also offer many intrapsychic interventions for the individual participant, but always with a keen awareness of the presence of the others.

Interpersonal interventions

Consistent with the above-mentioned revised concept of the self, I am equally inclined to look for the manifestations of the dependent, social self within the group process. Like the leading exponent of group therapy, Yalom (1995), I am struck by how often the interpersonal problems of the participants are played out in the here-and-now interaction. Since the origin of psychopathology is often social, the group is a most congenial arena where the healing of many interpersonal problems can take place.

Some illustrations of interpersonal interventions might be: 'When you talked about the violent streak in you, I must admit that I felt quite frightened.' 'You appear to be so overly self-sufficient that it seems almost impossible for you to accept our advice.' 'When you are challenged by our questions, you have these quick, pre-fabricated answers, which appear without any attempt to think about them here and now.' I often exploit the live, dynamic group interaction in the present, because such material carries more weight than reports about the there and then somewhere else.

Group-as-a-whole interventions

Some group therapists on the current scene advocate a systems approach, that is a consistent focus on what goes on in the group as a whole (Klein, 1992). This Bion-inspired T-group approach looks at the group as if it were an organism or a person. To the great frustration of many group members, such group leaders refuse to offer comments to individuals. Nevertheless, they claim that you cannot individuate unless you see yourself in relation to the others in the group. They are concerned about the boundaries between the group and the outside. They assume that the total group typically moves through certain, predetermined phases. They trust the group to do most of the work, but claim that only the group leader is in a position to actually observe group-as-a-whole phenomena.

Quantitatively speaking I do not engage in a lot of group-as-a-whole interventions. However, I have learned that *interventions about the total group are at times essential in order to facilitate the group process.* Here are some examples of such process comments: 'At this early stage, the group seems to be quite provoked by the lack of structure that is offered by the leadership.' 'Now the group appears to be concerned about good old power, that is who is at the top and who is at the bottom.' 'It's fascinating to me that it is as if you have exported your major personal problem into the group, so here we are feeling stuck with your impatience, guilt and hopelessness.'

Unique person-centred contributions

Over the last 15 years I have been a regular participant in all kinds of groups at institutes, workshops and seminars sponsored by the American Group Psychotherapy Association, the International Group Psychotherapy Association and the Norwegian Group Psychotherapy Association. From a broad perspective, I am more struck by similarities than by differences between group therapy colleagues. Most group leaders are persons of high integrity, who listen well, try to understand, and are dedicated to be helpful to their clients or patients.

For what it is worth, however, some differences between person-centred practitioners and others have impressed me over the years. Inspired by the concept of congruence/genuineness we allow ourselves to be more transparent than many colleagues, especially psychoanalysts, who advocate neutrality in order to promote transference. Again, the psychoanalysts especially are afraid of being too responsive to certain wishes of their clients, whereas we have always emphasized the significance of acceptance, positive regard and affirmation. It is only in recent years that Kohut (1977) has argued that all clinicians have to openly affirm clients when there are deficits of empathic mirroring in their childhood history. Finally, whereas most clinicians struggle to offer accurate empathy, only person-centred clinicians make a habit of actually checking out their understanding. I have grown so accustomed to this procedure that I often feel frustrated when people refuse to acknowledge whether a communication has been successful or not.

Effects on personal and professional lives

There now follows an exploration of how group processes have affected the lives of a number of participants in the leaders' groups. A more structured evaluation of the effects of person-centred group psychotherapy can be found in Braaten (1989a).

A successful male's lessons from the group process

This particular client was an especially eager 'student', who sat down at his personal computer after each session, and tried to extract some lessons meaningful to him.

During *session 1* he pondered the question of being successful. He listed the following criteria: obtain one's goals, earn a lot of money, have a good marriage, see that others think you are great. He decided to give this theme a lot of thought, in order to become more goal oriented.

Other themes from the initial session were formulated as important self-instructions: Take better care of your employees. Reserve more time for what you really enjoy. Reserve space to be alone to make time for reflection.

From *session 2* he gleaned: Take time to listen and analyse before you respond. Become more open to asking forgiveness when you have wronged a person. Keep normal working hours with the emphasis on quality performance. Try to develop a good, loyal team. Avoid weak, chaotic leadership.

Lessons from *session 3* were the following: openness and trust are required for a good team spirit. It is OK to be hurt, because it proves that you have feelings. Keep a certain distance from your employees. We are what we are doing.

Insights during *session 4*: Try to really understand what others are saying and check it out. For better or worse we are victims of our own self-images. Confront a conflict at once; do not postpone it. Too many employees are scared of the leader. A good leader is well prepared.

Material from *session 5*: It is OK to have other interests than your job. Do not stay too long in the same job. You must learn to work within your own limits. Become more aware of your true values. To enjoy being alone presupposes excellent company. We all perform better with recognition and affirmation.

Session 6 lessons: Take responsibility when you have done wrong. Be professional as a leader; don't let your feelings dominate. If you are strong, you must expect rivalry. A self-starter is a gift to every company.

Finally, during *session 7* he made note of these self-instructions: Even if you feel you are going to win, you may lose. Follow up and find out how others react to your criticisms. It is important to make decisions, and stand by them. You do not get responsibility, you have to take it. Nobody is going to destroy my day. Take responsibility for yourself.

From this point in the process this participant more or less dropped his impressive, but somewhat compulsive, note-taking and spent much time working through some underlying themes with much affective experiencing.

A *young leader learns about leadership and team-building*

In one group I challenged the participants to write a couple of pages about the topics generated by the above heading. This young leader had been fairly successful, but had quit his job during the process of the group. He was probably quite motivated as a result to think through what kind of leader he aspired to be. Here are some extracts from his report:

> Leadership is to make your employees accept and understand what has to be done, and motivate them to actually do it. They must feel responsibility for the work and be trusted.
>
> In order to develop a good team spirit certain preconditions have to be present: The leader must be able to feel into the situations of others, that is to show empathic understanding. He must train himself to read between the lines, and also to interpret body language. Conflicts must be faced, not pushed away. This requires an openness of mind and behaviour. A good leader must convey his great dependence on his collaborators to get the work done.
>
> Finally, our group work has shown quite convincingly that our private lives do indeed influence our work performance. Therefore, it is important to develop a total vision for the triangle – job, family, and leisure time activities, and use good judgment to find the proper balance.

These quotations show that this young leader has learned a lot from the group, but obviously he was quite sophisticated already when he first entered our fellowship. However, the group often inspires us to make more explicit our views of ourselves and our work performance.

A *mature leader's learning about leadership and team-building*

There now follow extracts from a report written by an older, more established leader:

This program has given me lots of feedback, time to think, and an opportunity for self reflection about personal issues. During this year my view of myself and my life situation has changed quite drastically, especially in relation to my wife. Here the contributions of the others have been quite helpful, when we have compared notes about our private lives. The effect has been that I have eliminated several non-important problems, and thus made it possible to focus on those aspects of the relationship which required personal changes.

Another area which has been very useful is the learning from the actual group process. The interaction between the participants and the leader has at times been heavy, because we were invited to generate our own problems and via the group process arrive at personal solutions. The effect of this indirect leadership style has dramatized the need to take personal initiative, both through self disclosure and compassion for the problems of the other participants in the group. This has amounted to a training in empathic listening and understanding, as well as the development of one's own capacity to offer constructive help.

Furthermore, this program has revealed the great complexities of cognitive and affective matters. The willingness and capacity to really change are not very well developed in most of us, even within this motivated group. As a result of this group process, we have demonstrably improved. On the other hand, change and self development take time. We have realized the significance of establishing a long-term view of learning for life.

The group process has been a journey in self discovery, facilitated by the group leader's competence, but also by the open-minded contributions of the members. We have had both sunny weather and rain en route. We have felt joy and pride when the participants actively used the group, and depression when things were moving too slowly.

You get the kind of group you deserve, what you creatively make of it. The course is equipped with a leader, but is directed by the participants. The strategic, long-range goal is to learn to cope with a life which is continuously undergoing change.

This older member clearly gained much from the group, both for his private life, and his work situation. He also improved somewhat in respect of his inclination to use overly complicated language, in order to impress himself as well as the group. It is interesting to note that members, according to him, have to learn to take more explicit responsibility for themselves in order to promote positive self-development.

Toward a tentative theory of group work with leaders

Thorne (1992: 24–43) has reviewed Rogers's major theoretical contributions: theory from experience, the actualizing tendency, conditions of worth, locus of evaluation, the fully functioning person, the core conditions, and the therapeutic process. On the whole I agree that this is an accurate summary of person-centred theorizing. Because of space limitations I shall now restrict myself to a few supplementary theoretical contributions which originate from my person-centred group work. Although leaders as clients are somewhat special as a group, they are actually more similar than different when compared to other client categories. Therefore, my somewhat innovative contributions probably hold for such person-centred group work in general.

Trusting the healing power of the group

In a similar way as in one-to-one therapy, it is assumed that each individual in a group is by nature motivated by the same actualizing tendency. In addition many group practitioners have learned to trust the healing power of the group itself. Again and again I have experienced that *as a total group we truly possess healing power*. The group leader is not the only facilitator; group members join in and contribute equally to whatever progress is made. A group, like an individual, has considerable healing and growth power. Learning to trust this power develops gradually throughout one's career as a group therapist and facilitator.

The false self and the real self

Even if Rogers himself did not make exactly this distinction, I have found it perfectly in harmony with the person-centred approach to postulate a real or true self behind a mask of falsehood and incongruity (Masterson, 1988). Typically in the group, as in individual therapy, the client becomes aware of the many conditions of worth which are introjected in childhood in order to maintain the love and affirmation of significant others. Many business leaders, in their forties especially, discover with horror the price they have paid for their often considerable material success. Significant aspects of the self have been minimized or denied, but within the optimal group climate these dormant qualities and needs surface and demand to be taken seriously.

The primacy of affective experiencing

Therapy is no intellectual matter. Even Ellis (1962), the father of cognitive therapy, who originally called his brand of treatment rational therapy, later had to rename it rational-emotive therapy. Rogers (1942, 1959) recognized early both clinically and theoretically how important the feelings are. He was especially skilful at drawing out the affective dimensions of his clients. There was much sadness, anger, guilt, shame and joy in his therapeutic work. Gendlin (1981) talks about focusing on felt experience, a significant theoretical concept which is wholly supportive of the notion of affective experiencing.

Group cohesion as the working alliance

Previously some psychoanalysts claimed that everything that took place between the therapist and the client was either transference or counter-transference. However, for many years now both psychoanalysts and other therapists have emphasized the importance of the working alliance. This is the more conscious contract between the two parties to be faithful to their common task, that is to make the unconscious conscious for the client. For most of us group cohesion is regarded as the equivalent of the working alliance in the group context. The primary task for the group leader is therefore to develop an optimal group climate, high in cohesion.

I have reviewed 30 years of theoretical and empirical work on this concept and have developed a new multidimensional model based upon 136 references (Braaten, 1991) . This model consists of certain pregroup, early group, and ingroup conditions or dimensions. The *pregroup conditions* are selection of suitable participants, a balanced composition of the group, and effective orientation, training and contracting. The *early group conditions* are resolving conflict and rebellion, constructive norming and culture-building, and reducing avoidance and defensiveness. Finally, the *ingroup dimensions* are attraction and bonding, support and caring, listening and empathy, self-disclosure and feedback, and process performance and goal attainment. The alert reader will recognize among the ingroup dimensions the classical person-centred triad of necessary conditions, expressed in generic language in order to have a broader appeal. Interestingly, this model adds to the old client-centred model two conditions which also foster group cohesion: attraction and bonding, and process performance and goal attainment.

From group cohesion to self-cohesion

For many years I have offered a half-day workshop at professional fora in Europe, the USA and Canada (Braaten, 1986b). The title of this presentation is 'The restoration of self-cohesion in group psychotherapy', and it proposes an integration of the self theories of Kohut (1977) and Rogers (1959). In analytical terms, because of pre-Oedipal injuries, mainly due to the lack of empathic mirroring from care persons, the self has been fragmented and falsified. The purpose of treatment then, is to restore self-cohesion, to assemble and integrate the fragmented parts of the self into a consistent whole. Through a series of sequences in the group process each participant is helped by the total group to discover or rediscover the real or true self. Yalom (1995: 50), a leading international exponent of group therapy, has recently offered support to this approach, arguing that one useful way to view this group process is to see how the internalization of a cohesive group augments a process of self-acceptance or 'self cohesion' in each individual group member.

Self-autonomy and solidarity with others

In 1996 I was invited to give a major plenary address at the opening session of the European Congress of the German Society for Client-Centred Psychotherapy (GwG) in Aachen, Germany (Braaten, 1996). I proposed on that occasion my revised concept of the self. In essence a distinction was drawn between the two major, and equally significant dimensions of the total self: *the unique, private self and the dependent, social self*. It follows that the person-centred challenge is to concentrate, in a balanced way, on developing both self autonomy and solidarity with others. Thus person-centred theoreticians (Braaten, 1996; Schmid, 1994) are in good company with the self psychology theory of Kohut (1977) and the object relations theory of Kernberg (1976). Whereas the old client-centred self concept was more intrapsychic, the revised concept incorporates the formidable accomplishments of attachment research and theory, with their emphasis on connectedness and bonding as the second basic dimension of human nature.

Conclusion and applications

The work reported here shows that the person-centred perspective is eminently suited to helping top and middle management leaders with their self-development and team-building. This client group is, usually, not heavily burdened with psychopathology. This particular contribution continues some of the work which Rogers himself undertook with its emphasis on the essentially *educational* thrust of the person-centred approach.

More specifically the following discoveries are of special interest: because of the shame connected with weakness such leaders are often badly in need of assistance; it is especially hard for them to ask for help. Since they are key people responsible for an organizational culture, their improvements in personal qualities, leadership traits and interpersonal competence will create synergy effects throughout the whole social system. Living the group process for a year with an experienced person-centred leader and motivated colleagues teaches them how to build a good team spirit, a learning which is transferred to their organizations. Because the person-centred approach emphasizes the individual as a whole person, many participants also reap benefits for their private lives.

Summarizing my own person-centred group work, I have considerable experience with student-centred teaching, group therapy with students and staff in a university setting, leaders within the mental health field, and, as addressed here, leaders in business and industry. Within all these areas I am convinced that there is room for continued engagement and development.

Finally, I would like to offer some reflections on other possible applications of the kind of group work which has been described in this chapter. I visualize great opportunities for internal leadership training and team-building in large and smaller companies. More experimentation needs to be done with median groups, that is groups with 12–50 participants. There is much to be done in understanding better the dynamics and change processes of staffs, communities and other large groups. Group therapy with couples and families could well be exploited more fully. I have little doubt that the person-centred group experience could be powerfully effective in fostering creativity in many areas – in the workplace, in society generally, and in the sphere of private life. What is more, my experience suggests that prospective group members are eager to seize the opportunities for creative growth if we are bold enough to offer them.

References

Braaten, L.J. (1974) *Psychotherapeutic Learning through the Group Process*. Oslo: Oslo University Press.

Braaten, L.J. (1986a) *Group Climate Questionnaire – Person-Centred Form*. Oslo: Institute of Psychology.

Braaten, L.J. (1986b) 'The restoration of self-cohesion in group psychotherapy'. Three-hour demonstration workshop, Annual Conference of the American Group Psychotherapy Association.

Braaten, L.J. (1989a) 'The effects of person-centred group psychotherapy', *Person-Centered Review*, 4: 183–209.

Braaten, L.J. (1989b) 'The Self Development Project List-90: a new instrument to measure positive goal attainment', *Small Group Behavior*, 20: 3–23.

Braaten, L.J. (1991) 'Group cohesion: a new multi-dimensional model', *GROUP*, 15: 39–55.

Braaten, L.J. (1994a) 'To what extent do clients discriminate between the group leader's basic therapeutic attitudes? A person-centred contribution'. Oslo: Institute of Psychology, mimeographed report.

Braaten, L.J. (1994b) 'Predicting changes in symptomatology and self development from early group anxiety'. Presentation at the Third International Conference on Client-centred and Experiential Psychotherapy in Gmunden, Austria, 5–9 September.

Braaten, L.J. (1996) 'Competition and solidarity: an evolving person-centred model for self development based upon theory and empirical research', in U. Esser (ed.), *The power of the person-centered approach*. Cologne: GwG. pp. 91–105.

Braaten, L.J. (1997) *Leader Development and Team-building in Norwegian Organizations*. Oslo: Oslo University Press.

Ellis, A. (1962) *Reason and Emotion in Psychotherapy*. New York: Lyle Stuart & Citadel Press.

Gendlin, E. (1981) *Focusing*. New York: Bantam.

Kernberg, O. (1976) *Object Relations and Clinical Psychoanalysis*. New York: Jason Aronson.

Klein, E.B. (1992) 'Contributions from social systems theory', in R.H. Klein (ed.), *Handbook of Contemporary Group Psychotherapy*. Madison, WI: International University Press. pp. 87–123.

Kohut, H. (1977) *The Restoration of the Self*. New York: International University Press.

Lietaer, G. and Dierick, P. (1996) 'Client-centred group psychotherapy in dialogue with other orientations: communality and specificity', in R. Hutterer, G.

Pawlowsky, P.F. Schmid and R. Stipsits (eds), *Client-centred and Experiential Psychotherapy: A Paradigm in Motion*. Vienna: Peter Lang. pp. 563–83.

Masterson, J. (1988) *The Search for the Real Self*. New York: Free Press.

Meador, B.D. and Rogers, C.R. (1979) 'Person-centred therapy', in R.J. Corsini (ed.), *Current Psychotherapies*. Itasca, IL: Peacock. pp. 131–84.

Mearns, D. and Thorne, B. (1988) *Person-centred Counselling in Action*. London: Sage.

Prouty, G. (1994) *Theoretical Evolutions in Person-centered and Experiential Therapy*. Westport, CT: Praeger.

Raskin, N. (1985) 'Client-centered therapy', in S.J. Lynn and J.P. Garske (eds), *Contemporary Psychotherapies*. Columbus, OH: Bell & Howell.

Rogers, C.R. (1942) *Counseling and Psychotherapy*. Boston: Houghton Mifflin.

Rogers, C.R. (1957) 'The necessary and sufficient conditions of therapeutic personality change', *Journal of Consulting Psychology*, 21: 95–103.

Rogers, C.R. (1959) 'A theory of therapy, personality, and interpersonal relationships, as developed in the client-centered framework', in S. Koch (ed.), *Psychology: A Study of a Science, Vol. 3: Formulations of the Person and the Social Context*. New York: McGraw-Hill. pp. 184–256.

Rogers, C.R. (1969) *Freedom to Learn*. Columbus, OH: Merrill.

Rogers, C.R. (1970) *On Encounter Groups*. New York: Harper.

Rogers, C.R. (1980) *A Way of Being*. Boston: Houghton Mifflin.

Schmid, P.F. (1994) *Personzentrierte Gruppenpsychotherapie. Ein Handbuch Vol. I: Solidarität und Autonomie*. Cologne: Edition Humanistische Psychologie.

Thorne, B. (1992) *Carl Rogers*. London: Sage.

Watson, N. (1984) 'The empirical status of Rogers's hypotheses of the necessary and sufficient conditions for effective psychotherapy', in R.F. Levant and J.M. Shlien (eds), *Client-centered Therapy and the Person-centered Approach*. New York: Praeger. pp. 17–40.

Yalom, I.D. (1995) *The Theory and Practice of Group Psychotherapy*, 4th edn. New York: Basic Books.

14 'Anchorage' as a Core Concept in Working with Psychotic People

Dion Van Werde

The image of the tree

When somebody is admitted to our unit, the psychotic problems and the associated suffering are usually obvious. Our first response is to long to relieve all the suffering, and the quicker the better. Experience, however, shows that our good intentions are hard to realize. Sometimes the problems are so severe and consequently the feelings of helplessness so great that we have to let go of our aspirations and learn a lesson of humility.

A first step is 'just' to accept that what we see is what we get, and that even the person suffering is an eyewitness to the whole event rather than an active participant/player. In this statement there is implied some of the philosophy that we work from. I came to discover this philosophy better myself by working with the parents and relatives of patients admitted to the ward. They suffer the same helplessness and are at least as motivated as we are to try to remove the suffering. At a first contact (if asked for), the only advice we can give, the only practical hint we can offer, is that maybe trying to live with the fact that their relative is in the grips of a psychosis is the first necessary step in the process of dealing with the suffering. Everything else comes later.

In our conceptualization of psychosis, we do not automatically see the psychotic symptomatology as the main problem. The real difficulty lies in ascertaining the balance between healthy and problematic functioning. This implies that we always presuppose a healthy part in the person we are dealing with, a core that can be reached and can be strengthened, however relatively small it may be. For us, there is always somebody we can address! When talking about all this to the people mentioned earlier, we present the image of the tree. The upper part, the top (branches, leaves . . .) represents everything that is in the air, meaning things like thoughts, dreams, daydreaming, nightmares, delusions, hallucinations of any mode, even clairvoyance and extrasensory perceptions and so on. The lower part (roots) represents everything that is grounded, rooted, solid, firm and offering foundations. We associate the latter with things like healthy food, a good balance between night and day, constructive social contacts, a place in society, physical health, a balance between work and leisure activities, careful grooming and so on.

When reasoning further along the lines of our image, we would say that it is essential that there is a balance between the upper and the lower parts of the tree. More specifically, if you have a large top to carry, you also need a vast bed of roots. Psychotic people are victims of their thoughts, fantasies, delusions and so on. They are overwhelmed by them and lack firm ground under their feet. They often do not sleep, their feeding habits and grooming habits deteriorate, they retreat/withdraw from social contact. As caregivers, we tend to be exclusively attentive to psychotic symptomatology. In our work, however, we experience the relevance of also working on the restoration and strenghtening of a patient's contact functions in order to prepare ourselves for addressing the psychotic content later. We explain to people that when you have poor or inadequate roots, it only takes a small wind to blow your tree down. The vast top is not so much the problem as the poor anchorage. Certainly seen from a therapeutic point of view, this represents a positive image of man and raises not only hope but also some handles to grasp on to as one embarks on a therapeutic journey.

The importance of the roots

Sometimes, as 'healthy' persons, we may have experienced strange things ourselves. Who isn't familiar with the phenomenon of hearing his or her own name called in the street? If rendered curious, maybe even rendered suspicious to the point of checking out where the call came from and who was yelling, one discovers that it was a misunderstanding, that the sound was similar, but not a name at all or maybe that it indeed was a name like our own, but that somebody else was meant. For a split second, we have had the opportunity to realize what it can mean to live in a world that is continuously filled with such 'misunderstandings'. A 'healthy' person can easily gear back to his or her common sense without losing control or without becoming flooded by this kind of singular and time-limited experience. We can say that such a person, notwithstanding a possible moment of existential doubt, manages to stay rooted in everyday reality, in the world as 'we' know it, in the 'shared' reality. Hearing one's name called is a relatively easy situation. What about hearing it during the night, disturbing sleep and starting off a circle of anxiety and restlessness that provokes even more auditory turmoil? What if the calling is very loud and hostile? What if it happens during a quarrel with your husband or at a party where you are supposed to be welcoming the guests? Numerous examples of such contact-endangering experiences can be given. The point is always: are you rooted enough to be able to balance these experiences with healthy functioning? Can your system of roots carry such a vast top?

If not, is it a momentary and occasional problem (not slept enough, on drugs, an emotional episode . . .) or is it a structural one, meaning that you are bound to collapse since your level of psychological resources is so low that any extra stress will trigger off more psychotic experiencing, whatever happens?

For all these reasons, we are not automatically in favour of instantly and iatrogenically cutting off the top of the tree when people seek help. At best, we see these kinds of intervention as an attempt to manage the problematic situation. In a medical setting and within the limitations of the system (number of personnel, responsibilities of taking care of 20 'beds', and so on), the compromise is made to use drugs since the resources for offering therapeutic relationships are limited and who are we to say that the latter would always be sufficiently therapeutic anyhow? So, when somebody hears voices for example, we try to engage with this client in a relationship so that we can find out together what the problem is, how a workable distance from the problem can be achieved, what is the most urgent thing to do and how the future needs to be designed.

About the top

Of course, if the patient wants to, he or she can be freed from psychotic symptomatology relatively easily. Medication or electroconvulsive therapy can do the job. The price that is to be paid for such an operation is almost always a severe cutting of the top and the loss of inherent life quality that could be drawn from it. This links up with Prouty's notion of pre-expressive functioning. Psychotic behaviour is seen as meaningful, as a way of dealing with something and a way of expression, without, however, reaching the communicative level that is required for congruent communication. Nevertheless, if one ignores, denies, neglects or fails to listen carefully to these ways of functioning, one underestimates their power in psychotherapeutic process. As Prouty describes it theoretically and illustrates with case examples, the hallucination can be the royal road to the unconscious (Prouty, 1994: 88). It is our conviction that science is still limited in understanding all the dynamics involved in such ways of functioning. Furthermore the relationship between psychotic and extra- or supra-sensory functioning is relatively uninvestigated. It is striking that Carl Rogers, towards the end of his life, started to make room for such aspects of life (cf. Thorne, 1992: 22). My learning has been that only if you can be really open will people begin fundamentally to trust you and accept you as a companion on their journey. Prouty documents several cases of visual hallucinations that were tracked to the core experience, which proved to be their originating point. Not many of us I believe have accomplished this kind of therapy. For me, it has to do with the level of congruence of the therapist. People suffering psychosis are particularly skilled at knowing from a distance the difference between those who are rooted enough in themselves, sincere and really containing and those who are going to play tricks on them. Only if the conditions are optimal, I think, do people dare to take the risk of really looking at their experiences, especially when these are so private, delicate and anxiety provoking as are those experiences that are proven to be generators of psychosis.

The treatment of choice is to contact and work with that part of a person that is still rooted and functional and to form an alliance with that part that can congruently deal with the situation or that still has some strength left. As a psychotherapist or contact-facilitator, we try to make contact with that part, accompany it, strengthen the anchorage and help the person gradually to master the situation again. Maybe later, the person will become strong enough to permit the therapist to work towards integrating the horrible or threatening experiences. Realism is necessary, though. Each person is unique and some persons can make much more therapeutic progress than others. Some have more courage, others have more strength, others again have had more suffering and are really damaged by it, others have people who support them, others have never experienced the feeling of trusting someone, a further group doesn't want to give up an established equilibrium since the actual psychotic suffering seems far less damaging than experiencing an underlying traumatic reality. Each process is different. Every quest for strength and health is unique. So is every therapeutic process. Helping somebody is a creative act. The therapist really has to look assiduously for a way to reach this particular fellow human being, how to form a relationship and how to strengthen a sense of being anchored. It sometimes means engaging in a lifelong project.

This way of looking at problems can be very powerful. If we look at person-centred and certainly at experiential literature, the things that we try to do fit the general line of theory. It is possible to conceptualize therapy as finding distance from problems. If our clients can join us in the image of the tree, this means that a distance from their psychotic functioning is already established. You are looking at your problem. 'You' doesn't equal 'problem' any more. This is an excellent starting point for further therapy. The therapist may be allowed to become an ally of the 'you' of the patient and perhaps in a 'trialogue' between patient, therapist and 'problems', things can be worked out. Maybe, and probably only very gradually, clients can become themselves again, decoding and integrating their psychotic experiencing. What we say to people, however, is that extremes need to be balanced and that everyone needs to find out for himself or herself how strong he or she is, what the therapeutic priorities for the moment are and how vast a top can be carried with the given roots. In almost every case, accepting the fact that they are losing control and understanding that strengthening anchorage has the priority is the main project for people who are admitted to our ward. After a while, they find out that maybe they don't need to be exclusively concerned with their problems any more, but can work on the balance between anchorage and alienating experiences of different kinds. In other words, we try to find out how remedial attempts at contact can be undertaken.

Pre-therapy inspiration in praxis

The starting point for our thinking about the full meaning of contact work as an answer to the need and even to the right for anchorage was pre-therapy as formulated by Dr G. Prouty. Even the awareness of the concrete surrounding reality can sometimes be problematic in itself. All too often, an admission to a hospital increases this kind of alienation and strengthens or exacerbates this kind of contact loss. We wondered how and in what way giving attention to anchorage could reverse this tendency in a therapeutic way. The question which faces us is what needs to be restored/anchored first (the cake) if we want to do (psycho)therapy later (the icing).

Theoretically, we can speak about different layers of anchorage that go hand in hand with different kinds of remedial contact efforts. We talk about four different types and these can serve as reference points in deciding the kind of contact we wish to offer to the clients with whom we work.

1 Existential contact: the right simply to exist and to be recognized as a member of humanity. This right is supposedly guaranteed by society.
2 Psychological contact: the concrete awareness of reality (people, places, events and things), of affective states and the ability to communicate about all this in a congruent and socially understandable way. When absent, individual pre-therapy can be used to restore this kind of contact.
3 Consolidation and strengthening of the restored contact functions. This can be done through individual exercises or together with other people in a so called 'contact-facilitating' milieu as, for example, the ward setting of the residential psychiatric hospital where my colleagues and I work.
4 Cultural contact. Feeling ourselves part of a larger group can (re)build our cultural identity. We will illustrate how this can be done through participating in thoughtfully designed leisure activities and through encountering culturally anchoring objects.

We will only expand at length on how we work with the last category. Illustrations of contact efforts in the other areas have been provided extensively in other publications.

The right to exist

The right to exist, to be a member of the human family, and the right to receive therapeutic assistance can be considered fundamental, but is seldom explicitly referred to and is not automatically granted everywhere. It is not so evident we all have the right to exist. As Dr Henriette Morato (São Paulo University, Brazil) points out (private communication), the street children of Brazil who become autistic and live in the sewers crave for everything, including even the basic right to exist. Their life is continuously in danger. Dr Morato has undertaken pilot work with pre-therapy applied to these children and finds it a very powerful and often successful tool in making contact with them. Nonetheless, we have to be aware that individual pre-therapy only makes sense if the first and fundamental right to exist has been secured. Therapeutic interventions in these cases need to go hand in hand with a radical sociological analysis and political action. The children are totally disconnected from everything (genealogical roots, family ties, natural habitat, economic resources of any kind, education, care, security) and are 100 per cent on their own, trying to survive minute to minute.

The fundamental right to exist is the right for contact in its most basic and universal form. When we consider the Belgian situation, we see that this first level of contact is almost always evident, even for groups that are not so 'profitable' or 'interesting' for society. Structurally (through a state social security system or by spontaneous solidarity), these people get help. It is interesting to record that in my country and in the Netherlands, therapists who work with this kind of population have recently discovered and come to recognize Dr Prouty as one of their sources of inspiration. They include Peters (1992) in the care of mentally retarded children, Verdult (1993) in working experientially with dementing elderly people and Van Werde and Willemaers (1992) in working with chronic psychotic people.

Psychological contact

Every human being has the right to contact with people, places, events and things, the right to be aware of his or her own feeling processes and the right to contact other people through congruent communication. In pre-therapy language, the fundamental right to exist psychologically means the right to reality-, affective- and communicative contact. To that end, the therapist, as a kind of *alter ego*, reflects in an existentially empathic way the things that happen with and around the patient. The therapist makes an offer for more relating and more feeling. As Prouty says – and in doing so he refers to Rogers (1966) and Gendlin (1968) – 'Pre-Therapy is a pre-relationship and pre-experiencing activity' (Prouty, 1994: 36).

Disconnecting psychologically from other people and from the surrounding reality can often be seen in the behaviour of those living in a hospital room. A room with no decoration, nothing personal in it, nothing referring to anything else, with just a bed and a table present, can hypothetically be interpreted as signalling psychic disturbance. It gives the idea that 'nobody is at home'. On the other hand, a room with a teddy bear, birthday cards, children's drawings, layouts or schematizations of how a problem is analysed and dealt with hanging on the wall, clearly indicates the presence of a person who has outside and inside points of contact. 'Outside' in this context means connections with the social and material environment, while 'inside' means awareness of his or her private psychological space.

The organization of a contact milieu

The notion of individual pre-therapy sessions for reasons of contact-restoration (see Prouty) can be developed. Theoretically important is the step from an individual to a team approach and the difference between pure contact-restoring efforts and contact-strengthening ones. This is elaborated in Van Werde (1995, 1998). The first kind of effort is more connected to individual pre-therapy – even when it does happen in informal and short interactions between nurses or therapists and patients – the second takes place in the form of exercises that can be done either individually or in a group, for example in a weekly ward meeting (Van Werde, 1994) or a perception training group (Deleu, 1995). The essence of the therapeutic 'milieu' is that the staff pay attention to psychotherapeutic process as well as to consolidating and enlarging the area of so called 'healthy functioning' while recognizing that in daily practice the two are constantly intertwined and very much resemble each other. Such work requires a high degree of professionalism and a phenomenological, welcoming attitude (Deleu and Van Werde, 1998).

Working on cultural anchoring

If the kinds of contact mentioned above are all present, that is if the right to exist is secured, existence isn't threatened from inside or outside, contact is made with the concrete here and now and there is a regular chance to strengthen anchorage, then we can look at if and how a person is a member of a group. The fact that I, as an inhabitant of Belgium, live in this region, at this moment, gives me something in common with other people from the same country, from the same region. This identification (as a kind of anchorage) also helps me to define my own individuality. In a way, this is obvious. As members of the same nation, we probably speak the same language, we have the same rituals, we often go to the same places for our holidays, have the same history, have the same memories and so on. For instance, 'our' Belgian King Boudewijn I, was very popular and loved when he died some years ago. People of all kinds were grieving, talking about nothing else apart from this event and everybody felt connected. We can compare it with the day when JFK was shot or when Martin Luther King died. Those memories are not even limited to nations. They are part of Euro-American or collective memory. They can serve very well for grounds of identification. They can therefore be of help in reconstructing one's own history and in strengthening one's identity as a person.

In our ward setting, we deliberately work on these ideas. Gradually we became aware of how subtly this kind of anchoring plays its part in everyday life. For instance, who isn't touched when travelling abroad by hearing in the corner of the hotel his or her own language spoken? It can mean a boost for our anchoring. This may be even more powerful for somebody from Flanders Belgium, whose native language is spoken only in the northern part of Belgium, the Netherlands and South Africa. The same thing happens when we come across a newspaper in our own language or when we manage to get to a phone and talk to our relatives at home. Such moments can also give a tremendous sense of anchoring. Other things that help us in our day-to-day anchoring are the seasons, religious and secular holidays and so on. They implicitly serve as anchorage points throughout the year. In the same way, when we are stressed, we choose a known, predictable and thus safe and anchoring environment in which to relax. The theme of anchorage is often prominent, even when we don't fully realize it and are not constantly aware of it. We noted that being admitted to a hospital can serve as an illustration of how alienating a move to another environment can be. We walk in a corridor, and the corridor looks the same as the one of the hospital nearby, and much the same as in any hospital in Belgium. Everything looks alike, everything smells alike, everyone is dressed alike, everyone is behaving alike. The total impact is sterile, not personal. Hospitals often have little identity and little specificity . . . it could be any hospital anywhere.

Since we make a point of strengthening cultural anchorage on our ward, it is clear that we have to offer the patients something that by definition can be beneficial for every individual in the group. An interior decoration project and the way we organize leisure activities illustrate the point.

We designed an interior decoration project and decided to place different culturally anchoring objects in the living rooms (see also Van Werde and Van Akoleyen, 1994). We had, for example, jars with shells from the Belgian North Sea beach – Belgium has a coast and most people go there for holidays and come across shells and sometimes collect them. We also had jars with Belgian stamps. We had some replicas of Belgian monuments like the Lion of Waterloo – a statue in memory of the defeat of Napoleon in Belgium – and the 'Atomium', the Belgian pavilion from the World Exhibition that took place in Brussels in 1958. We had an old map of Belgium on the wall with every small village mentioned. In this way everybody had the chance to reconnect with the village/town where he or she was born or once lived. We had original Belgian comic books of the Smurfs, Lucky Luke, Kuifje (Tintin) and so on. We had books about famous Belgian people like Eddy Merckx, the cyclist and Father Damian, who worked with lepers in Molokai and who was declared blessed by Pope John-Paul II in Brussels recently. We had a piece of famous Belgian lacework framed on the wall.

These objects did what they were supposed to do, that is they offered a way to contact a larger (cultural) identity. People – patients as well as staff members and visitors – said things like 'Oh yeah, when I was a child we visited the Lion of Waterloo with our class', or 'My grandmother lives near the sea and she has a collection of shells that is similar to the one here', or 'I used to own a lot of comic books before I got ill.' So the project stirred up individuals by confronting them with culturally relevant things. There was a great deal of communication, much identification took place, and considerable contact was facilitated. In people who were not so verbal, we could see faces change when they came into contact with one of these objects. We could reflect their facial expressions and start from there, working towards affective contact through responding at and connecting with such low-level and yet very concrete aspects of their being.

Another example of how we try to counter unnecessary alienation by offering the possibility for anchorage is the way we organize the ward's leisure activities. These activities consist of visiting a museum, playing games, taking a walk, and so on. We gradually became aware of the contact-enabling possibilities of these activities. For instance, near the village where our hospital has its grounds, the university of the city of Ghent has tropical glasshouses in its botanical garden. We used to go there, but don't do so any more because this milieu isn't the kind of place that anchors our patients. They already have so much difficulty staying in touch with 'normal' surrounding reality that we don't wish to confront them with an artificial, tropical environment with strange exotic vegetation, high temperatures and a high degree of moisture that is very unusual, not to say unknown in our climate. Nowadays we go regularly to a woman two blocks away from the hospital who has a very pleasant herbal garden and cultivates bees and honey. She shows us around her garden and shares with us her expertise on nature. By doing this, we are working with what is growing here and now and this sharpens contact with everyday reality. It also opens up people to all kinds of cyclical processes that are visible in nature. We return regularly so that not only our knowledge of botany, but also our personal relationship with the woman, her garden and her pets can grow. She sometimes comes over to our hospital to walk in our gardens and to talk about 'our' plant life. These are experiences that we value very much because they are so anchoring.

Since we work with a group of 20 patients, from the acutely psychotic to those recovering, we always have to design a contact offer that appeals to people on whatever level they are functioning. People who are in an acute state need only a very concrete activity. Others need more. They are encouraged to reproduce some artwork that we have seen or to prepare a speech on a topic that they are especially interested in or have expertise about. We have to be aware of different levels of anchoring and start from there. We don't want to appear exotic or extreme, but on the other hand we don't want to get trapped in nationalism. We have had people on our ward from other cultures and we offered them the chance to anchor themselves back in their native culture too. One patient's second language was English. She was Belgian but raised in England. When she was staying on our ward – and responding to a request from several patients – we got her to give some lessons in basic English language to her fellow patients and nurses. For her, that was anchoring since she could live again a part of herself that had been hidden for so many years. For other people in our programme who were sufficiently anchored, it was a challenge to try out their notions of English. Another patient, with grandparents in India, led a cooking activity. She made a rice dish with specific herbs that she brought along. For the woman herself, it meant anchoring her back in her native culture since she was born and lived for some years in India. For some interested others, it was enriching to meet her as a person and through her to meet another culture.

Planning these initiatives, whether the project of culturally anchoring objects or the leisure activities, is done in the weekly ward meeting (Van Werde, 1994). This produces many anchoring dynamics on the ward. It brings in the time factor: next week we are going to do this, last week we did that, who is going to take care of this? Who is interested in that? When things like this happen, we offer material to make contact about. We support and strengthen already restored awarenesses of reality and affect and we foster communication. It is only in such a way that a contact milieu can originate and have its impact. On the other hand we try to make sure that we don't overdo it. So we organize only one leisure activity a week. If we go out, we try not to combine this with other things. If visiting the museum in itself takes a lot of energy, we use our own transportation to get there and avoid complicated bus changes and so on. We try not to overload the programme because the people who need anchoring most are the people who function at the lowest level.

Conclusion

In this chapter I have attempted to explore central approaches in the treatment of people with psychotic problems. 'Contact-facilitating work' and 'offering anchorage' are terms that try to make these approaches more explicit. Anchoring starts with the right to be taken care of and, even more basically, with the right to exist. In addition to that and in different layers and ways, we can offer things of a similar kind, such as individual pretherapy, to restore psychological contact. We can combine this explicitly with exercises and initiatives to strengthen anchorage collectively. We have called this the organization of a contact milieu. Parallel to all this we can use elements from our cultural surroundings to build up an identity: cultural anchorage. Who is that? Where am I? How do I do this? What does it mean? What do I feel? What did I experience? Where do I come from? What do my people do? What do I have in common with others and how do I differ? How do I develop my own projects, my own future?

Aren't these the things that we all are working on constantly as part of being human?

References

Deleu, C. (1995) 'Buiten zinnen: persoonsgerichte waarnemingstraining voor psychosegevoelige mensen', *Psychiatrie en Verpleging: Tijdschrift voor Hulpverleners in de Geestelijke Gezondheidszorg*, 71 (5): 287–93.

Deleu, C. and Van Werde, D. (1998) 'The relevance of a phenomenological attitude when working with psychotic people', in B. Thorne and E. Lambers (eds), *Person-centred Therapy: A European Perspective*. London: Sage.

Gendlin, E. (1968) 'The experiential response', in E. Hammer (ed.), *Use of Interpretation in Treatment*. New York: Grune & Stratton. pp. 208–27.

Peters, H. (1992) *Psychotherapie bij Geestelijk Gehandicapten*. Amsterdam/Lisse: Swets & Zeitlinger.

Prouty, G. (1994) *Theoretical Evolutions in Person-centered/Experiential Therapy: Applications to Schizophrenic and Retarded Psychoses*. New York: Praeger.

Rogers, C. (1966) 'Client-centered therapy', in S. Arieti (ed.), *American Handbook of Psychiatry*. New York: Basic Books. pp. 183–200.

Thorne, B. (1992) *Carl Rogers*. London: Sage.

Van Werde, D. (1994) '"Werken aan contact" als leidmotief van de wekelijkse afdelingsvergadering in residentiële psychosenzorg', *Tijdschrift voor Psychiatrie*, 36 (8): 46–53.

Van Werde, D. (1995) 'Contact-faciliterend werk op een afdeling psychosenzorg: een vertaling van Prouty's Pre-Therapie', in G. Lietaer and M. Van Kalmthout (eds), *Praktijkboek Gesprekstherapie*. Utrecht: De Tijdstroom. pp. 178–87.

Van Werde, D. (1998) 'Prä-Therapie im Alltag einer psychiatri-schen Station', in G. Prouty, D. Van Werde and M. Pörtner, *Prä-Therapie*. Stuttgart: Klett-Cotta. pp. 85–158.

Van Werde, D. and Van Akoleyen J. (1994) '"Verankering" als kernidee van residentiële psychosenzorg', *Tijdschrift Klinische Psychologie*, 24 (4): 293–302.

Van Werde, D. and Willemaers R. (1992) *Werken aan Contact: Een Video-illustratie van Pre-Therapie met een Chronisch Psychotische Vrouw*. Ghent: Rijksuniversiteit Gent, Seminarie en Laboratorium voor psychologische begeleiding (with brochure).

Verdult, R. (1993) *Dement Worden: Een Kindertijd in Beeld – Belevingsgerichte Begeleiding van Dementerende Ouderen*. Nijkerk: Intro.

15 The Relevance of a Phenomenological Attitude when Working with Psychotic People

Chris Deleu and Dion Van Werde

Introduction: two complementary approaches

In this chapter we present how an explicitly phenomenological way of thinking and working is integrated into the life of a ward for people with psychotic behaviour.

> *A middle-aged man who hears voices, spends hours and hours keeping notes on everything that happens around him on the ward. He thinks that he is under the control of 'telephats' and demands that his doctor interfere to get rid of them. His awareness of time has narrowed to a never-ending paranoid here and now.*

> *A young woman continuously complains about growing distortions and the disintegration of her body. She has had a pigment stain removed from her hips and since then, a dread over losing her physical integrity has emerged. For weeks she couldn't make time or space for anything else.*

> *A young man silently pronounces words about God and the devil. He can only stay in the living room for the time needed to smoke a cigarette. He hears voices that order him to do harm to his fellow patients. He always flees to his room and tries to fight these impulses there.*

The relevance of the phenomenological inspiration to a somewhat traditional and medically oriented hospital will be illustrated by small vignettes from our daily psychotherapeutic practice. After an introduction we will discuss a four-step process that ideally unfolds when working along phenomenological lines. This process is a therapeutic one, and we shall illustrate how Prouty (1994) and Van den Berg (1989) conceptualize it and how in our daily practice the process can be recognized, even if only partially.

Making explicit our way of working stems from recent developments in person-centred/experiential psychotherapy (Lietaer and Van Kalmthout, 1995; Lietaer et al., 1990; Swildens et al., 1991). We also try to translate/

apply the Rogerian core conditions (empathy, unconditional positive regard and congruence) to our specific setting and target population. We work in residential psychiatric care for psychotic people (Van Werde, 1995). For us, this work essentially situates itself between two poles: following the experiential process of the client on the one hand and offering and working with the shared reality on the other. That is to say, we hold the tension between 'being with the client' and 'doing with the client'. We shall try to show that this opposition is in fact a false one. In our contact milieu we daily attempt to transcend it.

Since 1988, at the Kliniek St-Camillus Gent (SDW), Belgium, we have been working inspired by a phenomenological attitude and responding to people who are recovering from a psychotic episode in a ward setting. This inspiration finds its chief expression in Prouty's Pre-therapy (Prouty, 1994; Van Werde, 1989, 1994, 1998) and in the observation-training group (Deleu 1990, 1995; Van Dam, 1981).

As an evolution of 'classical' client-centred therapy (Mearns and Thorne, 1988; Rogers, 1957, 1966; Rogers et al., 1967), Prouty applies in his 'Pre-Therapy' the Rogerian core attitudes to his practice with severely contact-disturbed people. By reflecting the situation (Situational Reflection, SR), the face (Facial Reflection, FR), the body posture or body movement (Body Reflection, BR) and the words of the client (Word-for-Word Reflection, WWR) in combination with the repetition of the reflections that establish contact (Reiterative Reflection, RR), it becomes possible to re-anchor a person in a shared reality, to enable him or her to re-establish contact with affective life and to communicate these discoveries in a congruent manner (see Van Werde and Prouty, 1992). This way of implementing a phenomenological attitude has proved effective in healing florid psychotic episodes, and in alleviating bizarre or disorganized so-called 'positive' symptoms.

In the observation-training group, the participants learn how to connect with reality in a phenomenological manner. They become more than passive observers of the world. Usually people restrict themselves to a mere sum of what is offered to their senses and mind. In phenomenological observations there is a participating awareness, based on an openness oriented towards the world.

Training exercises are offered once a week in a 90-minute group session and they are aimed in the first place at awakening/arousing the capacity for observing in a healthy manner. Not only hearing and seeing are addressed, but also, and especially, those senses we need in order to be aware of our own corporeality, our personal physical space (Soesman, 1987). In so-called negative symptoms but also in the side-effects of neuroleptic medication, we see how poorly anchored psychotic people are in their bodies. Strengthening this anchorage is done through different kinds of exercises (tactile, motor, balancing, auditory and visual).

Approximately half the number of patients in the ward regularly participate. The group is open and heterogeneous: those who have experienced their first psychotic episode and are recovering, chronic sufferers, incipient psychotic persons. . . . Some have only recently been admitted, others have been in the hospital for months. This brings a complexity which demands a highly personalized approach, a basic phenomenological attitude and more than a little common sense. The exercises take place in different locations, even during one session: in the therapy room, in the garden or the wood of the hospital, in a nature resort nearby and so on. Different kinds of resources are used: sticks, little bags filled with rice, drawing material, Orff musical instruments, minerals, reproductions of artwork, participants' own bodies, plants, clay, sand and a Cretan labyrinth 26 metres in diameter. Exercises can be accomplished alone, in twos, in small groups or in the whole group. Short intensive-concentration exercises can be done, but a quarterly walk of a whole afternoon is often scheduled. The theme varies, but it is always connected to the rhythm of the year (seasons, Christian holidays and so on). During each session, people are free to drop out and to watch for a while if they feel like it, for not everybody is capable of actively participating for the whole 90 minutes.

It is significant how intertwined the pre-therapy and observation group approaches can become as they are implemented in our residential thera-peutic programme. We find them complementary in the sense that both work with observations; the first focuses on strictly private and psychotic observations and the latter on 'realistic' ones. Pre-therapy helps to re-establish contact with reality, emotions and other people, whereas obser-vation training supports and strengthens this anchorage and builds up healthy functioning further. Both are essential if we are to address psychotic experiencing in a therapeutically fruitful manner.

We would like to compare the two approaches presented – pre-therapy and observation training (with their respective focus on following the process and offering exercises; or in other words on being with and on doing with) – and point to a striking similarity. A similiar four-step process reveals itself if one manages faithfully to go all the way in the phenom-enological listening mode (Van den Berg, 1989), even with psychotic material – as in Prouty's Pre-therapy. The latter's approach came directly out of his praxis of working with visually hallucinating people. Later, we will illustrate this four-step process with vignettes from our personal practice. Even when the full process does not take place, the implicit therapeutic relevance can be demonstrated.

When we speak of phenomenology, which we illustrate here mainly in relation to its therapeutic and psychohygienic implications, we mean phenomenology as a scientific method. This way of approaching things essentially implies an optimal encounter between the 'observer' (the ther-apist) and the 'observed' (not only the private experiences of the client, his or her hallucinations and so on, but also the shared and admissible every-day reality). When approaching somebody or something, the researcher moves between being externally observing and internally imagining. When practising such an attitude, a desire for more knowledge about the person or object arises in the researcher. The phenomenon in turn invites us to be observed and welcomed in a particular way so that it may unfold its secrets. A phenomenological process of knowledge exchange is bound to happen. This process is a therapeutic one (Van Dam, 1981).

In a philosophical essay on perception and art by the French philosopher Merleau-Ponty (1964), we find the words to describe the difference between positivistic science and the way of studying things described here. He states that modern science manipulates things and refuses to dwell in them. It talks about 'objects in general', as if we have nothing to do with them and as if things were inevitably predestined to be mediated by our artifices/tricks. Such scientific knowledge is considered absolute, as if everything that was, or is, had been created for the laboratory. The artist's work, however, convinced Merleau-Ponty of the inseparability of the act of seeing and what is seen, of the impossible split between spectator and spectacle, the interwovenness of appearance and being.

Prouty's four-step process

The therapist systematically uses pre-therapy, a disciplined and client-centred way of offering empathy for these troublesome ways of functioning. It is an essentially phenomenological method, since there is deep respect for and a sensitive tuning into the client's world as he or she lives it. Prouty describes the four stages of hallucinatory experiencing as follows: the self-indicating, the self-emotive, the self-processing and the self-integrating (Prouty, 1994: 78–81). During this process, the hallucination moves from fixity and remoteness to a clear, alive, immediate and integrated self-experience.

1 The *self-indicating* phase. The therapist reflects the phenomenological qualities of the hallucination: what does it look like, where is it, distance, shape, form, colour. . . . The 'me' of the therapist continuously invites the 'me' of the patient to become interested both in what is experienced as belonging to himself or herself and in those things that are hallucinatory, alien and experienced as not-me.
2 The *self-emotive* phase. At this point, affect has developed in or around the hallucinatory image as part of its own self-signification or as a result of reiteration. Reflecting in this stage is toward both the image and the feelings. Later, often after a lot of trial and error, an image with an emotional undertone emerges, but it is still perceived as outside the client's own core.
3 The *self-processing* phase. Both the image, and its affect develop. Instead of merely describing the qualities of an externally perceived and hallucinatory image, the patient increasingly contacts affective qualities within himself or herself.

4   The *self-integrating* stage. In this stage, affect shifts from the hallu-
    cinatory image to the person's own self, and is integrated, owned, and
    experienced as self.

Van den Berg's four-step process

The phenomenological attitude as practised in the observation-training
group can be characterized as an activity in which the whole person is
involved: with body, life forces, psychic abilities and spirituality. Related to
this, Van den Berg (1989) delineates four steps or levels in the phenomenological method. The formulation of these steps is derived mainly from
the way Goethe (1981) studied plant life, but can equally well be applied to
phenomena other than plants. As we saw in Prouty's work, even a
hallucination demands a radical phenomenological approach. Each step
seeks to elicit a specific basic mood and attitude. The observer always tries
to be in tune with the object under observation. The steps are strikingly
similar to those formulated by Prouty.

1   *Creating an exact spatial representation.* The basic mood is a wondering
    one, receptive, unprejudiced, an unconditional positive regard towards
    the spatial qualities of a phenomenon. When constructing such an
    image, the processes of imagining, describing and comparing are
    interdependent and strengthen each other.
2   *Creating a living image (the element of 'time').* This step requires the
    observer to be respectful, open to beauty and unconditionally positively
    regarding of the developmental qualities of the phenomenon. These
    kinds of activity enable the phenomenologist to move from being a
    detached and intellectual observer to an active, engaged and
    participating one.
3   *The opening of oneself towards the physiognomy of the phenomenon.* The
    third step in the phenomenological method is about being receptive to
    the self-revealing quality of the image. This calls for a basic sense of
    harmony, for an attitude of empathy. The purpose of this step is to
    learn consciously to bridge the gap between object and subject.
4   *The encounter with the very being, the core of a phenomenon.* The fourth
    step – which we can only mention here – is about experiencing an
    encounter with the authentic essence of a phenomenon. This requires a
    basic desire for conscious surrender and for a sense of authenticity and
    moral growth.

Description of our own praxis

The thread running through these following examples – others could be
given – is the translation of a phenomenological attitude into the daily

praxis of how a therapist or client can work with material that presents/ announces itself, be it a hallucination, a disturbing sound or something in the natural environment. We will try to evoke something of the way in which we as psychotherapists approach this. In practice, we continuously have to choose between reflecting and offering opportunities to engage with (the shared) reality. The first vignette especially illustrates that in daily practice the two are interwoven. The opening remark of the therapist is a question. It is not a reflection but an attempt to initiate congruent communication with the patient. It is checking out if the patient is functioning on an expressive level. We see that the patient answers from his psychosis and that the therapist consequently shifts back to pre-expressive interaction and starts to use Pre-Therapy reflections. When the patient reports on his hallucinatory image, they both pause and start to question this phenomenon: yes, he sees her, no, she is not dressed in white but in colours, she doesn't speak and so on. One could call this a kind of observation-training exercise. It means questioning the perceptual qualities of what presents itself, but from a welcoming attitude (cf. phase/step 1). This way of working, which combines reflecting and questioning and finds its synthesis in the phenomenological attitude, enables a bridging of the supposed contradiction between 'being with' and 'doing with'. It fosters the further phases/steps of the therapeutic process and – if applied on a large scale – it establishes a contact milieu (cf. Van Werde, 1995).

'I want to return to my wife'

The vignette comes from a session with Dennis (D), a borderline-psychotic young man. The therapist (T) and D know each other well and up to this point in the session, communication has been on a congruent level. It is nearing the end of the calendar year . . .

T: D, is there something you wish for next year? You don't have to say it if you don't want to, of course. . . .

D: Yes, I want to go back to my wife [*with a big smile, moist eyes and looking very happy*].

T: [*perplexed because T knows that there is no woman at all in D's life at the moment and touched by this New Year's wish*]
    (FR) We are about to cry the two of us! [*in saying this, also indicating his own wet eyes*]

D: [*keeps smiling and is obviously enjoying the idea of a meeting with his wife and its quality*]

T: (WWR) You want to return to your wife. [*reflecting word for word and psychologically fully present at that imagined and experienced reunion*]

D: [*stares at a point to the side of T*]

T: (BR) [*points at the place that D is addressing – by doing so, accepting client's reality – and asks*] Do you see her? [*T wants to inform himself about the sense impressions of what the client perceives (cf. phase/step 1) as a way of making contact. This contact may reveal or accompany emotions (cf. phase/step 2) that can be reflected in their turn, so that both the image and the affect can begin to develop) (cf. preparing for phase/step 3). [During a previous conversation, D had also perceived his loved one. She was dressed in shiny white, with gloves on her feet and she invited him to return to a hospital where he had been before. She had also promised that she would be waiting for him. . . .]*

D: [*nods his head affirmatively*] Yes.

T: Is she in white? [*again referring to previous information*]

D: No, in colour.

T: Is she saying something? [*The therapist afterwards regrets that he changed the topic to a different sense field. Probably it would have been better to have stayed closer to the given and asked more about the colours.*]

D: No. [*staring more and more and then looking at T. D holds his eyes and looks at T.*]

T: (FR) You look surprised.

D: [*nods his head*] Yes. [*obviously contacts his feelings: Affective Contact*]

T: (BR) You nod 'yes'. (RR) Just a while ago, you looked over here . . . [*points again at that hallucinatory place beside him*] (SR) and now you're looking at me.

D: [*nods affirmatively. D keeps looking at T – so does not follow the pointing at the place of the hallucination – and looks as if he himself is surprised that such a thing as a hallucination has occurred. He clearly doesn't know how to handle it and seems willing to try anything to keep his eyes grounded in reality.*]

T: (BR) [*also nods his head – as a way of communicating his understanding*]

D: Can I go upstairs?

T: [*T interprets this as a congruent request and implicitly agrees to stop and to let the psychotic content drop. Probably continuation would have endangered the newly regained contact with reality and with the affective state.*] OK, I'll walk you to the ward.

'A deafening noise'

During one of our conversations in which Agnes is once more upset by a disturbing noise, I propose a short listening exercise. I invite her to listen actively to sounds she can distinguish in her surroundings, starting with those close by and then moving away to the most remote one and to return 'the same way' (cf. phase/step 1). She does the exercise in silence and reports afterwards that to her surprise the deafening noise hadn't been present during the exercise. The patient had made a journey in space (from close by to further away and back) and in time (one step after the other). Doing so, she was able to identify sounds and could afterwards describe their different qualities: the sound of the barking dog far away, steps in the room above our heads, the roaring sound of a jet flying over and so on. The point, however, was not that she could name the sounds, but that she was able to register the different qualities of what she perceived.

Although these kinds of exercise are beneficial for training attention and concentration (patient aims her attention at – in this case – audible phenomena), the basic attitude is crucial: to listen quietly in a receptive manner. This small exercise taught Agnes that she herself, at least temporarily, could monitor/direct her attention herself and by doing so, master – if only temporarily – the disturbing sounds that she thought uncontrollable.

October: month of the mushrooms

Each year in September and October, the wood in our grounds is full of mushrooms that grow on fallen trees and cut wood. Each year during this period we take the same walk every Friday afternoon and do observation exercises. The first week we mainly pay attention to where the mushrooms grow, what they look like, how they smell, taste and feel. Different senses are addressed (cf. phase/step 1). Every participant can stop the group when he or she runs into something interesting. The second and third week the attention automatically shifts to how the mushrooms are changing in form, colour, size and so on (cf. phase/step 2). The basic attitude is again a phenomenological one and can be summarized as being quiet and 'listening'. The effect of these walks is remarkable and contrary to the so-called 'negative' symptoms of psychosis and other forms of alienation (cf. Van Werde and Van Akoleyen, 1994). Participants become expectant and attentive to new and changing things (cf. phase/step 3). Not infrequently, people experience joy and feel encouraged since their own willpower is being addressed.

Concluding remarks

The phenomenological method as we have described it plays a key role in our daily work. It can ignite processes that are therapeutic. We recognize some of the four comparable phases/steps as defined by Van den Berg and Prouty, applied in daily working.

In our examples, the immediate impact was limited, though significant: Dennis who shares his hallucination with the therapist contacts his astonishment (affective contact). He is empowered to choose whether or not he is willing to explore (phase/step 1) his hallucination. He prefers not to, protects himself from becoming flooded (that would mean entering phase/steps 2 and 3 unprepared) and returns to the ward. In the second example, the woman succeeds in putting aside the disturbing noise through responding to the therapist's suggestion to do a listening exercise (cf. phase/step 1) and through the anchorage that subsequently follows. Maybe this will prove to be the first step of a therapeutic process that will lead her to master or even to decode or understand the deafening noise (that would mean phase/step 4). The mushrooms in our third example are first spotted, then exactly described (cf. phase/step 1) and investigated by means of a welcoming, observing and listening attitude (cf. phase/step 2). A shuttle between looking and seeing arises and different feelings can be tapped into and expanded (this would mean moving to phase/steps 2 and 3).

To move between 'contacting' and 'revealing' is essential. We are receptive to what's coming, go towards it and, by our attitude, invite it to disclose itself (finally, this would imply phase/step 4). As Goethe said: 'You can only know the things you love'. We want to encounter the particular, the essence. . . . We find in our way of working a therapeutic potentiality that demands further exploration. Pre-therapy and the observation-training exercises as we have described them have common roots. We call it applied phenomenology – not unknown in person-centred therapy. Rogers (1966), Gendlin (1968) and Prouty (1994) are our historical reference points.

Finally, it is our view that both pre-therapy and observation training are aimed at awakening and mobilizing clients' own proactive forces. Medication that deadens or exhausts these forces needs to be used in a restricted, limited way, if at all. We consider that the development and use of medication that is free of this kind of (iatrogenic) negative side-effects would be an important contribution by the medico-pharmaceutical world to the realization of holistic phenomenological healthcare.

References

Deleu, C. (1990) 'Luisteren naar de overstemde: over stemmen horen en andere hallucinaties', *Tijdschrift voor Sociale Hulpverlening Vanuit de Antroposofie*, 3: 26–37. Translated into German as Deleu, C. (1992) 'Hören und Überhören . . . Über das Hören von Stimmen und andere Halluzinationen', *GWG-Zeitschrift*, 23 (86): 10–14.

Deleu, C. (1995) 'Buiten zinnen: persoonsgerichte waarnemingstraining voor psychosegevoelige mensen', *Psychiatrie en Verpleging: Tijdschrift voor Hulpverleners in de Geestelijke Gezondheidszorg*, 71 (5): 287–93.

Gendlin, E. (1968) 'The experiential response', in E. Hammer (ed.), *Use of Interpretation in Treatment*. New York: Grune & Stratton.

Goethe, J.W. (1981) *De Metamorfose van de Planten*. Rotterdam: Uitverij Christofoor.

Lietaer, G. and Van Kalmthout, M. (1995) *Praktijkboek Gesprekstherapie*. Utrecht: De Tijdstroom.

Lietaer, G., Rombauts, J. and Van Balen, R. (eds) (1990) *Client-centered and Experiential Psychotherapy in the Nineties*. Leuven: Leuven University Press.

Mearns, D. and Thorne, B. (1988) *Person-centred Counselling in Action*. London: Sage.

Merleau-Ponty, M. (1964) *L'Oeil et l'esprit*. Paris: Gallimard.

Prouty, G. (1994) *Theoretical Evolutions in Person-centered/Experiential Therapy: Applications to Schizophrenic and Retarded Psychoses*. New York: Praeger.

Rogers, C. (1957) 'The necessary and sufficient conditions of therapeutic personality change', *Journal of Consulting Psychology*, 21 (2): 95–103.

Rogers, C. (1966) 'Client-centered therapy', in S. Arieti (ed.), *American Handbook of Psychiatry*. New York: Basic Books. pp. 183–200.

Rogers, C., Gendlin, E., Kiesler, D. and Truax, C. (eds) (1967) *The Therapeutic Relationship and its Impact: A Study of Psychotherapy with Schizophrenics*. Madison, WI: University of Wisconsin Press.

Soesman, A. (1987) *De twaalf zintuigen*. Zeist: Vrij Geestesleven.

Swildens, H., de Haas, O., Lietaer, G. and Van Balen, R. (eds) (1991) *Leerboek Gesprekstherapie: De Cliëntgerichte Benadering*. Amersfoort and Leuven: Acco.

Van Dam, J. (1981) *Fenomenologie en Therapie*. Oegstgeest: Bolkbericht 2.

Van den Berg, B. (1989) 'De stappen in de fenomenologie', *Drieblad*, 10 (2): 15–17.

Van Werde, D. (1989) 'Restauratie van het psychologisch contact bij acute psychose', *Tijdschrift voor Psychotherapie*, 15 (5): 271–9.

Van Werde, D. (1994) 'An introduction to client-centred pretherapy and dealing with the possibility of psychotic content in a seemingly congruent communication', in D. Mearns, *Developing Person-Centred Counselling*. London: Sage. pp. 121–8.

Van Werde, D. (1995) 'Contact-faciliterend werk op een afdeling psychosenzorg. Een vertaling van Prouty's Pre-Therapie', in G. Lietaer and M. Van Kalmthout (eds), *Praktijkboek gesprekstherapie*. Utrecht: De Tijdstroom. pp. 178–87.

Van Werde, D. (1998) 'Prä-Therapie im Alltag einer psychiatri-schen Station', in G. Prouty, D. Van Werde and M. Pörtner, *Prä-Therapie*. Stuttgart: Klett-Cotta. pp. 85–158.

Van Werde, D. and Prouty, G. (1992) 'Het herstellen van het psychologisch contact bij een schizofrene jonge vrouw: een toepassing van Prouty's Pre-Therapie', *Tijdschrift Klinische Psychologie*, 22 (4): 269–80.

Van Werde, D. and Van Akoleyen, J. (1994), '"Verankering" als kernidee van residentiële psychosenzorg', *Tijdschrift Klinische Psychologie*, 24 (4): 293–302.

16 Empathy and Empathy Development with Psychotic Clients

Ute Binder

This chapter explores the connection which can be demonstrated in cases of severe mental disorder between a lack of empathy in a child's primary carer and later pathological developments. A knowledge of these pathogenic factors makes it possible to activate constructive, healing developmental processes through a specific therapeutic empathic understanding of the disorder. Without such a knowledge of these aetiological connections it is more difficult to develop an adequate empathic therapeutic procedure.

Commonly experienced phenomena in psychotherapy with psychotic persons

In all positive psychotherapeutic experiences with psychotics I find a remarkable degree of confirmation of the appropriateness of the person-centred approach. Frieda Fromm-Reichmann (1976), Hilde Bruch (1980), Otto Allan Will (1980), Theodor Lidz (1980) and many others emphasize the importance of authenticity in the relationship. Acceptance as a core condition, the absence of which has a considerably more negative impact on these patients than on neurotics, is not only stressed in theoretical papers, but has also been confirmed by empirical research (Tourney et al., 1976; Whitehorn and Betz, 1975). Stephen Fleck (1980) and W. Mendel (1974) consider the establishment of a stable therapeutic relationship both to be the biggest problem and to have the greatest curative power.

Whitehorn and Betz (1975) emphasize that certain aspects of a real relationship are essential and that successful therapists are more interested in the personal meanings and the motives of the patient, show themselves as strong, active personalities with clear boundaries and radiate kindness, friendliness, clarity, honesty and tolerance. A central result of Rogers's Wisconsin project was the following:

Neurotic clients appear to perceive the understanding and genuineness of the therapist and thus it is natural that their central focus appears to be on self-exploration. Our schizophrenic patients on the other hand perceived primarily the levels of warm acceptance (positive regard) and genuineness. Their focus appeared to be on relationship-formation. (Rogers, 1967: 75–6)

Furthermore, we find running like a thread through the literature an insistence that therapists manifest respect, optimism, an absence of power-seeking, and a refusal rigidly to submit the patient to particular techniques, methods, goals and values. There is an insistence, too, on openness, tolerance for deviant behaviour or experience, intuition, moment-to-moment clarity, open-mindedness and accurate listening. At the same time we find that interpretations, insight-oriented clarification of so-called 'wrong' attitudes and techniques for working with transference, resistance phenomena and early childhood conflicts take a lower profile in the literature relating to work with psychotic persons.

In the Wisconsin project it was clearly demonstrated that in successful cases the patients were able to discern the presence of person-centred attitudes in their therapist. In the majority of patients, however, it was found that such an awareness was minimal. This, among other things, was the result of the interpersonal experiences in their personal histories. Their disorder and their symptoms generally produced an extremely low degree of acceptance, congruence and empathy in those whom they met (Binder, 1990). Many patients can give us various degrees of difficulty as we try to meet them with acceptance, congruence and empathy. The effect of this difficulty on neurotic patients is less evident and less disastrous than on psychotics. I think that psychotic patients not only become aware of these conditions belatedly and to a lesser degree, but also that therapists generally do not display these attitudes to the same degree.

Empathy is always dependent on signals; the fewer, the more unclear, strange and confusing the signals, the weaker or even simply the less accurate the empathic understanding becomes, irrespective of the efforts of the therapist, and the more frequently it is based on a different dimension of social understanding. Viewed in this light it is not so much a question of whether empathic understanding is useful in working with persons with psychotic disorders, but whether what is understood by empathy is really empathy in the sense of contact which connects people on an emotional level. Prouty (1994) claims that psychological contact is the necessary condition for psychotherapy to occur at all.

Dimensions of social understanding

Empathy

If empathy refers to a sensitive sharing in the state of being of another person as this is expressed in his or her behaviour, situation and communication, and by what we grasp from his or her personality and its distinctive features from moment to moment, then it embraces a large spectrum of therapeutic behaviours which have in common a specific kind of contact, motivation, social relationship, understanding and emotionality. This contact occurs through many forms of verbal and non-verbal communication but it only succeeds if the therapist not only understands empathically what is happening in the patient, but also what he or she wishes and is able to communicate and what he or she understands and what he or she needs and when. In this way the manifestation and function of empathy are multidimensional and involve much more than simply the clarification of the inner frame of reference (Binder, 1994b). Batson and Oleson write:

> the most frequently proposed source of altruism has been what we shall call empathy – an other-oriented emotional response congruent with the perceived welfare of another person. If the other is in need, then empathic emotions include sympathy, compassion, tenderness, and the like. These empathic emotions can and should be distinguished from the more self-oriented emotions of discomfort, anxiety, and agitation, often called personal distress . . . it often seems that we must take steps to avoid feeling empathy. This apparent necessity to defend ourselves against feeling empathy suggests that our potential for such feelings is strong indeed. (Batson and Oleson, 1991: 63, 81–2)

Empathic understanding is an interpersonal process whose level depends on emotional amenability to the perceived feelings of another person, i.e. one assumes for the moment a person is capable of receiving the signals of the other person and that the other is capable of sending these signals. The closer the two persons are in their experience, the easier this process becomes. Empathy doesn't occur at random, but in the context of a frame of reference which is structured according to the dimensions closeness–distance, known–unknown, friend–foe, clarity–confusion. It is in its original nature socially communicative (Bavelas et al., 1990). Empathic processes and their succcessful realization in understanding, communication and action lead (for both transmitter and recipient) to increased well-being and self-esteem, to a more optimistic view of the world and to stronger contact and trust. Batson and Oleson continue:

> If the empathy-altruism hypothesis is true, there are broad implications . . . we must radically revise our views about human nature and the human capacity for caring. To say that we are capable of altruistic motivation is to say that we can care about the welfare of others for their sakes and not simply for our-own. And if this is true, then we are far more social animals than our social psychological theories would lead us to believe. (Batson and Oleson, 1991: 81)

So here we have – and with empirical validation – a confirmation of Rogers's conception of man. If, however, empathy and altruism were the only behaviours available to us our ability to protect ourselves and our own territory would be under threat. We would be permanently and totally overwhelmed both emotionally and socially and no longer able adequately to regulate our own needs, interests and desires. What is more, empathy can lead to aggressive reactions. Many a being-for-a-specific-person is automatically accompanied by a being-against-another-person i.e. with empathic anger (Hoffmann, 1990). Furthermore, empathy, being an emotional process which has to be genuinely experienced, requires – in comparison with routinely accessible knowledge – a high degree of intensity and mental energy and, no matter how spontaneous and fresh it is experienced, it still takes place in a comparatively complicated, hesitant and ponderous way (Wilson and Klaaren, 1992). Therefore we still need and have another species-specific disposition of social understanding which is just as vital but whose emotional/affective structure is neutral and motivationally different.

Cognitive/social perspective-taking

Cognitive/social perspective-taking is a rationally focused putting-oneself-into-somebody's-position. It assumes a cognitive understanding of the feelings and the motives of the other person and is a practical and technical skill oriented towards objective classification and assessment (Bryant, 1990). It has the function of environmental and social control. It decreases anxiety and makes forward planning possible. It can produce, on the one hand, flexible and quick decisions and evaluations, which are based on life experience, and on the other hand rigid, narrow-minded patterns of expectation and judgement which block access to genuine experiencing.

Apart from its function in promoting social learning through the observation and interpretation of meaningful patterns of cause and effect in human behaviour, it can serve also to ensure the fulfilment of individual interests and needs in social interaction. The capacity to see through other persons, to deceive and cheat them for one's own interests, is compatible with an image of man which is in its own terms just as plausible as the altruistic model outlined above. If we consider it neutrally as a useful instrumental skill, cognitive social perspective-taking serves primarily to give us experience and insight which will enable us to improve our self-control and control of our environment by constructing consistent expectations with regard to the patterns of human behaviour. The tendency to take such a rational, interpretive understanding of significance and motive, with its accent on both immediate relevance and future consequences, understandably increases in interpersonal relationships, wherever competitive ambitions and conflicts of interest predominate. Furthermore, it occurs very markedly in conditions which are characterized by fear, uncertainty, inferiority, confusion, helplessness, dependence and weakness, that is to say in cases where there is a lack of confidence and trust in oneself and in others.

Fluctuation between the dimensions of social understanding

In reality, both dimensions of social understanding are usually combined, complete each other and displace each other. Different people – dependent on the context, the relationship, the situation and the condition – have different priorities regarding understanding and communication in interpersonal relationships. It seems to be precisely this appropriate fluctuation between more emotional and more cognitive ways of understanding which constitutes congruent mental functioning, manifested in more flexible, autonomous self-control and in the control of the environment in the interpersonal field. Mental disorders can be considered as an inability to be flexible and autonomous in the perception of and adaptation to intrapsychic and external reality.

A core problem for psychotic persons is the fact that they have not developed adequate discrimination in the understanding dimension. Because of the intractable ambivalence of their need for closeness and their simultaneous mistrust, there exists an unintegrated and confusing (for both partners in the interaction) readiness for empathy, which is oriented towards connecting and opening up on an emotional level while at the same time there is a need for self-protection and dissociation which generates interpretive social cognitions. A consequence of this is the interpretation of all signals from the other person as secret, but significant, relationship messages.

Implications for psychotherapeutic understanding

In a constructive therapeutic procedure, as the therapist seeks access to understanding, each step is always empathic. We must establish an emotional contact with the experiencing of the other person which is often different to our own, inaccessible and disordered. This is necessary in order to maintain an empathic connection with the other person and his or her specific disorder through those aspects of their experience which are accessible, perhaps via their fantasies. We do this by moving within our personal world of experience and/or if need be by means of a general empathic responsiveness relating to conditions such as inner emptiness and confusion. Only later is it advisable by empathic active searching for meaning-contexts to edge closer to a way of understanding which creates meaning (Finke, 1994).

Here we need to acknowledge clearly that even client-centred psychotherapists rarely work according to an exact definition of empathy construed as an essential agent of change. Empathy, as a basic element of social understanding and action, forms, both ontogenetically and in the practice of social communication, the basis of all processes of social understanding. It serves as an affective-motivational frame of reference and gives these processes, which trigger and reinforce each other, their due significance. From the point of view of client-centred theory it is a step backward in our understanding to subordinate both emotions and cognitions to a concept derived from information theory and then to equate them as different aspects of the same thing. Implicitly, however, we proceed from the assumption that the actual processes which are essential to human beings take place on a cognitive level. The differences which we cannot deny and which are experienced at a phenomenal and functional level are acknowledged as an unpleasant, disturbing concomitant. Recent debate on the notion of emotions as epiphenomena has elucidated this idea. Tucker, Vanatta and Rothlind remind us that 'at each level, emotional and motivational processes exert specific controls on the cognitive representational system. The biological view shows that emotions are not just epiphenomenal, subjective products of the mental apparatus. They are indeed the engines of the Mind' (1990: 164). Even though thinking about another person and empathizing with this person are actually different mental processes, they can certainly be compatible. They are only in opposition when they establish motivationally contrasting priorities, and not when they are complementary modalities referring to the same objective (Binder, 1996).

Empathy in the child's primary carer and its impact on the development of the person

Typical interactions

If we look at the normal development of the self in early childhood we find common characteristics of the mother–child interaction throughout all cultures. These are clearly equivalent to what Prouty calls 'psychological contact'. The tendency to imitate and to comment on the behaviour of the child is recognized as early empathic reflection, motor mimicry and affect attunement. These are considered to be primitive forms of communicative empathy (Bavelas et al., 1990).

In early empathic reflection the reference person is aware of and understands the feelings of the child and shows the child, by imitating it, how it feels and which expression belongs to which feeling. In such a way the perceived feelings and their expression and communication are connected. With communication and reaction a further dimension comes into play; the reference person stimulates, regulates, reassures and converts the interaction into an emotional process or into a concrete need-satisfaction. Here, as a first step, empathic participation is communicated through imitation and then smoothly passes into modes of behaviour which are based on empathy: arousing interest, sharing attention, cheering up or distracting, soothing and offering concrete help. Early mother–child interactions do not always take place without words; in all cultures if they are verbalized this is done in a relatively high voice and, depending on the situation, in an exaggerated or a monotonous tone. All over the world babies pay more enthusiastic attention to 'baby language' than to adult language (Fernald, 1992). By speaking baby language the primary carer makes it easier for the child to distinguish which messages are relevant to the relationship and which are neutral and in this way helps the child to develop a selective perception of environmental stimuli.

The functions of early mother–child interactions

The empathy of primary carers is most significant in the development of the self, the self-concept, the capacity for bonding and social understanding and in the acquisition of self-control and control of the environment (Hattie, 1992). As the primary carer not only imitates, but also comments, reacts and acts, he or she anticipates later processes: self-regulation, prioritization of emotions and motives, discrimination between external and internal attention (which includes the discrimination between discrete feelings, emotional attunement and reaction on the one hand and purely subjective responses on the other) and the ability to shift between them, control over one's social interaction and control of one's environment. Thus, early empathic interactions are of great significance in the social/emotional development of the self even before the establishment of a self-concept, a clear I–others differentiation, and before verbal symbolizations and cognitions.

If we look at the interactions described above we see that this early empathic contact shows several distinctive features which correspond, even if on a different level, with the characteristic disorders of our patients (though these will have different significance and different manifestations, depending on the nature of the disorder).

Psychotic disorders as possible consequences of inadequate development

We know that a deficiency in empathic ability on the part of the child's primary carer correlates with a deficiency in the empathic development of the child. We also know that a deficiency in the development of a mature empathic ability is connected with deficiencies in the regulation of emotions, in the capacity for spontaneous social behaviour, in social competence and in the capacity for emotional expression. There is also a lack of self-confidence (Eisenberg and Fabes, 1992) and of self- and environmental control.

We find disorders, problems and deviances in patients with schizophrenic tendencies in all these respects. They often do not have a sufficiently structured, stable self-concept or, in apparent contrast to this, they manifest a rigid, not easily comprehensible distortion of their self-concept. They desperately enter into binding relationships with great intensity or they avoid them with equal intensity. They take things personally and develop vehement reactions to others where no rational basis for such a reaction can be discerned. They seem to be at the same time highly empathic and completely indifferent. They also have difficulties in assigning, controlling and structuring their experiences, thoughts and feelings. They oscillate between 'excessive actualising tendency' (Speierer, 1994)[1] and inner emptiness. They are not able to influence either the inflation or the deflation of their experiencing sufficiently. They also have difficulty in co-ordinating, in a future-oriented, goal-directed way, their ability to influence relationships in their social milieu on the one hand and their actual behaviour on the other. Their capacity to structure, differentiate, select and hierarchize motives is reduced in both their internal awareness and in their understanding of the external social world. Their lack of a sufficiently stable, structured self-concept and perception of others – whether or not these are congruent or realistic – also has an impact on their agonizing ambivalence. Furthermore their consciousness of time goes astray. They can seem trapped for ever in the past, but it is not unknown for them to speak as if they have no past at all. Mendel (1974) refers to this as the 'historicizing deficit'.

What went wrong in the social-emotional development of our psychotic patients, and why and how and with what consequences, we are only just beginning to understand. We do know, though, from research (Cicchetti and White, 1990; Feshbach, 1990) that parents who maltreat their children show a significant difference in empathic ability from parents who don't but are otherwise comparable. We also know that maltreated children show similar behaviour and social-emotional problems in their observable psychopathological deviances as other children who grew up with a primary carer who was lacking in empathic capability. And we know from such research (Cicchetti and White, 1990) that these problems relate to disorders in the social-emotional development and not to impairments in the cognitive field. This is in agreement with many on research-based results concerning the primacy of emotional affective processes regarding both healthy and disordered developments (Damasio, 1994).

Development of empathy

The developmental steps of the child

Empathic ability in the child develops via pre-forms like emotional contagion and imitation, emotional attunement and emotional reactions (Binder, 1994a). These pre-forms occur automatically and immediately. They are not dependent on a goal-oriented intention. They cannot function without a responsiveness to feelings. Empathy in the usual sense of the word only becomes possible with the ability to differentiate between I and others, which occurs at the age of 16–20 months (Bischof-Köhler, 1989). When the moment arrives, empathy occurs immediately and with full intensity in the context of the child's world of experience.

Generally, intensive empathic excitability decreases in the course of development in favour of situation-specific and relationship-specific empathic processes in which the pre-forms – excitement, contagion, identificatory understanding – are always passed through very rapidly and sometimes only partially and finally, either through actualization and action or through refusal and avoidance, are transformed into differentiation and coping. The empathic pre-forms are maintained as possible modes of reaction throughout life. At best, they are integrated as a necessary element of the empathic process. At worst, they are maintained without being integrated.

The development of cognitive/social perspective-taking occurs at about the same time, but it is subject to different developmental conditions (Bryant, 1990). The development from a purely affective empathy in early childhood to empathic experiencing goes along with the development of time consciousness (Melges, 1982) and identity consciousness. Being able to empathize with another person and thus with this person's different way of experiencing, with his or her felt sense and motivation, requires a sufficiently stable identity. Empathizing with the personality of another person, based as it is on both stable and changing factors, is also a condition for flexibility in the selection of appropriate dimensions of social understanding. Empathy makes it easier to oscillate appropriately and realistically between cognitive/social perspective-taking and empathy itself.

Intentionality of focused attention through the example of role-playing in childhood[2]

The high intensity of empathy in early childhood is not merely the product of an immature, incomplete transitional stage, but also aids self-experience and environmental experiences which stimulate orientation and control in the intrapsychic and interpersonal field and in the environment as a whole. In role-playing the child, in endless variations, experiences a differentiation between the manifold forms of emotional exchange as well as an understanding of another person's way of being through an identificatory understanding. The feelings represented in the role-playing can certainly be experienced, but the child is aware of the fact that he or she has adopted them consciously and produced them himself or herself; that is, they remain subject to self-regulation. Thus, the I–others differentiation and the outside–inside differentiation are maintained analogously to mature empathic processes.

Role-playing serves to enable an understanding of the environment at a pre-verbal level and in a concrete and holistic fashion. In this way the environmental circumstances are experienced for oneself through an identificatory empathic understanding and then become experiential patterns which can be retrieved without the emotional energy originally attached to them. Emotional experiencing is triggered and acted out through intentional imitation and identification. The process-nature of experience and the ability to exercise skill in action and control are maintained, so that the emotional intensity stays in the experience and through insight, and the person is not overwhelmed and distressed.

Reflections upon disorder-specific consequences of impaired development processes

Disorder-specific deficiencies, such as an inadequate integration of emotional and cognitive functional systems and the consequent inability to shift between different dimensions of social understanding (empathy and social/cognitive perspective-taking), and the dominance of empathic pre-forms and thus deficient perception and behaviour, especially in the interpersonal field, lead to a specific vulnerability in psychotic persons. Apart from certain dispositional factors, this vulnerability can be attributed to interpersonal processes in the early empathic developmental stage and in the early relationship with the primary carer. It usually becomes relevant only during a later adolescence stage, because only then, as in non-pathological development, does the person become capable of experiencing mature social understanding and mature interpersonal relating.

Empathy is an active mental procedure which is based on motivation, specifically on a conscious control not of the perceived contents, but of the direction towards them. It involves the intentional activation of certain emotional dimensions of experiencing. Emotional contagion and imitation, however, are unintentional, passive events without a specific goal. Depending on the quality of the infected or imitated feeling, this can be positive or negative. Absolutely negative, so to speak, is the lack of active, competent interpersonal influence which is experienced in psychosis. Empathy, in principle, evokes field-specific emotions via the I–others differentiation; emotional contagion, on the other hand, generates global conditions. Such global conditions which take place passively are of an absolute nature and are not adequate materials from which to construct a sufficiently differentiated self-image.

If it is not embedded in a frame of reference, empathy can become an agony: one cannot charge oneself continuously and without impairment with someone's feelings and state of mind nor can one cope with the idea of being emotionally transparent to everybody without becoming frightened. Apart from that, in the case of an indiscriminate, unspecific empathic receptivity one cannot structure the inevitable ambivalences and turbulences on an experiential level, nor can one control one's own feelings and actions in a realistic way. Where signals and their communicative direction are vague and unclear the task of deciphering messages which are relevant for the relationship in principle has priority over empathic participation, which only takes place after classification in a fixed friend–foe, familiar–unfamiliar frame of reference and a corresponding motivation, and also always depends on whether the perceived signal refers to the interaction, to the inner psychic experience or to an external event which both partners in the interaction are aware of.

Therapeutic implications

In the therapeutic procedure, it is essential in working with psychotic patients always to be aware of the fact that in spite of all their disorders and problems, they have access to behaviours where they function as adults and in a differentiated way. In stable periods they know very well how they feel and understand and they also know – and to them this is a shameful and well-kept secret – that in some fields and phases of their experience they abandon the adult way of feeling and understanding, as we all do at certain exceptional moments. This means that if, together with them, we always empathically search for the experiential point of development in which they are situated, and react in a way which corresponds to their immediate state of need and their ability to understand the process in which they are involved, we have to do this with the respect appropriate to equal, adult persons. We can communicate this respect by not necessarily pushing them to explore their inner frame of reference, but by admitting content which in the normal therapeutic process is seen as less constructive, for instance conversations about general, intellectual and philosophical subjects. In such conversations the patients can experience self-respect as well as feel themselves valued in the relationship and thus, while maintaining the connection with themselves and with the therapist, they have a break from psychotic experiencing during which they can recover structure and differentiation on the emotional and on the cognitive level (Binder and Binder, 1994b).

Empathy, at least in work with these patients, is not an accessory to the relationship; it is, so to speak, the method itself which runs analogously with the early childhood development of self-structure, self-experience, I–others differentiation, social frames of reference and the shaping of central, motivational, emotional, affective and cognitive structures (Brooks-Gun, 1992; Lewis, 1992) within a secure relationship. In concrete terms, this procedure can be activated by establishing a psychological contact (Prouty, 1994) through imitation, comment and active, positive emotional reference. In this way the patient doesn't experience himself or herself simply as part of an interpersonal relationship, but experiences his or her self through the ability to influence and control the process. This means that self-control and environmental control are reinforced.

By evoking a state of emotional attunement without emotional entanglement, for instance through joint attention to the shared environment (noises, temperature, objects and so on), within a sufficiently secure, but not constricting bond, structure and orientation as well as control of attention are facilitated (Binder, 1994b). This security without constriction occurs because, among other things, the therapist discloses concerns to the patient by articulating experience of their common environment. If the therapist reflects his or her thoughts aloud in front of a silent patient, as Rogers does in the sessions with Mr Vac, this fulfils the same function (Rogers, 1967). Emphasizing continuity (past), predictability (future) and moment-to-moment empathy (present) helps to give a time structure to experience and to maintain the process (Swildens, 1991).

If we understand a patient's demanding behaviour to be an expression of their need for a bond and at the same time a maintenance of their need to control the interaction within the relationship,[3] then we can react in a therapeutically constructive way first by understanding this empathically and then, while maintaining an affirming attitude, by fulfilling this need or not according to our own differentiated needs which we communicate to the patient. If the patient's time consciousness is confused, he or she comes to imagine that thinking is the same as having done, and external and internal occurrences which are accidentally simultaneous become meaningfully connected. If we view these phenomena in terms of the dominance of empathic pre-forms, combined with a sensitivity (which goes far beyond the childish world of experience) to signals which make the I–others and the outside–inside differentiation fragile and inconstant, we can understand them as something which is subjectively real for the patient in their situation. Then we can react to these phenomena without developing negative affect ourselves with which we might infect, frighten and confuse our patients.

Because there is a dominance of unintegrated empathic pre-forms and a tendency to reach a state of extreme stress with high ambivalence between fearful, confused and vulnerable withdrawal tendencies on the one hand and a longing for harmonious and strong emotional bonds on the other, with such patients there is a danger that they will react to barely conscious minor facial expressions and irrelevant gestures by the therapist as if these were meaningful messages regarding the relationship. It is necessary to establish an emotional relationship in which both partners can be so secure, free of anxiety and confident that in the immediate interaction the relationship either is in the foreground and acknowledged as such, or can be, as it were, set to one side. Against the self-evident background of the relationship it is possible that patient and therapist can pay close attention to the patient's experiences as a common third element (Pfeiffer, 1993).

Emotional, affective and cognitive self-experience without isolation (that is, with emotional resonance with a partner) always frees the experience from the consequences of external social evaluation which threaten the relationship, and thus enables the person to have internal, organismic experiences which certainly have a social dimension. Thus the experience of the relationship is disconnected from the conflict between the tendencies to autonomy and dependence (Searles, 1976), and there is a reinforcement of the experience of identity and the constructive control of self and environ-ment. An understanding of development stimuli in the early mother–child relationship can assist us to support the patient in developing their identity and in learning to send and receive messages adequately with the goal of an empathic and cognitive social understanding within their present frame of reference.

In work with severely disordered psychotic patients it is essential that we make our interactions, as well as the source of our empathic understanding and knowledge, transparent to the patient. In order to be able to do so, we have to be accurately and congruently aware of our own experiencing and reflect it with regard to its implications for the therapeutic relationship and the therapeutic process from moment to moment on the basis of our understanding of the particular disorder and of our concrete experience with a particular client. Then there is also a possibility that the client can experience in a positive way – and this is often a really new experience – that human beings can open themselves up and can become as familiar with each other as they want to within a specific time-frame and in a goal-oriented and co-ordinated approach of differentiation, self-control and control of others and without damage or offence (Binder and Binder, 1994a).

Even though from an external point of view the therapeutic process in work with these patients often seems to develop in an unconventional way, it generally follows the same principles as other empathic processes of understanding and intimacy. Overall we support Buck and Ginsberg who say: 'The capacity for altruism and communication, having an affective foundation, requires, if impaired, an affective approach to restoration that precedes the rational-cognitive in both human and animal therapy' (1991: 160).

Final remarks

In all mental disorders – not only in schizophrenic disorders – the outcome of the therapeutic treatment offered by all psychotherapeutic schools is by no means satisfactory and there is much need for development. The fact that client-centred psychotherapy once turned its back on the psycho-pathological field (for good historical reasons) can no longer serve as a legitimate reason for neglecting work with psychotic people. There is a crying need for study and innovative practice, and the person-centred approach has shown itself to be wholly compatible with recent discoveries in developmental psychology and psychopathological research. We need to establish clinical hypotheses and to set about research which is appropriate to the person-centred paradigm.

Notes

This chapter was translated by Elisabeth Zinschitz.

1 This is the technical form for a phenomenon which can be described as excessive impulsivity.

2 Selective perception: in Germany the psychiatric technical term is the ability to 'actualize' and 'disactualize' (Janzarik, 1959) which means to be able to intentionally focus on or put aside a certain affective, emotional, cognitive or perceptional aspect of a total experience.

3 In autistic children we find adequately developed request behaviour alongside the lack of social emotional communication (Cicchetti and White, 1990).

References

Batson, D. and Oleson, K. (1991) 'Current status of the empathy-altruism hypothesis', in M.S. Clark (ed.), *Prosocial Behaviour*. Newbury Park, CA: Sage.

Bavelas, J.B., Black, A., Lemery, C.R. and Mullet, J. (1990) 'Motor mimicry as primitive empathy', in N. Eisenberg and J. Strayer (eds), *Empathy and its Development*. New York: Cambridge University Press.

Binder, U. (1990) 'Einige Thesen zur personzentrierten Psychotherapie mit Schizophrenen', in G. Meyer-Cording and G. Speierer (eds), *Gesundheit und Krankheit*. Cologne: GwG.

Binder, U. (1994a) *Empathieentwicklung und Pathogenese in der klientenzentrierten Psychotherapie*. Eschborn: Dietmar Klotz.

Binder, U. (1994b) 'Klientenzentrierte Psychotherapie mit Patienten aus dem schizophrenen Formenkreis. Ein systemimmanentes, störungsspezifisches Verstehens- und Handlungskonzept', in E. Hutterer-Krisch (ed.), *Psychotherapie mit psychotischen Menschen*. Vienna: Springer.

Binder, U. (1996) 'Die Bedeutung des motivationalen Aspektes von Empathie und kognitiver sozialer Perspektivenübernahme in der personenzentrierten Psychotherapie', in R. Hutterer, G. Pawlowski, P. Schmid and R. Stipsits (eds), *Client-centered and Experiential Psychotherapy*. Frankfurt-on-Main: Peter Lang.

Binder, U. and Binder, J. (1994a) *Klientenzentrierte Psychotherapie bei schweren psychischen Störungen*, 3rd edn. Eschborn: Dietmar Klotz.

Binder, U. and Binder, J. (1994b) *Studien zu einer klientenzentrierten störungsspezifischen Psychotherapie – Schizophrene Ordnung – Psychosomatisches Erleben – Depressives Leiden*, 2nd edn. Eschborn: Dietmar Klotz.

Bischof-Köhler, D. (1989) *Spiegelbild und Empathie*. Bern: Hans Huber.

Brooks-Gunn, J. (1992) quoted in Hattie (1992).

Bruch, H. (1980) 'Psychotherapy in schizophrenia', in J.S. Strauss, M. Bowers, T. Downey, S. Fleck, S. Jackson and I. Levine (eds), *The Psychotherapy of Schizophrenia*. New York: Plenum.

Bryant, B.K. (1990) 'Mental health, temperament, family and friends: perspectives on children's empathy and perspective taking', in N. Eisenberg and J. Strayer (eds), *Empathy and its Development*. New York: Cambridge University Press.

Buck, R. and Ginsberg, B. (1991) 'Spontaneous communication and altruism: the communicative gene hypothesis', in M.S. Clark (ed.), *Prosocial Behavior*. Newbury Park, CA: Sage.

Cicchetti, D. and White, J. (1990) 'Emotion and developmental psychopathology', in N.L. Stein, B. Leventhal and T. Trabasso (eds), *Psychological and Biological Approaches to Emotion*. Hillsdale, NJ: Erlbaum.

Damasio, A.R. (1994) *Descartes' Error. Emotion, Reason, and the Human Brain*. New York: Avon Books.

Eisenberg, N. and Fabes, R. (eds) (1992) *Emotion and its Regulation in Early Development*. San Francisco: Jossey-Bass.

Fernald, A. (1992) 'Human maternal vocalizations to infants as biologically relevant signals: an evolutionary perspective', in J. Barkow, I. Cosmides and J. Tooby (eds), *The Adapted Mind*. Oxford: Oxford University Press.

Feshbach, N.D. (1990) 'Parental empathy and child adjustment/maladjustment', in N. Eisenberg and J. Strayer (eds), *Empathy and its Development*. New York: Cambridge University Press.

Finke, J. (1994) *Empathie und Interaktion*. Stuttgart: Thieme.

Fleck, S. (1980) 'Some observations of the nature and value of psychotherapy with schizophrenic patients', in J.S. Strauss, M. Bowers, T. Downey, S. Fleck, S. Jackson and I. Levine (eds), *The Psychotherapy of Schizophrenia*. New York: Plenum.

Fromm-Reichmann, F. (1976) 'Heilung durch Wiederherstellung von Vertrauen', in P. Matussek (ed.), *Psychotherapie schizophrener Personen*. Hamburg: Hoffmann & Campe.

Hattie, J. (1992) *Self-Concept*. Hillsdale, NJ: Erlbaum.

Hoffmann, M.L. (1990) 'The contribution of empathy to justice and moral judgement', in N. Eisenberg and J. Strayer (eds), *Empathy and its Development*. New York: Cambridge University Press.

Janzarik, W. (1959) *Dynamische Grundkonstellationen in endogenen Psychosen*. Berlin, Göttingen and Heidelberg: Springer.

Lewis, M. (1992) *Shame*. New York: Free Press.

Lidz, T. (1980) 'The developing guidelines to the psychotherapy of schizophrenia', in J.S. Strauss, M. Bowers, T. Downey, S. Fleck, S. Jackson and I. Levine (eds), *The Psychotherapy of Schizophrenia*. New York: Plenum.

Melges, F.T. (1982) *Time and the Inner Future*. New York: Wiley.

Mendel, W.M. (1974) 'A phenomenological theory of schizophrenia', in A. Burton, J. Lopez-Ibor and W.M. Mendel (eds), *Schizophrenia as a Lifestyle*. New York: Springer.

Pfeiffer, W.M. (1993) 'Die Bedeutung der Beziehung bei der Entstehung und der Therapie psychischer Störungen', in L. Teusch and J. Finke (eds), *Krankheitslehre der Gesprächspsychotherapie*. Heidelberg: Asanger.

Prouty, G. (1994) *Theoretical Evolutions in Person-Centered/Experiential Therapy*. Westport, CT: Praeger.

Rogers, C.R. (ed.) (1967) *The Therapeutic Relationship and its Impact: A Study of Psychotherapy with Schizophrenics*. Madison, WI: University of Wisconsin Press.

Searles, H.F. (1976) 'Volle Einsicht in das Abhängigkeitsbedürfnis', in P. Matussek (ed.), *Psychotherapie Schizophrener Personen*. Hamburg: Hoffmann & Campe.

Speierer, G.W. (1994) *Das differentielle Inkongruenzmodell*. Heidelberg: Asanger.

Swildens, H. (1991) *Prozeßorientierte Gesprächspsychotherapie*. Cologne: GwG.

Tourney, G., Bloom, V., Lowinger, P.L., Schorer, C., Auld, F. and Grisell, J. (1976) 'Neurotiker müssen anders psychotherapiert werden als Psychotiker', in P. Matussek (ed.), *Psychotherapie Schizophrener Personen*. Hamburg: Hoffmann & Campe.

Tucker, D.M., Vanatta, K. and Rothlind, J. (1990) 'Arousal and activation systems and primitive adaptive controls on cognitive priming', in N. Stein, B. Leventhal and T. Trabasso (eds), *Psychological and Biological Approaches to Emotion*. Hillsdale, NJ: Erlbaum.

Whitehorn, J.C. and Betz, B. (1975) *Effective Psychotherapy with the Schizophrenic Patient*. New York: Jason Aronson.

Will, O. (1980) 'Comments on the elements of schizophrenia, psychotherapy and the schizophrenic person', in J.S. Strauss, M. Bowers, T. Downey, S. Fleck, S. Jackson and I. Levine (eds), *The Psychotherapy of Schizophrenia*. New York: Plenum.

Wilson, T. and Klaaren, K. (1992) 'Expectation whirls me round: the role of affective expectations in affective experience', in M. Clark (ed.), *Emotion and Social Behavior*. Newbury Park, CA: Sage.

Postscript: Person-Centred Therapy: an International Force

Brian Thorne

The first International Forum for the person-centred approach (as opposed to the first conference) took place in 1982 and the venue was Oaxtepec in Mexico. This year's (1998) Forum is to be held in South Africa. It is the contention of this book that the approach is alive and well in Europe and that European scholars and practitioners are currently making major contributions to its increasing influence and development. Be that as it may, Europeans need to guard against *folie de grandeur*. It is a remarkable fact that the approach has made considerable inroads into such widely differing cultures as those of the South American continent and of Japan. The South African venue for the next Forum also serves as a powerful reminder that Carl Rogers and his colleague, Ruth Sanford, made a significant contribution to the emergence of democracy in that country by their courageous visits in the years leading up to the bloodless revolution and the abolition of apartheid.

It is undoubtedly a tribute to the genius of Carl Rogers and his associates that the approach to therapy which they developed in the context of American society in the 1950s and 1960s, encapsulates a truth about human beings and their yearnings for a better world which finds a resonance in almost every part of the globe. Person-centred practitioners who now regularly come together to exchange their discoveries and experiences at international gatherings are no longer astonished that what goes on in consulting rooms in Chicago, London, Vienna, Berlin, Paris, Tokyo, Mexico City, Johannesburg and countless other locations throughout the world bears witness to a common humanity and to a universal longing both for individual fulfilment and corporate identity. It is difficult to imagine a therapeutic approach of which the world stands in greater need as we move towards the new millennium.

Appendix: European Associations, Societies and Training Institutes for the Person-Centred Approach

Austria

Österreichische Gesellschaft für wissenschaftliche, klientenzentrierte Psychotherapie und personorientierte Gesprächsführung (Ö GwG)

Altstadt 17
A–4020 Linz
(Society and Training Institute)

Arbeitsgemeinschaft für Personenzentrierte Psychotherapie Gesprächsführung und Supervision (APG)

Währingerstraße 50–52/1/13
A–1090 Vienna
(Society and Training Institute)

Vereinigung Rogerianische Psychotherapie (VRP)

A–1091 Vienna
Postfach 33
(Society and Training Institute)

Person-Centred Association in Austria (PCA)

PCA, c/o Institut für Psychologie
Universität Wien
Liebiggasse 5
A–1010 Vienna
(Association providing training seminars and workshops)

Belgium

Associations

Vereniging voor clientgerichte psychotherapie
Zeelse baan 52
B–9200 Grembergen

Association francophone pour la psychothérapie non-directive ou centrée sur le client (AFPC)
Avenue Sainte-Alix 60
B–1150 Brussels

Training institutes

Counseling Centrum (K.U. Leuven)
Blijde Inkomststraat 13
B–3000 Leuven

Faculteit voor mens en samenleving
Stationsstraat 82
B–2300 Turnhout

Postgraduate studies in Experiëntiële Therapie (R.U. Gent)
Faculteit voor Psychologische en Pedagogische Wetenschappen
H. Dunantlaan 2
B–9000 Ghent

Czech Republic

Training institutes

PCA Institute
Plavecká 2
12800 Prague 2

Czech PCA Institute
Brno

Charles University
Faculty of Letters and Faculty of Medicine
Prague

France

Training institutes

Groupe d'étude Carl Rogers (modules in Paris and in Dijon)
9 avenue de la Motte-Picquet
75007 Paris

Institut du Développement et de la Formation à la Communication des Personnes (IDFCP)
25/27 rue Pigalle
75009 Paris

Centre de Développement de la Personne (La Maison des Bois)
158 avenue Sidi Carnot
91160 Les Rochers de Saulx les Chartreux

Person Centered Approach Institute France
22 Chemin des Creux
74140 Veigy-Foncenex

Germany

Associations

Gesellschaft für wissenschaftliche Gesprächspsychotherapie e.V. (GwG)
Bundesgeschäftsstelle:

Richard-Wagner-Straße 12
D–50674 Cologne

Ärztliche Gesellschaft für Gesprächspsychotherapie e.V. (ÄGG)

c/o Dr Jobst Finke
Rheinische Landes- und Hochschulklinik
D–45147 Essen

Training institutes

Akademie für Gesprächspsychotherapie GmbH (AGB), Berlin
Ausbildungsinstitut für Gesprächspsychotherapie GmbH Essen (AiG), Essen
Ausbildungsinstitut für klientenzentrierte Psychotherapie und Beratung Schleswig-Holstein und Mecklenburg-Vorpommern, Kiel
Ausbildungsinstitut für personenzentrierte Psychotherapie und Beratung im Rheinland, Rheinbach
Ausbildungsinstitut Landau, Heidelberg
Ausbildungsinstitut Münster (aim), Nordwalde
Bergische Universität Wuppertal – Fachbereich 3, Wuppertal
Bielefelder Ausbildungsinstitut für personenzentrierte Gesprächspsychotherapie, Beratung und Supervision (BAIG), Bielefeld
Bremer Institut für Gesprächspsychotherapie und Gesprächsführung, Bremen
Carl Rogers Akademie Ruhr, Essen
Deutsche Akademie zur Verbreitung für personzentrierte und experientelle Psychologie und Psychotherapie e.V. (DAPEPP), Heidelberg
Fachhochschule Frankfurt, Frankfurt-on-Main
Focusing-Zentrum Karlsruhe, Weingarten
Fortbildungsinstitut Engelshof, Cologne
Hessische Akademie für personzentrierte Psychotherapie, Beratung und Supervision e.V., Marburg

Humboldt-Universität Berlin, Berlin
Institut für personzentrierte Beratung und Gesprächspsychotherapie, Hannover
Institut für personzentrierte Psychotherapie, Beratung und Supervision (IPP), Bielefeld
Institut für personzentrierte Beratung und Supervision, Rhein/Ruhr (IBS), Dortmund
Institut für Gesprächspsychotherapie und klientenzentrierte Beratung e.V., Saarbrücken
Institut für klientenzentrierte Gesprächspsychotherapie und Beratung Freiburg (IKGB), Waldkirch
Institut für personzentrierte Beratung und Gesprächspsychotherapie (IGB), Stuttgart
Institut zur Verbreitung des klientenzentrierten Ansatzes (VkA), Bad Waldsee-Osterhofen
Institut für personzentrierte Kinder- und Jungendlichenpsychotherapie (KJPT), Munich
Institut für Gesprächspsychotherapie (IGT), Schrobenhausen
Institut für psycho-soziale Gesundheit (IPSG), Weitransdorf-Weidach
Institut für Gesprächspsychotherapie (Franken), Bamberg
Institut für personzentrierte Beratung, Reutlingen
Kölner Institut für personale und professionelle Entwicklung e.V., Cologne
Kölner Therapeuten Kollektiv, Cologne
Lehrinstitut für Kindertherapie, Berlin
Regensburger Akademie für Gesprächspsychotherapie e.V., Regensburg
Zentrum für personzentrierte Pädagogik e.V., Cologne
Zentrum für personzentrierte Pädagogik e.V., Bremen
Zentrum für personzentrierte Pädagogik e.V. (ZPP), Marburg

Great Britain

Associations

British Association for the Person-Centred Approach (BAPCA)
BM–BAPCA
London WC1N 3XX

Association for Person-Centred Therapy, Scotland
40 Kelvingrove Street
Glasgow G3 7RZ

Training institutes

Person-Centred Therapy (Britain)
40 Kelvingrove Street
Glasgow G3 7RZ
(Supervision and Advanced Training)

Institute for Person-Centred Learning
220 Ashurst Drive
Barkingside
Ilford
Essex IG6 1EW

Person-Centred Approach Institute International (Northern Britain)
11 St Mary's Avenue
Mirfield
Yorks WF14 0PX

Metanoia Institute
13 North Common Road
Ealing
London W5 2QB

Sherwood Psychotherapy Training Institute
Thiskney House
2 St James Terrace
Nottingham NG1 6FW

Counselling Unit
Faculty of Education
University of Strathclyde
76 Southbrae Drive
Glasgow G13 1PP

Centre for Counselling Studies
School of Education and Professional Development
University of East Anglia
Norwich NR4 7TJ

Centre for Counselling Studies
Department of Applied Social Studies
University of Keele
Keele
Staffs ST5 5BG

Temenos
13A Penrhyn Road
Sheffield S11 8UL

Greece

Association

Hellenic Person-Centred Approach Association
PO Box 21001
114 10 Athens

Training institute

Centre for Education in the Person-Centred Approach
11 Antinoros Street
Athens 11634

Italy

Association

Società Italiana per il Counselling,
Via Cà Bianca 5
40131 Bologna

Training institutes

Centro Di Psicologia Clinica
Piazza di Porta
Maggiore 6 – 00185 Rome

Istituto di Psicologia della Persona e della Personalita
Via Cà Bianca 5
40131 Bologna

Istituto dell'Approccio Centrato della Persona
P. Vittorio Emanuele, 00100 Rome

Luxembourg

Association

Gesellschaft fir Psychotherapie a Forschung – Lëtzebuerger
Gesellschaft fir wëssensschaftlech
Gespreichpsychotherapie (GPG-LGwG) B.P. 54
L-8005 Bertrange

The Netherlands

Association

Vereniging voor Cliëntgerichte Psychotherapie (VCgP)
Emmalaan 29
3581 HN Utrecht

Training institutes

Postdoctoral training programmes in client-centred psychotherapy are offered by the Regionale Instellingen voor Nascholing en Opleiding (RINOs).

Centrale RINO-groep
St Jacobsstraat 12–14
3511 BS Utrecht

RINO Noord-Holland
Leidseplein 5
1017 PR Amsterdam

RINO Zuid Nederland
Postbus 88
6200 AB Maastricht

Pre-doctoral training and research programmes are offered at:

Vrije Universiteit Amsterdam
De Boelelaan 1109
1081 HV Amsterdam

Catholic University Nijmegen
Montessorilaan 3
6525 HR Nijmegen

Portugal

Society and training institute

Soceidade Portuguesa de Psicoterapia Centrada no Cliente e Abordagem
  Centrada na Pessoa
Rua Prof. Simòes Raposa, 4–6 A
1600 Lisbon

Portuguese Association for Person-centred Psychotherapy and Counselling
(APPCPC)
Av. 5 de Outubro, 204–5° – 13
1050 Lisbon

Republic of Slovakia

Training institute

PCA Instituté – Ister
Lipova 1
81102 Bratislava

Spain

Training institute

Instituto de Interacción y Dinámica Personal
Hortaleza 73, 3° izda
28004 Madrid

Switzerland

Society and training institute

Schweizerische Gesellschaft für Gesprächspsychotherapie (SGGT)
(Société Suisse pour l'approche et la psychothérapie Centrées sur la personne – SPCP)
(Società Svizzera per l'approccio e la psicoterápia centrata sulla persona – SPCP)
Schoffelgasse 7
CH–8001 Zurich

Training institute

(For French speakers particularly in Switzerland and France)

Association Francophone de Thérapie
Centrée sur la Personne
15 avenue du Lignon
CH-1219 le Lignon-Genève

European Association

Moves are now afoot (1998) to found a European Association for the Person-Centred Approach following a recent meeting in Belgium of practitioners and scholars from several countries.

Website

http://users.powernet.co.uk/pctmk

Index

acceptance, 150, 216, 217
actualizing tendency, 15–16, 18, 92, 96, 106, 113–14, 119, 121
acute stress reaction, 122, 123, 124–5
adolescents, developmental phases, 148–9, 160–1; therapy with, 159, 161–6, 168–74
affective experience, 190
altruism, 218
anchorage, 195–7; and types of contact, 199–204
anxiety, 112, 115, 122, 127, 182–3
attachment, 112–13
Austria, person-centred approach in, 8–9
authentic communication, 143–4
autonomy, 56, 192
awareness, 107

Batson, D., 218
Belgium, person-centred approach in, 3–4
bodily sensations see focusing
Braaten, L., 8
Buber, Martin, 43, 49, 77–8, 80
Buytendijk, Frederik J.H., 77

Carkhuff, R.R., 70
childhood, empathy in, 221–5; see also development of person
client-centred approach, to neurosis, 127–8; non-directivity of, 64–6; to psychopathology, 119, 128, 129–30; see also person-centred approach
cognitive/social perspective-taking, 219, 220, 224
conditioning, 54–6
conditions of worth, 113
congruence, 114, 121, 143–4, 164, 217; see also incongruence
consciousness, 107
contact, types of, 199–204

contact-restoration and strengthening, 199, 201
cosmic meaning, 15–16, 17–18, 19
Crouan, M., 101
cultural contact, 199, 201–4
Czechoslovakia, person-centred approach in, 1–2

Daly, M., 98–9
de Peretti, André, 7
decision-making, 150–1
Deikman, A., 60
desires, 29–32, 33
development of person, adolescent phases, 160–1; anxiety and congruence in, 112, 114, 115; attachment research, 112–13; client-centred concept of, 129; and conditions of worth, 113; emotional experience, 111, 113, 114, 115–16; empathy in, 221–5; fully functioning person, 114; impact of incongruence and trauma, 121–5; phases in development of self-concept, 114–17, 125–6; self-defending tendency, 113–14; self-development in childhood, 109–10, 111; tenderness in, 111–12; UPR and integration of self-experience, 119–21; see also personality development
Devonshire, C., 2, 6, 7
dialogical thinking, 42, 76–7
Dinacci, A., 7
directivity, 62–4, 68–70, 71; see also non-directivity
discourse, 91, 93–6; see also language
Dyckman, J., 59

Eastern Europe, person-centred approach in, 1–2
ego-psychology, 128, 129

emotions, 107–8, 110–11, 120, 190, 221
empathic regard, 110–11, 184
empathy, definition and dimensions of, 109, 217–19; and development, 110, 111, 120, 221–5; in therapy, 135–6, 166, 184, 217, 220, 226–8
encounter, approaches to, 76–9; meaning of term, 75; person-centred theory of, 79–87; as personal relationship, 74–5; in therapy and groups, 83–4, 86–7
encounter philosophy, Other in, 75–6
evil, 56
existential contact, 199–200
experience, affective experience, 190; of bodily sensations, 135, 136–41; concept of person based on, 45–6; definition of, 107; and formation of self-concept, 111, 113, 114, 115–16; and incongruence, 121–3; monitoring of, 126; and personal meaning, 14–15; symbolization of, 107, 141–7; *see also* self-experience
experience-orientation, 66–70
experiential change, 57–8
external desires, 30

fathering, 141–3, 144–7, 148
feminist discourse theory, 93–6, 100–3
first-order desires, 29–32
focusing, and cosmic meaning, 19; and distance to bodily sensations, 135, 136–41; finding own direction, 149–50; friendly interest of therapist, 150–1; good father and authenticity, 141–7; good mothering and empathy, 135–6; hindrances in puberty, 148–9; inner critic, 151–4; interpersonal conditions for, 134–5; link with person-centred approach, 133–4; maturity and spiritual awareness, 154–6; nature of, 131–2; processes and life stages, 133
formative tendency, 15–16, 18
France, person-centred approach in, 7
Frank, J., 20
Frankfurt, H., 29–30
Freud, S., 94, 107–8
fully functioning person, 114, 119, 121

Gendlin, E.T., 3, 7, 65, 69, 131–2, 134, 135, 152, 153
genuineness, 164–5, 183, 184
Germany, person-centred approach in, 2–3
Great Britain, person-centred approach in, 5–6
Greece, person-centred approach in, 7
Griffin, S., 93

groups, encounter in, 83–4, 86–7; person-centred approach to, 177–8, 192–3; *see also* cultural contact; leaders
Guardini, R., 76

Hallidie Smith, W., 6
hallucinatory experiencing, 209–10
Heuves, W., 170
Hlavenka, V., 2
Hollway, W., 94–6

Iberg, J.R., 134
incongruence, 112, 114, 115, 121–3, 124, 125–7; *see also* congruence
individualistic concept of person, 41–2, 44–5
inner critic, 151–4
innocence, 29
insight, 59–60
interactional approach, 166–74
interpretations, 172
Iossifides, P., 7
Irigaray, L., 93–4
Italy, person-centred approach in, 7

Kegan, R., 106
Kierkegaard, S., 48–9
Kratochvil, S., 1–2

Lambers, E., 5, 6
language, 93–4, 99–100; *see also* discourse
leaders, as clients, 176–7, 192; effects of therapy for, 187–9; process and personal themes of, 178–81; theory of group work with, 189–92; therapy conditions and techniques, 182–7
Leijssen, M., 4, 19
Lévinas, E., 43, 78–9
Lietaer, G., 3, 4
love, 25–6, 58, 83
Luckmann, T., 20

manipulation, 63–4
Marcel, G., 77
meaning, cosmic meaning, 15–16, 17–18, 19; link with clinical practice, 12–14; person-centred approach as system of, 16–20; personal meaning, 14–15; psychotherapy as system of, 11–12, 20; understandings of meaning of life, 12
Mearnes, D., 5, 6
Merleau-Ponty, M., 209
Mittlefehldt, P., 100
Morato, H., 199–200
mothering, 135–6, 148

Netherlands, person-centred approach in, 4–5
neurotic patients, 127–8, 216–17
non-directivity, 64–70; *see also* directivity
Norway, person-centred approach in, 8
Nuttin, J.R., 3

object relations, 129
observation-training groups, 207–8, 210, 213
observing self, 60
organism, 92
Other, in encounter philosophy, 75–6

Pagès, M., 7
person, client-centred ideal of, 114, 119, 121; experiential concept of, 45–6; individual and relational concepts of, 41–5; person-centred concept of, 38–9, 45–6, 48–50; philosophical concept of, 39, 40–4, 48–50; psychological approaches to, 38–9, 49–50; Rogers' concept of, 41–2, 44, 46–8; tree image of, 195–8; use and meaning of term, 39–40; *see also* development of person
person-centred approach, applications of, 2–3, 4, 5; group work, 177–8, 186–7, 192–3; international context of, 1–9, 231; as system of meaning, 16–20; training in 2, 3, 4–5, 6, 7, 8, 9, 101–2; *see also* client-centred approach
personal meaning, 14–15
personalism *see* dialogical thinking
personality change, and concept of self, 57–9, 61; and insight, 59–60; person-centred concept of, 54, 55–6, 60–1, 182–4; primacy of therapeutic relationship, 56–7; process of, 57–8; role of conditioning, 54–6
personality development, Rogers' theory of, 92–3; through encounter, 79–83
phenomenological approach, 208–9; Prouty's process, 209–10; with psychotic people, 206–8, 210–14; Van den Berg's process, 210
philosophy, concept of person, 39, 40–4, 48–50; encounter philosophy, 75–6
Poland, person-centred approach in, 1
Portugal, person-centred approach in, 1
post-traumatic stress disorder, 123–5
pre-therapy, 199–204, 207, 208, 209–10
presence, 82, 85–6
Prouty, G., 4, 7, 197, 207, 208, 209–10
psychoanalysis, 64, 128, 129
psychogenic illness, and incongruence, 125–7
psychological contact, 199, 200–1, 221, 226

psychology, concept of person, 38–9, 49–50
psychopathology, concepts of, 119, 128–30
psychotherapy, link between meaning and practice, 12–14; Rogers' definition of, 108–9; as system of meaning, 11–12, 20
psychotic disorders, features of therapy, 197–8, 216–17, 226–8; phenomenological approach to, 206–8, 210–14; as result of inadequate development, 222–3, 225; social understanding, 220; tree conceptualization of, 195–8; types of contact, 199–204
puberty *see* adolescents

reinforcement, selective, 68–70
relationship, concept of person based on, 42–6; conditions for focusing, 134–5; connection with encounter, 74–5; role in personality change, 56–7, 58; *see also* development of person; therapeutic relationship
religion, 19–20, 42; *see also* spirituality
respect, 23, 25
Rogers, Carl, concept of person, 41–2, 44, 46–8; definition of psychotherapy, 108–9; on encounter, 74, 79–81; on meaning, 15–16, 18–19; model of personality change, 182–4; on non-directivity, 64–5, 67, 68; on 'the self', 59, 92–3, 96–7, 98; visits to Europe, 1, 3, 5, 8
role-playing in childhood, 224
Rombauts, J., 3
Rosenbaum, R., 59

Scandinavia, person-centred approach in, 8
schizophrenic disorders, 222–3
Schmid, P., 9
second-order desires, 29–32, 33
selective reinforcement, 68–70
self, characteristics and dimensions of, 29, 58–9, 96–7, 185, 190, 192; discourses of, 95–6; impact of conditioning on, 54–5; observing self, 60; and personal meaning, 14–15; and personality change, 57–9, 61; recovering lost aspects of, 100; Rogers' theory of, 59, 92–3, 96–7, 98; social reality and construction of, 93–4; and transcendent awareness, 97–9, 156; UPR and aspects of, 27–8; *see also* development of person
self-acceptance, 150
self-actualization, 92, 106–7, 114
self-cohesion, 191

self-concept, and conditions of worth, 113;
development of, 114–17, 125–6;
experiences at core of, 111, 113, 114,
115–16; integration of self-experience into,
119–21, 125–6; and schizophrenic
disorders, 222–3; threat of incongruence
to, 121–3
self-defence, 113–14, 121–3, 124
self-experience, integration into self-concept,
119–21, 125–6, 127–8; subjective and
objective, 108
sexuality, discourses of, 94–6
social reality, and construction of self, 93–4
social understanding, 217–21
Solms, M., 107
Sommeling, L., 19–20
spirituality, 32–5, 155–6; see also religion
Stern, D., 116, 126
stress, 121–5
substantialistic concept of person, 41–2, 44–5
Sullivan, H.S., 111–12, 166
superego, 152–4
Swildens, H., 124, 128
Switzerland, person-centred approach in, 9
symbolization of experience, 107, 111,
141–7

Tausch, R., 2, 3
tenderness, 111–12
therapeutic relationship, conditions for
focusing, 134–5; directive and non-
directive, 62–70; encounter as form of,
74–5, 79–81, 83–4; as medium of change,
56–7, 172–3; with psychotics, 216–17,
226–8; Rogers' concept of, 109
Thorne, B., 19

Tillich, P., 77, 97, 98, 102
Tomada, F., 98
Tomlinson, T.M., 65–6
training, 2, 3, 4–5, 6, 7, 8, 9, 101–2
transcendental experience, 97–9, 156
trauma, 121–5
tree, image of, 195–8
Truax, C.B., 70

unconditional positive regard (UPR), in
childhood development, 110, 111, 115, 117;
definition of, 23–4, 109; and integration of
self-experience, 119–21; and neurosis,
127–8; problem of unconditionality, 26;
and second-order desires, 31, 32, 33; and
self-concept, 113, 117, 122–3; and
spirituality, 32–5; as therapy condition,
165–6, 183–4
unconditional valuing, 25–7

Van Balen, R., 3
Van Belle, H., 18
Van den Berg, B., 210
van der Linden, P., 169
Van Kessel, W., 169
vulnerability, 182–3

warmth, 23–4
Weiser Cornell, A., 132, 139, 150
Welte, B., 77
Whitney, R.E., 65–6
Wiltschko, J., 134
working alliance, 191

Zucconi, A., 7